SHATTERED SILENCE:

A JOURNEY OF SURVIVAL

AND HEALING

Nanice Munoz -Formerly Nicola Nooks

DEDICATION

This memoir is dedicated to those who have endured abuse in silence, whether as children, as young people, or as adults still carrying the weight of unspoken pain. To those who feel voiceless, trapped, and unseen, I hope my story will offer you courage, healing, and the reminder that your experiences matter. To the young hearts who suffer in silence, and to the adults whose pasts continue to shape their present, I dedicate these words. May you find strength in your own journey toward healing and know that you are not alone.

I also dedicate this book to my husband, whose own unique experiences have shaped him in ways words can't fully capture. Your strength, understanding, and unwavering support have been my foundation, and I'm grateful for you every day.

ACKNOWLEDGEMENTS

I would like to begin by thanking my grandmother, the woman who was my mother in every way that truly mattered. From the moment my mother entrusted me to her care at just one year and six months, my grandmother became my protector, my nurturer, and my guide. She shaped me with her wisdom, her unwavering love, and her quiet strength. She was the mother I needed when I had none, and I will forever be grateful for the years we spent together, from my childhood into my teenage years. Her love and sacrifices have had an immeasurable impact on my life, and her spirit lives on in everything I do.

I also want to acknowledge my mother. While our relationship has been fraught with pain and distance, I acknowledge the role she played in my life, however complicated it may have been. I recognize that she carried me, and for that, I am thankful. The experiences we've shared, though difficult, have shaped who I am today. I have found healing in accepting the complexities of our bond, and I offer my forgiveness and gratitude for the lessons learned along the way.

To the prophets who spoke into my life over the years, your words of encouragement have had a lasting impact on me. You saw books inside me before I even knew I had a story to tell. Your prophetic messages gave me the courage to embrace my voice and my calling to write. For your insight, your faith in me, and your guidance, I am truly thankful.

To my husband, thank you for being my unwavering source of strength and encouragement. Your support has allowed me to find the courage to share my story, and for that, I am forever grateful. Your belief in me has been a beacon of light through the darkest moments.

To my dear friend, who is both a social worker and a leader in the church, your words of wisdom and encouragement have been a guiding force. You helped me see the importance of sharing my story, and for that, I thank you.

Finally, to anyone who has supported me on this journey, whether through prayer, understanding, or simply by being present, I am deeply thankful. Your love and kindness have meant the world to me, and I carry each of you in my heart as I continue to walk this path of healing and self-discovery.

Table of Contents

DEDICATION iii

ACKNOWLEDGEMENTS iv

PREFACE viii

INTRODUCTION ix

PROLOGUE x

CHAPTER 1 1

   The Beginning of Separation: A Mother's Decision 1

CHAPTER 2 27

   New Beginning, or So I Thought 27

CHAPTER 3 61

   The Church Argument 61

CHAPTER 4 93

   Leaving Home and the Silence That Followed 93

CHAPTER 5 120

   Breaking Free 120

CHAPTER 6 166

   Navigating the Complex Ties of Family and Forgiveness
   166

CHAPTER 7 195

   An Invitation to My Father's House 195

CHAPTER 8 218

   Introduction to the Visa and the Need for a Safe Haven
   218

CHAPTER 9 238

Crossroads of Faith and Destiny: Stepping into the Unknown 238

CHAPTER 10 271

Disconnecting from Family 271

CHAPTER 11 285

Seeking Independence and Reconnection 285

CHAPTER 12 316

Honoring Your Parents 316

CHAPTER 13 337

Mother's Day and birthday: Setting the Stage 337

CHAPTER 14 356

The Gift of Self-Discovery: Embracing My True Self 356

CHAPTER 15 362

Journey of faith 362

CHAPTER 16 376

Embracing New Opportunities for Growth 376

CONCLUSION 380

EPILOGUE 382

AUTHOR'S NOTE 384

PREFACE

Writing this memoir has not been an easy task. The truth is, there were times when I questioned whether I should even share the story. Was it too personal or too raw? Would it dishonor those I love? However, as I reflected on my journey, I came to realize that my story was never just mine. It is a reflection of countless others who have faced similar struggles, challenges, and heartaches, especially those tied to family, identity, and the enduring scars of difficult relationships.

This memoir includes honest and unflinching depictions of the trials I faced, including experiences of abuse, neglect, and trauma. These parts of my story are not shared lightly. Some passages may be disturbing or triggering to certain readers, and I encourage you to proceed with care if these topics may be difficult for you.

I did not write this memoir to implicate anyone or place blame. My intention is to share my story as a testament to the resilience of the human spirit and to offer a voice to those who feel silenced by their own struggles. This memoir is for anyone who has ever felt lost, broken, or unseen. I hope it provides a sense of hope and reminds readers that no matter the pain, there is always room for healing, growth, and reconciliation.

INTRODUCTION

This is the story of a young girl who learned to navigate the complexities of family, faith, and survival after feeling like an outsider in her own life. It is a story of love that was never fully given and of a heart that, despite its brokenness, found a way to heal.

The pages that follow explore the mother-daughter bond, the struggles of growing up in an environment that didn't always feel like home, and the search for meaning in places where it seemed absent. These experiences are shared not to seek sympathy but to illuminate the courage it takes to rise from the ashes of pain.

As you read, expect moments of sadness, anger, and sorrow, but also moments of light, grace, and undeniable hope. This memoir is more than my story. It is a reflection of the universal battle for self-identity, healing, and the courage to speak truth even when silence feels safer.

PROLOGUE

There is a saying that our greatest battles often happen in silence. In the quiet moments, when no one is watching, the weight of our struggles bears down the hardest. For many years, I fought battles no one knew about, buried beneath a facade of normalcy. But what happens when the pain, the shame, and the silence become too much to carry alone? What happens when the journey toward healing begins not with an outward confrontation, but with the decision to speak?

This memoir is an attempt to share the story of my heart, a story shaped by wounds that no one could see and struggles that were rarely voiced. It is a story of survival, of over—coming fear, and of embracing the truth that healing begins when we stop pretending everything is okay. This book is not just about me, but it's about all those who have lived through pain, trauma, and silence, wondering if their story could ever matter.

My story is not a typical tale of triumph. It is one of deep questioning, raw emotions, and moments of realizing that honoring the past does not mean accepting its pain as a per—manent part of who we are.

It is a journey toward understanding that acknowledging our hurts and choosing to heal is an act of courage. As you turn these pages, I invite you to walk with me through the anger, the grief, the struggles, and the eventual peace that I found not through external validation, but through the strength of choosing my own voice. The road to healing is never easy, but it is one worth traveling.

In sharing my story, I hope you will find hope, healing, and the courage to embrace your own

CHAPTER 1

The Beginning of Separation: A Mother's Decision

I can't recall the exact moment my mother handed me over to my grandmother, but that handoff is one of the first pivotal moments in my life. I was only a year and a half old when it happened. At that age, memories blur easily, fleeting like whispers carried off by the wind. Still, some events, no matter how faint, linger in the heart and carve out scars that never fade.

The Mystery of My Mother's Absence

I was sent to live with my grandmother, a decision that, in the world of an infant, could only be felt, not understood. My mother's reasons for this choice were never explained to me, but that single act shaped much of my childhood. Even as a small child, I carried the weight of absence, though I couldn't yet name it.

The reasons behind her decision, or the emotions she might have felt, remained hidden from me for years. What I did know was that my grandmother became the foundation of my world. She loved me fiercely, stepping into the role my mother had left behind. In her care, I found a sense of safety, nurturing, and stability that my young heart so deeply needed. Her home became my home, the only one I truly knew. Still, the question of why I wasn't with my biological mother lingered, haunting me like a silent presence I could never shake.

A Grandmother's Love, Not Spoken but Shown

Living with my grandmother became my world. Her home, her voice, and her rules shaped the foundation of my earliest memories. My grandmother wasn't someone who expressed love through words. She never said, "I love you." But her actions spoke louder than any phrase ever could. She cared for me with unwavering devotion, creating a sense of comfort and stability that I didn't even realize I craved. She made sure I was safe, always provided what I needed, and supported me in ways that went beyond words. Her love was constant and deep, filling the unspoken spaces where verbal affirmations might have been.

The Unspoken Questions: The Longing for Connection

As I grew older, questions about my mother began to surface, quietly stirring in my mind. Why had she made this decision? Why hadn't she kept me? The longing to understand her choices became an unspoken ache, a silent weight I carried. I didn't have the words to ask her, nor the courage to confront the unanswered questions.

I don't remember the moment she brought me to live with my grandmother. At just one year and six months old, I was far too young to grasp what was happening or why. There's no image of her face imprinted in my memory as she left me behind, no echo of her voice offering comfort or explanation. All I have is the knowledge passed down to me later: she made a choice, one that would alter the trajectory of my life.

The Painful Distance: Limited Contact with My Mother

Although I didn't live with my mother, her presence still lingered in my life. Distant, yet painful! The rare interactions we had never resembled the nurturing connection I imagined a mother and child should share. On my birthdays, I longed for a simple gesture, a phone call, or message but it never came. I would watch my cousin, who lived in the same home, celebrate with joyful birthday parties thrown by his mother. His father would take us both, and I would tag along, wearing the only dress I had, even though it wasn't the nicest. I enjoyed the celebration as his parties were the only birthday celebrations I knew. I yearned for a closeness with my own mother that always seemed out of reach, like something fragile and broken that I desperately wished could be mended.

Shyness and Isolation: The Unseen Impact of Separation

From as far back as I can remember, during my early school years, I was a shy and reserved child. While other children laughed and played together, I would sit quietly by myself, always on the edges of their joyful chaos. I'm not sure if my shyness was connected to my separation from my mother, but deep down, I felt different from the other kids. I yearned for connection, yet I couldn't find the words or actions to bridge the gap. In hindsight, that persistent sense of isolation may have been one of the earliest signs of how profoundly her absence shaped my inner world.

Endless Wonder: The Search for Answers

Despite the distance between us, despite the unanswered questions, I never stopped wondering about her. What had shaped her decisions? What caused the rift that lay between us?

Given Away but Not Forsaken

As I was only eighteen months old when my mother left me in my grandmother's care, I never fully understood the circumstances until much later. The story goes that my mother brought me to her amidst difficult times. The man believed to be my father had refused to take any responsibility. But my grandmother, deeply rooted in the belief of familial bonds, took me in without hesitation. She had her

4

reasons. As a baby, I sucked my thumb, a habit that, in her eyes, was a sign. Her son, the man believed to be my father, had also sucked his thumb as a baby. To her, this was undeniable proof that I was his child.

Rooted in Love and Sacrifice

Those early years were defined by love, protection, and the unspoken weight of hidden truths. My grandmother and her husband raised me with great care, ensuring I attended Early Childhood School, a crucial part of my early development. I can still vividly recall the small, yet warm home we lived in, a place that felt safe, where I never had to question whether I belonged.

But life changed when my grandmother and her husband divorced. The stable world I had known unraveled as we moved to a new home. It wasn't just a change of address; it marked a transformation in our entire way of living. We eventually settled into a new house where we stayed for many years. It felt like home, at least for a while. I lived there with my grandmother, her daughter (my aunt), and two cousins.

This house became the backdrop of my childhood memories. It was where I first began to understand the complexities of family: the love, the challenges, and the sacrifices that came with it. My grandmother was a woman of quiet strength, doing everything she could to provide for us. But nothing in life is permanent. When the landlord eventually reclaimed the house, our sense of stability was shaken once more. It felt as though a cycle of displacement had begun.

When Home Became Unsteady

We moved from place to place after that, always searching for a sense of home, though nothing ever felt as permanent as those early years. Each new location brought its own challenges, and with every move, I learned to adapt quickly. I became skilled at packing up, settling in, and making the most of my surroundings. It would take me years to understand just how deeply those early moves shaped my ability to navigate change later in life.

Despite the constant movement and uncertainty, I never forgot the feeling of being chosen by my grandmother. She believed in me when others didn't. She saw something in me, something as simple as a thumb-sucking habit, and turned it into a reason to love me. For that, I have always been profoundly grateful. Her constant belief became the lifeline I clung to through every storm, every new home, and every unspoken question about who I was and where I truly belonged.

Lessons in Hard Work and Discipline

Life with my grandmother was a blend of hardship and love, both deeply intertwined in the routines of our daily lives. Each morning, my cousin and I would set out on a long walk to school, our small feet trekking the sunbaked path under the relentless Caribbean heat. The journey felt endless, and yet, it was simply part of our rhythm. At lunchtime, my grandmother would meet us halfway, bringing meals she had cooked with care. We'd sit together for just a few moments, sharing the brief respite before heading back to school. The walk home always felt longer, the weight of the day pressing down on us, but even as a child, I could sense her effort and sacrifice, though I couldn't yet fully comprehend its depth.

Our home was small but sturdy, made of concrete walls and a zinc roof that turned every rainstorm into a symphony of sound. I can still hear the sharp, steady ping-ping-ping of raindrops hitting the roof at night, a rhythm that, though persistent, felt oddly comforting. That sound lulled me to sleep, a steady cadence that seemed to whisper assurances of safety. The house wasn't big, but it was solid. It didn't need to be grand to protect us. No matter how fierce the storm outside, I always felt safe beneath that roof, secure in the knowledge that it would hold. Life there was simple yet structured, anchored by routines that kept us grounded in love and discipline.

My grandmother was a woman of unshakable discipline. In her house, there were no "lazy days." Chores weren't optional; they were simply a part of life. Sweeping the yard with a bush broom, scrubbing clothes by hand, and hanging them on the line were all lessons in effort, self-reliance, and preparation for life. These tasks weren't punishments, they were life skills, gifts I carried with me long after I left her care. She carried herself with a quiet authority that demanded respect. She didn't shout often, but when she did, it was enough to make everyone pause and listen. My aunt, who also lived with us, had a different energy, a playful, sometimes lighthearted presence that balanced my grandmother's seriousness.

Yet, when it came to family responsibilities, my aunt was as firm as needed. When I was still young and attending basic school, another male cousin moved in with us. For a time, our lives settled into a delicate balance: a mix of family responsibilities, occasional bursts of laughter, and moments of quiet understanding.

But as much as our routines felt stable, change was on the horizon, bringing with it challenges I could not yet imagine.

Silent Storms: The Unspoken Chapter

Another male cousin moved in with us, and at first, I didn't think much of it. He was older, and I assumed that, like most adults, he would care for and protect me. Life continued as usual. The chores were done, school was attended, and our nights ended in a familiar rhythm: we gathered under the flicker of the kerosene lamp, said our prayers, blew out the light, and retired to bed.

My grandmother often filled those evenings with her stories, rich with lessons cloaked in tales of mystery and the supernatural. There was the one about a crow circling a coffin, searching for a man named Mr. Brown, or the story of the woman who heard a kitten crying in the night, took it home, and was shocked to hear it speak; "You better carry me back where you got me from." These were not just ghost stories, they were warnings, reminders that the world could be strange and unpredictable. Sometimes, she shared lessons from her own life, wisdom I didn't realize I would cling to until much later.

It was during these moments, listening to her, sitting in the comfort of her presence, that I felt safest. She had a way of making me feel seen, heard, and understood, something rare in a world that often felt too big and too uncertain.

But not everything about living with my grandmother was comforting. There were moments of unease I couldn't quite name, and feelings of confusion I didn't have the language to express. Much of it centered around my male cousin. Unlike my grandmother and aunt, he lacked their warmth, their steady presence. His presence unsettled me, though I couldn't yet articulate why.

A Fracture in Innocence

The incident that changed everything is something I carried in silence for years. It's strange how the body remembers even when the mind tries to forget. I won't go into the details now, but I will say this: in those moments, I learned what it meant to feel powerless. For a child who had been raised on self-reliance by my grandmother, it was jarring to face something beyond my control.

The silence afterward was just as loud. There were no words, no conversations, and no explanations for why things like this happen.

Looking back, I think about how children are taught to "be quiet." We're told to mind our manners, respect adults, and not make trouble. I took those lessons to heart, but over time, that "quiet" became more than just obedience. It became a shield, a place to hide the things I didn't know how to face.

I didn't tell my grandmother. I didn't tell anyone. Instead, I folded the experience up and buried it deep inside myself, like a note hidden under a mattress, a secret tucked away where no one would find it.

Life Goes On

Life went on, as it often does, with secrets buried in the quiet corners of daily survival. My grandmother never knew the full weight of my pain. She taught me the importance of self-respect, with lessons often delivered through tough love. Yet, at times, I wondered if she ever sensed that a small part of me was fading, slipping away like a shadow at dusk. I held onto the structure and routine of home, even though it was far from perfect.

The house where I lived with my grandmother before moving to live with my mother was modest, a humble board structure that bore the passage of time in its very bones. Unlike the neat, well-kept homes that surrounded us, ours showed its age in every crack and creak. The wooden walls were weathered, with gaps wide enough to reveal glimpses of the outside world. When the wind blew, it slipped through those openings, piercing the rooms with a chill no blanket could fully fend off.

Carrying Water and Carrying Shame

Water was always a struggle. We had no running water in the house, so I had to fetch it from a tap near an abandoned pig farm. I hated that task, not just because of the effort it required but because of the shame it carried. Schoolchildren would pass me as I balanced a bucket of water on my head, my heart sinking with every glance in my direction. I felt exposed, as if my poverty was laid bare for everyone to see.

Sometimes, in a futile attempt to avoid humiliation, I refused to carry the bucket on my head and gripped it with both hands instead. But that only made the task harder. My grandmother would tease me, calling me "Miss World" whenever I did this. "You want to look too cute to do hard work," she'd say with a smirk. It wasn't the work I minded; it was the fact that carrying the bucket made my family's struggles visible to everyone. I didn't want to be seen that way.

Fighting Injustice: The struggle of expectations and unequal responsibilities

My clothes had become a silent reminder of everything I lacked. They weren't new or fashionable, and every time I compared myself to the other children who lived in and around my community, I felt a pang of inadequacy. I was out of place, like I didn't belong. I tried to mask my discomfort by toughening up. I became something of a tomboy, running around and getting into mischief with my male cousin. But when it came to chores, the unease crept back in. Tying out the goats felt especially unfair. Why should I be the one to handle the animals? My cousin was a boy; shouldn't he be doing this instead?

I grumbled under my breath, stomped my feet, and let my frustration show. My grandmother didn't care for my protests. She snapped in Patois, flinging words like stones. 'Feisty Pickney'! her voice rose as she carried on about how stubborn and feisty I was. I suppose she was right, though at the time, I didn't think of myself that way. I wasn't trying to be rebellious. I was simply exhausted by what felt like unfair expectations. Tying out the goats always seems like a task my cousin, being a boy, should handle, Yet I was often assigned to do it. Even after he left home, the chore remained mine, a responsibility I neither liked nor ever grew accustomed to.

The struggle of unspoken longing

Growing up under my grandmother's roof was a journey defined by both love and longing. As a teenager, I often muttered under my breath, stomped around, and grumbled when I thought she was being "miserable." At the time, I didn't fully understand my own actions. To anyone watching, it might have seemed like typical teenage rebellion: a child pushing back against discipline. But beneath that behavior was a quiet ache I hadn't yet learned to name.

I had been given to my grandmother at just one year and six months old, too young to understand what was happening but old enough for the loss to leave its mark. Even without the words to articulate it, I wondered why my mother didn't want me. My grandmother did her best, pouring her steady and unwavering love into me. Now, as an adult, I see that clearly. But back then, my view was clouded by the unmet need for a mother's affection.

Every rule she set felt heavier, and every punishment seemed sharper, not because of what she did, but because of what I was missing. My backchatting wasn't just about testing boundaries; it was a silent protest against the invisible weight of abandonment. It was my way of asking, "Am I really wanted here?

Hard Work and Determination

My grandmother worked tirelessly to ensure we had everything we needed. Her main crop was lettuce, though she also grew other vegetables to sell at the market. When the crops were ready, my cousin and I would carry heavy baskets of lettuce on our heads up the steep hill to our house, where my grandmother prepared them for market day. The baskets were burdensome, but we managed by using a cotter, a piece of cloth twisted into a ring to cushion the weight on our heads. It wasn't a daily task, but it was one that demanded patience and perseverance.

Before dawn, my grandmother would catch a truck to the market, her produce carefully packed and ready to sell. In the evenings, my cousin and I would wait for her return at the bus stop, using a bottle torch to light our way through the darkness. The air was cold, but we didn't mind. We passed the time running and playing with other children until we saw the market truck finally pull in. Then, we'd help her carry what was left of her produce and head home together as a family, tired but fulfilled.

In addition to selling lettuce, my grandmother would often travel to her mother's house in St. Thomas, another parish. I remember walking home from school in the late afternoon, knowing we had a long journey ahead of us. The walk to St. Thomas took hours, and we often didn't arrive until nightfall. Sometimes, we'd have to stop and rest along the way, our legs weary from the endless stretches of road. Trucks and other vehicles would pass us by, and every so often, we were fortunate enough to catch a ride for part of the journey.

Those walks tested my patience and endurance in ways I didn't fully understand at the time. They were tiring, even frustrating. But they also taught me a lesson I carried with me to this day: the value of perseverance.

Discipline from My Father and Uncle

My father and uncle would visit from time to time; though never at the same time. These visits didn't bring joy or gifts; they brought discipline. If my grandmother mentioned that we had been misbehaving, we already knew what would follow. They would sit and listen to her recount stories about me and my cousin, nodding in quiet agreement, as if the verdict had already been decided. Whichever one had come would grab a belt. My cousin and I would both get spankings no questions asked, no explanations given. It didn't matter who had done what.

Looking back, however, I don't remember my father ever disciplining my cousin. He only spanked me, since my cousin was not his child. My cousin's father, though, would spank both of us. That difference still lingers in my memory. In those moments, I learned that discipline wasn't about understanding or fairness. It was about submission and pain. I longed for something different: a relationship with my father built on connection instead of punishment. But this was all I knew. His visits, brief and detached, left me with more questions than answers. What did I mean to him? Did he even see me as his child? Those unspoken questions lingered well into my high school years. They shaped my perception of what it meant to be cared for or not, leaving me with a complicated understanding of love and belonging.

When One Cousin Left, Another Stayed

The cousin responsible for the incident that nearly changed my life was the first to leave the house. His departure felt like a storm passing. It wasn't completely gone, but heavy clouds lingered in its wake. Life around me didn't shift drastically, but his absence was palpable.

Later, my other cousin left too. He was the one I played with, laughed with, and got into mischief with. He went to live with his mother in Kingston. His departure felt different. This time, I wasn't relieved; I was sad. He had been my playmate, my partner in childhood adventures. Then suddenly, he was gone.

With both of them gone, I was left alone with my grandmother. The house grew quieter, and I felt the weight of solitude settle around me. The lively energy of playing, running, and laughing was gone. All that remained was stillness, a silence that made the days feel longer and the nights even lonelier.

The Warmth I Never Knew

There is another memory that has stayed with me. It revealed a stark contrast in how my cousin and I were treated. When his mother came to visit him at my grandmother's house, even after hearing that he had been misbehaving, she approached him with love and compassion. She spoke to him softly, her voice full of care and understanding. By the time she left, he was crying in the bathroom. He was overwhelmed by the warmth he had received.

In contrast, when my mother, who as far as I can recall, visited my grandmother once, was told that I had misbehaved, her reaction was harsh and cold. There was not even a flicker of love. I vividly remember climbing into a tree to hide because I didn't want to be spanked. Later, as I followed her to the bus stop, I kept my distance and walked far behind her. I was afraid. I wasn't just afraid of her stern demeanor, but also of her sharp words that cut deeper than any punishment. There was no warmth, no tenderness, and no trace of the love my cousin had received from his mother.

Hard Lessons and Unspoken Pain

One of the hardest nights I can remember was the evening I came home late. I hadn't been doing anything wrong; I was just spending time at the game shop, losing myself in the small escape it offered from the heaviness of home life. But when I walked up to the door and knocked that night, my grandmother's expression told me she didn't believe me. Her suspicion cut deeper than words. Maybe she thought I was out with boys or doing something wrong, and she let her anger spill out unchecked. Then, without warning, she spat in my face. But I had only been at the game shop.

The sting wasn't physical. It was emotional. A wound I couldn't rub away. I'd been trying so hard to follow the rules, to meet every expectation, to prove myself worthy of trust. Yet no matter how much I gave, it seemed like it was never enough. That night, the weight of that truth sank in. Sometimes, no matter how good you try to be, you'll still be misunderstood.

An Encounter at the River

One of the most defining moments of my childhood happened during a trip to the river. It was a place I often visited to bathe and find relief from the punishing heat. That day, I never imagined my life would change in a way I could never forget.

While I was there, an older man approached me. His intentions were unmistakable as he grabbed me. I tried to fight him off, pushing and resisting with everything I had, but he was stronger than me. For a moment, I froze, trapped between fear and instinct. But even in that terrifying instant, I knew I wasn't powerless. I quickly came up with a plan. I told him I needed to water my grandmother's lettuce so it wouldn't wilt.

My words came quickly, steady and convincing. I even promised I'd come back soon. To make my story believable, I left behind my underwear, my rag, and the soap, knowing they would serve as proof I wasn't running away for good. With that, I turned and walked away, my heart racing with every step.

While he waited for me to come back, I ran home as fast as I could, my heart pounding so hard it felt like it might burst from my chest. Once I reached the safety of home, breathless and shaking, I told my grandmother what had happened. Her reaction was immediate: furious, loud, and unrestrained. She caused a scene that drew the attention of the entire community.

She sent me to the police station. I was still too shocked to fully process what had just happened, but I followed her plan without question. At the station, the officers struggled to piece together the details, uncertain of exactly what had occurred. Later, I think it was my mother who took me to see a doctor for an examination. But since nothing physical had happened, there was no evidence to support the claim of assault.

Even before I could process my own emotions, the story had already shifted. My grandmother's version of events took on a life of its own. By the time I found the words to explain what had truly happened, it felt as if my experience had been taken from me. My truth was buried under the weight of their version, and I was left powerless to reclaim it.

Years later, I spoke with the young man's mother over the phone. I felt the need to bring clarity to what had happened or rather, what hadn't. I explained to her that it wasn't actual rape. He had tried to have his way with me, but I escaped before anything more could happen. I told her I was sorry for allowing the story to stand the way it did. She responded calmly, saying, "Well, if he hadn't interfered with you, then his name could not have been called,". And she assured me that it was well. Not long after that conversation, I learned that the same man had raped someone else; this time, he was sent to jail. That knowledge left me with a heavy mix of emotions: relief that I had escaped, guilt for what I had once said, and sorrow for the girl who hadn't been as fortunate.

The Dream of Living with My Mother

As the years went by, I began to dream of a different life. My cousin had moved to Kingston to live with his mother, and I longed for the same opportunity. I wanted to be with my mother. I believed she could give me more than my grandmother ever had: a better life, a home where I felt safe, and maybe, just maybe, a chance to feel a mother's love; to know what it was like to be loved by my own.

I was tired of the house we lived in, a place that seemed to be crumbling, barely standing against the test of time. I was tired of hauling water from the abandoned pig farm and tired of being mocked and called "Miss World" because I refused to balance a bucket on my head.

But the dream of living with my mother wasn't just about escaping discomfort; it was rooted in something deeper: a longing to belong. I yearned to feel like I truly belonged somewhere; to know I had a place where I mattered.

The thought of moving to Kingston felt like a chance to start over, to leave behind the burden of chores that seemed endless and unfair. I imagined walking down the streets without the weight of shame, without feeling like my poverty was a billboard for everyone to read.

A Missed Opportunity and a Leap Forward

I was an intelligent child, one who loved school and thrived in the classroom. My teachers saw my potential early on and in my final year at all-age school, recommended me for the position of Head Girl. It was an honor and a recognition of all my hard work: a big deal not just for me, but for what it meant in my small world.

But when the time came, my grandmother couldn't afford the expenses required for the role; the position was given to someone else. The disappointment hit me harder than I expected. It wasn't just about losing the title; it felt like I had lost a piece of myself. It was another blow to my already fragile sense of self-worth, a painful reminder that no matter how much I achieved, there were forces beyond my control that could strip it all away.

A Mind Beyond Limits

Despite the hardships I faced, there was one thing no one could take from me: my mind. I was sharp, quick to learn, and eager to understand the world around me. School became my sanctuary, the one place where I could escape the harsh realities of life at home. My teachers often recognized my potential, and I excelled in my studies. I was even bright enough to skip the 7th grade. That achievement wasn't just a mark of academic ability; it was proof of the resilience I had cultivated to survive.

Still, I refused to give up hope. I was determined to move forward, no matter the odds. When the opportunity arose to take the Common Entrance Exam, I believed it could be my chance to change my future. The exam was a gateway to high school and a stepping stone toward a better life.

But my excitement was short-lived. The children selected to take the exam were required to attend a special preparatory class, and their families had to pay for it. My grandmother couldn't afford the fees. Without the money, I couldn't sit the exam. I was devastated, watching yet another door close because of financial struggles beyond my control.

Then something unexpected happened: My Vice Principal selected three of us from among the top students in our class to travel to Kingston to sit for the entrance exam at a school there. I am deeply grateful I passed, and that success became my ticket to a new life.

With this achievement, I saw a window of possibility. I asked my mother if I could live with her so I could attend school in Kingston. For once, she said yes.

Moving in with my mother felt like the beginning of a new chapter, a chance to rewrite my story. For the first time, it felt as though the ending of my life wasn't set in stone, and I was finally in control of the pen.

Reflection: The Roots That Shaped Me

Looking back on my years with my grandmother, I now see how deeply those experiences shaped the person I've become. At the time, I didn't have the words to explain it, but her love was there: embedded in every quiet sacrifice she made. She didn't express affection through words like "I love you," but her actions spoke louder than anything she could have said. From the steady rhythm of daily chores to the shelter of a home that stood firm through every storm, her care was a constant I couldn't always recognize.

There were moments of frustration: back-chatting, stomping around, and rebellion born from an unspoken pain I didn't yet know how to name. But now I understand that her discipline wasn't about control; it was about preparation. She was teaching me to stand on my own, to rely on myself, and to endure even when life felt unfair. Her firmness, which I once resented, was her way of showing love. It was a love I didn't fully grasp as a child but have come to deeply respect as an adult.

Life under her roof wasn't perfect. It had its shadows: confusion, fear, and the painful loss of innocence. Those moments could have broken me, but they didn't. Instead, they gave me a quiet strength. I learned how to endure, how to keep hope alive even when the weight of the world felt unbearable. I realized that safety isn't always found in a place. Sometimes, it's found in the people who stand by you when life's storms rage.

The years I spent with my grandmother taught me resilience, resourcefulness, and the power of quiet, unyielding love. Her belief in me, seen even in something as small as how she claimed me as her son's child, stayed with me. It became a lifeline I held on to through every move, every heartbreak, and every unanswered question about belonging. In her own way, she answered the question that lingered in the back of my mind: Am I wanted? Her actions told me I was.

Living with my grandmother was a journey of love, hardship, and growth. Her house, with its concrete walls and zinc roof, became more than just a shelter. It was a space where I was shaped into someone who could face life's challenges. While I often longed for my mother's affection, I now realize I was never without love. It just came in a form I didn't recognize at the time.

CHAPTER 2

New Beginning, or So I Thought

At fifteen, I left the only home I had ever known with my grandmother and stepped into what I hoped would be a fresh start. Living with my mother felt like the long-awaited reunion I had dreamed of for years. It was a moment of reunion brimming with equal parts excitement and anxiety. Having spent most of my childhood without her, I imagined this would finally be my chance to feel the warmth and affection I believed only a mother could provide. My expectations were high, fueled by dreams of finally belonging somewhere.

But what I thought would be a new beginning quickly turned into a period of painful discovery. The day I moved in with my mother, it felt as though I had stepped into an unfamiliar world. I was old enough to understand that change was inevitable, but I was too young to grasp how profoundly it could unsettle me. This wasn't my first move, but it was the first time I truly felt like a stranger in my own home.

When I asked my mother if I could stay with her so I could attend school, since her house was closer, I didn't expect resistance. But she was clear and firm: she didn't want me there on the weekends. "You need to go to your yard," she would say, meaning I had to return to my grandmother's house. Yet, I didn't want to leave. I longed to stay near her, to live in Kingston, to feel like I finally belonged somewhere, not just physically but emotionally.

I remember how my sister was living with relatives in another parish, attending a good school. She would usually come home on weekends or during holidays, but when she saw that I was there to attend school, she suddenly wanted to transfer to the same school I was about to attend. Even though there was a bit of resistance, it didn't take much for my mother to agree to let her come.

I didn't think much of it at the time, but now I wonder why I was the one who was passed back and forth, while she was given stability? Why did I always have to fight for space, for belonging, even in my mother's house, even in my mother's heart?

The Slap That Stung More Than The Skin

One incident stands out as a pivotal moment during my time with my mother. It happened not long after I moved in with her and marked the first time she sat me down to discipline me. I don't remember what I was being reprimanded for, but I do remember the silent promise I made to myself beforehand: I would never respond to my mother with disrespect or irritation under my breath, as I had sometimes done with my grandmother. I would never stomp away in anger.

I was determined to be respectful, to show her I was different. But as she spoke to me, the moment escalated in a way I didn't expect. Out of nowhere, she slapped me across the face. The reason? She thought my mouth was trembling as though I were about to respond. But I hadn't said a word. I hadn't even intended to.

The slap shocked me. The sting on my cheek faded quickly, but the emotional pain lingered. It wasn't just the physical blow that hurt; it was the unspoken message it carried. In that moment, it felt like a confirmation of what I had feared deep down: no matter how hard I tried, I couldn't earn her love or approval.

That slap was more than just discipline. It became a physical manifestation of the emotional distance between us, a painful reminder that, in her eyes, I was someone to be controlled, not cherished. It deepened the divide between us in a way I couldn't have anticipated. The sting on my skin disappeared, but the mark it left on my heart remained long after.

A Love Unreciprocated

At that point, I loved my mother more than I loved myself. I wanted nothing more than to be close to her, to make up for the years we had spent apart. But her rejection began to erode that love, little by little. When she resisted my request to stay with her, I resorted to a quiet act of desperation. I deliberately let the last bus to the country pass, then lied to her, saying I hadn't caught it. It wasn't an act of rebellion; it was a small, desperate attempt to stay near her, to hold onto whatever closeness I could.

Over time, though, the love I felt for her became eclipsed by resentment. Her actions made me feel unwanted, like a burden she merely tolerated rather than a daughter she cherished. That resentment slowly hardened into hatred, a weight I could no longer carry alone. It was a burden I eventually had to lay before God. I prayed for help, asking the Lord to guide me in releasing the bitterness that had taken root in my heart, and he answered, lifting the weight I couldn't carry on my own.

Walking the Hard Road

Living with my mother was nothing like I had imagined. Her house, though slightly bigger than my grandmother's, felt hollow. At my grandmother's, the air carried echoes of spoken words: stories, laughter, and even struggles that somehow made the small space feel alive. It was a home filled with love and belonging. But my mother's house was different. It felt cold and unfamiliar, as if I were an outsider tiptoeing through spaces that never embraced me.

A Mother's Expectations

My mother even asked me to sell bagged juice and water, tasks that would have required me to trudge through the stifling heat of downtown Kingston or the crossroads area. I refused, unable to shake the heaviness of her request. It felt less like a practical necessity and more like an assertion of control. Though she framed it as a way for me to contribute, it only heightened my feeling of isolation in a household where fairness always seemed out of reach.

Hand-Me-Downs of the Heart

Even in the smallest details, the divide in our household was undeniable. I remember stopping at the Salvation Army to get clothes which made me feel small of course. It wasn't just about the clothes; it was the unspoken message they carried. While others were afforded the dignity of choice, I was left with secondhand remnants, a quiet reminder of how little my worth seemed to matter.

The Silent Struggles of Inequality

Living in my mother's home, I quickly noticed how different life was for my siblings and me. My sister and brother always had enough lunch money, provided by their father, who was also my mother's husband. They could easily afford to take the bus to and from school, while I had no choice but to walk long distances every day.

It wasn't just about the money; it was the decisions that were made. Even though my sister often helped herself to extra money from her father's pocket; my mother never made any effort to share the money my stepfather left for his children with me. And yet, I was the one doing his laundry and pressing his clothes for work. My needs seemed invisible, as though they didn't matter. I often wondered why things were made so much harder for me. Why wasn't the money divided more fairly? Why did it feel like I was always left out?

The small amount I received for lunch was barely enough. Sometimes, all I could afford was a single cone of ice cream. I would stand quietly in a corner, eating with my head down, hoping no one would notice I didn't have a real meal. I preferred the hunger over the shame of letting my classmates see the reality of my situation. In those moments, I learned to disappear, not out of fear but as a survival skill.

Despite the struggles, there were rare moments of kindness that reminded me I wasn't completely alone. As a cadet, I had an officer who would occasionally invite us to his home for lunch. Those meals, humble as they were, felt like a banquet to me. They nourished more than just my body; they nourished my spirit. The officer has since passed, but his kindness remains a vivid memory. Even now, it reminds me how a simple act of compassion can alter the course of someone's life.

The inequality extended to dinnertime. My sister often served the meal, and when it came to dividing the chicken, I always ended up with the "parson's nose," the part most people discarded. It wasn't just about the food. It was about what it represented. The constant reminder was that I was given the least of everything.

The Weight of Labor and Words

One of the most painful memories from my teenage years was the burden of weekly chores, especially washing clothes. Every Thursday, my mother would come home from work exhausted, claiming she wasn't feeling well. Without fail, she demanded that I do the laundry. What began as a one-time favor quickly became a routine expectation, leaving me without a voice or a choice.

But my mother wasn't the only one who was tired. I would come home from school drained, only to find that the responsibility of scrubbing the laundry by hand rested entirely on me. My mother's clothes, my stepfather's clothes, my little brother's clothes, and my own became my duty. On top of that, I was also expected to iron the clothes regularly. This added task only deepened my physical and emotional exhaustion.

My stepfather, a taxi driver, often brought home clothes stained from his long, grueling days of work. The dirt clung stubbornly to the fabric, and washing his clothes by hand felt like scrubbing away layers of cement. My fingers would ache by the time I was finished, and I couldn't help but wonder why this burden had been placed squarely on my shoulders.

Meanwhile, my sister, just two years younger than me, was only responsible for washing her own clothes. The imbalance was glaring, and I often felt like I was being punished for something I couldn't understand. If I washed the clothes and hung them out to dry, my mother would sometimes inspect them. If she thought they weren't clean enough, she would take them down and hand them back to me to wash again. It didn't matter how tired I was. What mattered was that it met her standard.

Years later, I tried to talk to my mother about it. I wanted her to acknowledge how unfair it had been. Instead, she denied everything. She claimed she had been paying me to do the washing, but I never saw it that way. It wasn't just about the labor. It was the unspoken expectations and inequities that seemed to define my place in the household.

It wasn't the washing itself that hurt the most. It was what it symbolized.

The Sting of Singling Out

One day, as my sister and I walked behind my mother on the street, chatting and laughing about something trivial, she suddenly stopped and turned to face me. Her sharp gaze pierced through me, and she snapped, "You are the one that something is on to laugh about."

Her words cut deeper than I could have anticipated. It wasn't just the statement itself; it was the tone, the coldness, and the weight of her disapproval. In that moment, it felt as though my very presence was an annoyance, as if my laughter and my joy were a provocation rather than a natural expression. I felt small and exposed, my happiness shrinking under her glare. The message was clear: any spark of joy I showed would always be met with dismissal or contempt.

A Test of Truth and Favoritism

My mother handed me money to go to the market, and I was desperate for a summer job. Determined to make the most of my trip to downtown Kingston, I set out under the blazing sun. The streets buzzed with activity: vendors shouting their prices, buses honking, and the constant shuffle of people navigating the chaos. It wasn't long before a man in a red shirt and jeans spotted me in the crowd. He approached with an air of confidence, speaking smoothly as he offered me a job. His words were so convincing that I found myself believing him, even when he said I'd need to pay for an ID photo before starting. The keys jingling in his hand, which he casually claimed were for his office, made him seem legitimate.

As we walked, he began talking about faith. I mentioned a well-known church and asked if he knew it, and he said he did. I was a young Christian, and his references to faith and religion, paired with his calm demeanor, made him seem trustworthy. His offer felt more and more genuine with every step, and I followed him eagerly, clinging to the hope that this would be my chance.

He led me to a photo studio conveniently located near a police station. That detail reassured me, it made everything feel secure, like this was meant to be. Inside the studio, he hurried upstairs, explaining that he needed to pay for the photos. By this point, I had already handed him the money.

A few moments later, he returned, his voice steady and his smile reassuring. He promised that everything was in order and told me to come back on Monday morning to take the photos before starting work. His words sounded sincere, and I trusted him. I was confident he would refund the money once we arrived at his office.

As we left the building, he started talking about security dogs and officers at his office, weaving a story so plausible that I didn't question him when he began walking. I had doubts, but I convinced myself he was leading me to the office. By the time I realized he wasn't heading there at all, it was too late. He kept moving farther away, and I began to notice that something was off. When I finally understood what was happening, he was already lost in the crowd.

The streets were chaotic, packed with people, and he disappeared without a trace, taking not only the market money but also my hopes with him. Panicked, I ran back to the photo studio, desperate to recover my money. But when I arrived, the building didn't even house a studio. It didn't exist. My heart sank.

As I stood there, overwhelmed and trying to make sense of what had just happened, a man approached me. He said he had noticed the scam unfolding earlier and had considered coming over to talk to me, but he hadn't acted in time. Then, unexpectedly, he suggested I lie to my mother and say I'd been held up and robbed.

It stung to hear this. He hadn't even realized it was a scam until I explained what had happened. He admitted that he'd seen me standing there and had thought about stepping in. But for whatever reason, he didn't.

"If I had come over earlier," he said, "you could've told me what was going on, and I would've told you there's no photo studio upstairs."

Hearing his words was both frustrating and heartbreaking. What might have been different if someone had stepped in sooner?

Looking back, I had wanted to go upstairs with the man; that was my plan. But when he rushed off, something didn't feel right. Chasing after him felt strange, so I stayed downstairs, waiting for him to come back.

It was during this moment of helplessness that I ran into my former cadet officer, the one who had once shared his lunch with me when I had none. Embarrassed and feeling hopeless, I explained what had happened. He listened carefully, without judgment, and when I finished, he simply handed me money to replace what had been stolen so I could return to the market and buy what my mother had sent me to get. His kindness was a small light in an otherwise dark moment, a reminder that not everyone in the world was out to take advantage of me.

When I got home, I was late, but I had the items my mother needed. I hoped the delay would be forgiven, but instead, her anger erupted like a storm. She cursed me, calling me "stupid," her words cutting far deeper than the loss of the money itself. I tried to explain what had happened, my voice trembling, but before I could finish, my sister interrupted. "The same thing happened to my friend," she chimed in, echoing each detail I shared, as though narrating someone else's life.

A tenant in the yard finally called her out, laughing and saying, "That happened to you, not your friend!" Only then did it come to light that my sister had been deceived in the exact same way before. Instead of telling the truth, she had rushed home breathless, spinning a story about the bus she was on being held up at knifepoint. Her lie had spared her from punishment entirely. The moment my mother realized the same thing had happened to my sister, her anger toward me disappeared. It was as if the scolding had never happened.

Relief washed over me, but it was quickly overshadowed by a bitter sense of injustice. If my sister's lie had shielded her from ridicule, why hadn't my honesty done the same? My mother didn't even acknowledge the unfairness, let alone apologize for her harshness. I wasn't sure what hurt more: the loss of the money, the sting of her words, or the realization that the truth didn't matter when it came from me.

Small Possessions, Big Losses

When my father brought me a typewriter for school, knowing I was studying typewriting, I was overjoyed. For once, it felt like I had something of my own: a small victory that felt deeply personal. But that feeling didn't last. One day, I offered to lend the typewriter to a friend, wanting to share something that brought me so much pride. My mother stopped me in my tracks. "That's not yours," she said sharply. "It's mine." Her words struck me harder than I expected. In that moment, the typewriter no longer felt like a gift. It wasn't mine after all. Instead, it became a symbol of what I was never truly allowed to have: ownership, autonomy, or even a simple token to call my own. I couldn't bring myself to use it after that. Each time I looked at it, I felt that pang of rejection, a reminder of the limits of my independence, even in something as seemingly insignificant as a school supply.

Unfair Rules and Unseen Scars

Discipline in my mother's house wasn't just a matter of rules; it carried both physical and emotional weight. When my brother and I sat watching television, her reaction always depended on who claimed responsibility for turning it on. If my brother admitted to it, she wouldn't say a word. But if I confessed, she would immediately order me to turn it off.

Her punishments went far beyond scolding or even spanking. She would bite. Those bites weren't just painful; they lingered, leaving marks on my skin and in my memory. A neighbor in the yard nicknamed her "Vampire." The nickname stung, not because it wasn't accurate, but because it captured the sharp reality of what I endured.

The Fridge Incident: A Cruel Reminder

There was one time when I went to the fridge to grab some water, only for her to stop me mid-step. " Go get water outside to drink" she said, her voice sharp with finality. Though we didn't even have running water, water was always stored in drums and other containers. Still, she insisted I drink from there. Then came the cutting words: "You didn't even have a fridge when you lived with your grandmother." I froze. Her statement hit me harder than I expected, not because of the words themselves, but because of the weight they carried. It wasn't just about the glass of water, it felt like a pointed reminder of where I came from, of how, in her eyes, I would never measure up. That moment, so small on the surface, stayed with me. It was one of those times when her disapproval felt like a wall I could never break through.

The Favoritism and Inequity

The favoritism in our family was an undeniable reality, one that left a lasting mark on my teenage years. One memory in particular stands out, sharp and vivid: my mother bought a shimmering gold fabric for my sister to sew a dress for my aunt's wedding. For me, she handed over a plain blue satin, a material far less elegant, almost an afterthought.

It wasn't the gold fabric itself that I longed for. What stung was what it represented: my place in the family. The choice was a reminder, subtle yet unmistakable, that I was always second in line, always less.

The Wedding Dress Incident

A kind woman, noticing my pain, spoke up on my behalf. She suggested that my mother buy the same material for me. At first, my mother resisted the idea, dismissing it as unnecessary. But after some coaxing, she finally relented.

On the day of the wedding, my sister and I wore matching gold dresses. Outwardly, I should have felt included, even equal. But as I stood there in that shimmering dress, the emotional wound remained raw. It was never about the material itself; it was about what it signified. It was another reminder of the recurring pattern in my life: being overlooked, being less.

The Impact of Words Unspoken

The favoritism in my family wasn't limited to material things; it seeped into relationships as well. My mother never allowed me to form a genuine connection with her side of the family. For instance, my aunt would visit our home but never spoke a word to me. Her silence felt deliberate, as if it had been shaped by whatever my mother might have said about me. These fractured relationships were not of my making, yet I carried their weight all the same.

I remember one moment in particular, a remark from my mother that cut deeper than most. She told me plainly that my sister would go further in life than I ever would. Those words sank into my mind, amplifying the favoritism I already felt and planting seeds of self-doubt. It wasn't just about the things my sister received; it was about the belief my mother seemed to hold: that I was somehow lesser.

As a teenager trying to navigate life's uncertainties, hearing that from my own mother was devastating. Her words didn't just sting; they lingered, leaving me to question whether my efforts would ever be enough in her eyes. No matter how hard I tried, it felt like I was fighting a battle I had already lost.

Words That Wounded

I vividly remember one birthday when my mother walked into my room. She didn't say "Happy Birthday" or acknowledge the day in any way. Instead, she looked at me and said, "People say you look like me, but you don't look like me because you're ugly." The sting of those words overshadowed what should have been a celebration.

It was my stepfather who broke the silence, offering a rare defense: "She's not ugly." His words were brief, but they felt like a lifeline, cutting through the deep hurt her remark had caused. That birthday, like so many others, was a painful reminder of how much I longed for her affirmation, and how profoundly her words could wound. Even in that moment, though, I clung to the glimmer of hope his kindness gave me: small but steady, like a flicker of light in the darkness.

My mother didn't wait for arguments to tear me down. She did it as part of her everyday routine. It was never about discipline or correction. It was simply the way she spoke to me. She'd look me straight in the face and say things like, "Your mouth big like," or "Your mouth is so big," as if it were an undeniable fact, she needed to remind me of again and again. Not as a joke or an offhand comment, but like she meant to wound me with it. Like it was something ugly I needed to be ashamed of. She said it with such disgust it felt like my face vexed her.

There was no context. No reason. Just regular, unprovoked humiliation. I became so ashamed of my lips that I started sucking in my bottom lip all the time. I would walk around with it tucked in, trying to make my mouth look smaller. I was painfully self-conscious, and not just in the usual way children can be. I was actively trying to hide what she made me believe wasn't attractive, like the very size of my mouth was something I had to apologize for

Studying in the Shadows

Balancing academics with my challenging home life was not easy. As a cadet, I was disciplined and determined to succeed. Most days, I carefully saved the little lunch money I received so I could afford extra lessons in Principles of Accounts, the only subject I could pay for. My sacrifices paid off when I graduated with distinction in accounts, proving to myself that determination could break barriers.

Yet, studying at home was a constant struggle. My mother would often demand that I turn off the light, claiming its glare bothered her from the other room, even though a curtain blocked the doorway. Electricity was free, but the peace I needed to study came at a price. Her voice, sharp and insistent, would interrupt me, commanding me to "hurry up and switch off the light." I found myself anticipating her interruptions, which made it nearly impossible to focus.

Desperate for a better solution, I tried studying outside in the yard with a classmate, but even that was met with disapproval. When we attempted to study at his uncle's house, where there was proper lighting, my mother forbade it entirely. Her restrictions felt suffocating, boxing me in and depriving me of the opportunity to prepare for my exams the way I needed. Despite my efforts and abilities, including earning a prefect badge and placing first in my graduating class, the lack of a conducive study environment held me back from excelling in all the exams I had set my heart on.

The Absence Felt

My achievements in school extended beyond academics. I felt immense pride in being a cadet, a role that demanded both discipline and dedication. Cadet parades were held regularly, and parents were invited to celebrate their children's progress. Each time, I scanned the crowd, hoping to catch a glimpse of my mother, but she never came. Watching my peers' glow with pride as their families cheered them on filled me with a deep sense of emptiness.

In those moments, I was transported back to being the little girl who cried quietly because the person I needed most wasn't there. That absence left an undeniable ache, but it also shaped me in profound ways. Even without her physical presence or encouragement, I learned to push through the pain. I found strength in that void, vowing to build a future where I could stand tall and be proud even when there's someone or no one is there to witness it.

A Shattered Truth: Discovering My Identity

My mother once revealed to me that the man I had always believed to be my father, the one who had gifted me the typewriter, was not, in fact, my biological father. The revelation came out of nowhere. One day, she took me to the airport, a place I had never visited before. There, she introduced me to a man and told me he was my real father. He greeted me warmly, embracing me with hugs and kisses. The entire moment felt unreal, as though I was watching someone else's life unfold. Later, when she asked how I felt about this discovery, I responded calmly, "I don't feel any way; it already happened."

But beneath that composed response, a storm of emotions churned. I had been nurturing meaningful connections with my cousins on my father's side; the man I had always known to be my father. Now, I faced the heartbreaking task of telling them we were not actually related. Losing those growing relationships felt like a betrayal layered on top of another.

Conflicting Messages

Even after revealing the truth, my mother still sent me to the man I had always known as my father to collect lunch money. The journey was long, and I often made the trip alone. Sometimes, I returned home late at night, only to discover he wasn't there. Each time, I was left with a nagging sense of confusion. If he wasn't my father, why did she continue to send me to him? The emotional toll was immense as I struggled to make sense of the two conflicting realities she had placed before me.

Violated Boundaries

Around that time, I began receiving letters from the man my mother had introduced as my biological father. These letters became my lifeline to understanding this new relationship, a small, private link connecting me to him. But any sense of privacy I thought I had was short-lived. Without my knowledge, my mother would go through my school bag and personal belongings.

One day, she confronted me with words that cut deep: "He's writing you the same things he's writing me." I don't clearly remember if she had asked to see the letters or if I had shown them to her as some memories blur with time but what stayed with me was the feeling of exposure. I felt violated, as though even the smallest corner of my life was no longer my own. It was a betrayal of boundaries I hadn't even realized I needed to guard.

A Dark Revelation

After I left my mother's house, life dealt me another devastating blow. The man who had claimed to be my father continued writing letters to me, their contents laden with unsettling undertones. He used biblical references, such as the story of Lot and his daughters, that seemed to justify inappropriate intentions. Each letter left me shaken to the core, forcing me to wrestle with emotions I wasn't ready to confront. The discomfort didn't stop there. He made similarly disturbing remarks during phone calls, deepening my unease and leaving me feeling trapped in a dynamic I didn't know how to escape.

One day, while I was in Jamaica, he called to inform me he was coming to Kingston to visit me at my house. Though he told his wife he would stay at his brother's house in Kingston, he arrived directly at mine instead. His arrival wasn't entirely unexpected, but it was deeply unsettling. It was New Year's Eve, and I had been preparing to attend church that evening when he showed up. We were in the room, and though we had already greeted each other, he kept trying to hug me and pull me close.

I embraced him, but I resisted getting too close, keeping a certain distance. There was something about the way he tried to hold me that felt off: too intimate, too uncomfortable. I didn't want to give the wrong impression or create a moment that felt inappropriate. Before leaving, I decided it was time to address the question that had been weighing heavily on my mind. Looking him in the eye, I asked directly, "Are you sure you're my biological father?" Without hesitation, he said yes, confidently claiming he remembered the exact moment it happened. I responded calmly, though my mind raced. "Then we should do a blood test to confirm," I said, holding my ground.

Before leaving for church, I asked if he wanted to come with me, but he declined. Feeling unsettled, I sought guidance from my landlord, whose advice was firm: "You don't know him well. You should not stay alone in the same room with him." She suggested I stay with her after church, and I agreed. With that plan in place, I left for church, determined to find solace in worship while he remained behind. When I returned later that night, I followed my landlord's advice and stayed in another room instead of my own. The next morning, I accompanied him to the bus stop. From that day forward, I never saw or heard from him again. Perhaps it was because he didn't get what he wanted, or maybe it was because he knew he wasn't truly my biological father. I will never know.

Reflections on Resilience

These experiences challenged me in ways I could never have anticipated, but they also became the foundation of my strength. Each revelation and betrayal, though deeply painful, taught me how to navigate the complexities of life. While I cannot control the actions of others, I've found healing in accepting my emotions and discovering paths **to move** forward.

Avoiding Home: A Place of Unease

As a teenager, I often looked for ways to delay going home. If I had cadet activities after school, I stayed as long as I could. On days when I finished early, I lingered in places like the National Heroes Circle, sitting quietly until nightfall. The thought of stepping through the door and facing my mother's accusations and belittling words filled me with a deep sense of dread. Home wasn't just a physical place I was avoiding; it was the emotional burden it carried.

A Vision of Despair

One day, as I was walking up the road, I had a vivid vision that shook me to my core. Ahead of me, I saw another version of myself, literally eating from a garbage bin. It felt as though my spirit was laying bare the depth of the despair I carried. The vision lingered, haunting my thoughts and serving as a stark reminder of how overwhelming the weight of my depression had become.

Prayers for an End

The emotional pain I carried often felt unbearable, pressing down on me in ways I couldn't explain. I prayed constantly not for courage to take my own life, but for something, anything, to release me from the suffering. As I wandered the streets, I prayed and asked the Lord for a stray bullet to find me, to bring an end to the pain I could not out-run. I wanted to die. I longed for relief; an escape from the weight of a life that felt too heavy to bear.

Lack of Support for Higher Education

When I graduated from high school, I remember my mother's disinterest in my future with painful clarity. "So, you want to go to college?" she asked, her tone heavy with indifference. It was painfully obvious she hoped I'd say no. Trying to ease the tension, I responded with a forced joke: "God soon come, I'm going to work." Her silence afterward was deafening, filling the space between us with everything she left unsaid. She didn't challenge me to think about col-lege, didn't encourage me, and didn't urge me to reach for something greater. It was as if she had already decided my future for me, a future without hope, growth, or expectation.

Prophecy of Evangelism

I'd never forget the day a man prophesied over me, tell-ing me that I would become an evangelist. That night, on our way home from church, I was elated and eager to share the news with my mother. But her response was immediate and sharp: "You're not becoming no evangelist." Her words cut deep, leaving me stunned. But they didn't stop me. Years later, I was not only ordained as an evangelist in Jamaica, but

I was also ordained as both an evangelist and a pastor in America. What she dismissed as impossible became my reality. Her disbelief, rather than breaking me, became my fuel.

Strength Amid the Storm

Looking back, I realize now that even in my darkest moments, I was still holding on to hope, quietly, almost unknowingly. My prayers, though desperate, were a reflection of my resilience, a silent refusal to let go completely. Deep down, I was searching for something greater: a sense of peace and purpose that could exist beyond the pain.

Understanding My Responses

Even though my mother often labeled me as stubborn and feisty, likely influenced by my grandmother's words, I believe my responses were rooted in the consistent provocation I endured. The Bible says, "Parents, provoke not your children to wrath," yet the relentless criticisms and accusations I faced naturally provoked a reaction. I wasn't trying to be disrespectful or confrontational; I was defending myself, questioning why I was treated the way I was. It wasn't defiance. It was survival.

Despite how she interpreted my actions, I can say with certainty that I was never rude to her. I never insulted her, attacked her, or called her names. I maintained a sense of respect, even when my heart ached from the wounds her words inflicted. Deep down, I still longed for her love and approval.

Even in moments when I felt unjustly treated, I often took the initiative to apologize, hoping to mend the relationship and earn her affection. I poured my feelings into letters of apology, carefully writing each word with the hope that it would soften her heart. In those letters, I expressed my love for her and my desire for peace between us. But despite my efforts, nothing seemed to change. If anything, my attempts at reconciliation may have reinforced her perception of me as the feisty daughter she believed me to be. Still, my intentions were sincere. I only wanted to bring harmony to a relationship that often felt fractured and distant.

A Silent Struggle

The three years I spent with my mother were the hardest of my life, filled with confusion and an aching sense of rejection. I tried to remain quiet, to fade into the background, hoping that my silence might somehow make her notice me. But I was wrong. It wasn't my silence that caught her attention; it was the constant reminder that I wasn't the child she had envisioned.

I struggled quietly, longing for the love that never came. Yet, amid the pain, I began to notice something else: a quiet resilience growing within me, like a spark refusing to be extinguished.

The Lasting Impact

Living in my mother's house from the age of fifteen to eighteen was a period of profound emotional challenge. During those years, I often felt unseen, unheard, and undervalued. My mother's words and actions left scars that still linger, but they also uncovered an inner strength I hadn't realized I possessed. That chapter of my life wasn't just about enduring pain; it was about learning to survive it and discovering my own light in the darkness. Though I couldn't always speak up back then, I can now. In finding my voice, I honor the strength of those who face similar struggles in silence.

Reflection: Moving Through the Shadows

This chapter explores one of the most turbulent periods of my life. It was a time when I was searching for my identity, grappling with the pain of favoritism, belittlement, and betrayal, all within the walls that were meant to protect me. This chapter isn't about assigning blame but about giving voice to the experiences that shaped me and, hopefully, offering a voice to others who feel silenced by similar

56

struggles.

It's for the countless sons and daughters who wrestle with the complexities of their relationships with their parents. For those who bear the conflict of loving someone who has also caused them deep pain. It's a reminder that you are allowed to speak your truth, even when it feels uncomfortable.

For years, I carried the weight of my mother's words, her actions, and her expectations. These experiences could have broken me, but they didn't. Instead, they revealed a strength within me. It was a determination not to be defined by neglect or harshness of others.

What I've learned is that healing doesn't mean erasing the past or pretending it didn't happen. Healing means facing those moments, acknowledging their impact, and still choosing to move forward. This chapter is a step in that journey, both for me and for those who see themselves reflected in these words.

If you've ever felt abandoned in a house full of people or longed for a love that never came, know this: your feelings are valid. It's okay to grieve. It's okay to hope. And it's okay to rebuild a life that isn't defined by the pain of the past.

This chapter reflects my growth and the strength I discovered to keep moving forward. It's a testament to the human spirit's ability to endure immense pain and still strive for something better. My prayer for you, as you read this, is that you find your voice, your courage, and your hope. And in sharing my story, I hope I've reminded you that you are not alone.

Finding Hope in the Struggle

For anyone who feels silenced, overlooked, or undervalued, know this: your worth is not determined by the opinions or treatment of others. During those difficult days, I often felt like my voice didn't matter, that my pain was invisible. But even in those moments of silence, I held tightly to the promises of God. Scripture reminded me that the One who created me sees every tear and hears every unspoken word.

Psalm 34:18 comforted me: "The Lord is close to the brokenhearted and saves those who are crushed in spirit." It became my lifeline in moments when I felt utterly alone. And when I questioned my own worth, Isaiah 49:16 reassured me: "See, I have engraved you on the palms of my hands; your walls are ever before me." Those words affirmed that I was never forgotten, even when it felt like the world had moved on without acknowledging my pain.

There were days when I wondered if my circumstances would ever change, if I would ever feel truly seen or heard. But Jeremiah 29:11 gave me hope for the future: "For I know the plans I have for you," declares the Lord, "plans to prosper you and not to harm you, plans to give you hope and a future." I clung to this promise, trusting that even when the present felt dark, God was working things together for my good.

Another verse that brought me peace was Matthew 11:28, where Jesus says, "Come to me, all you who are weary and burdened, and I will give you rest." When the weight of rejection and silence became too heavy, I found comfort in knowing I didn't have to carry it alone. In those quiet moments, I learned to lean on God's strength rather than my own.

I also found reassurance in Psalm 56:8: "You keep track of all my sorrows. You have collected all my tears in your bottle. You have recorded each one in your book." This reminded me that every tear I shed mattered to God. My pain wasn't overlooked; it was held tenderly by the One who knew me best.

To anyone walking a similar path, I encourage you to lean into these truths. You may feel unheard now, but God hears you. You may feel unseen, but God has not forgotten you. As Romans 8:28 reminds us: "And we know that in all things God works for the good of those who love Him, who have been called according to His purpose."

Your pain, though profound, has a purpose. God's plan for your life extends beyond what you can see right now. Trust in His timing, and hold onto the truth that brighter days are ahead. Just as He carried me through, He will carry you too. You are stronger than you realize, and though your voice may have been silenced for a time, it will rise again.

CHAPTER 3

The Church Argument

The End of Another Long Day

The day ended like any other. I had just returned from school after a long day. My school bag rested on the bed beside me, and the fading evening light cast long shadows across the room. I sat on the edge of my bed, my uniform slightly wrinkled from the day. Exhaustion weighed heavily on me, and it wasn't just physical. It was the burden of everything I carried inside. The thought of going to church that evening felt impossible, not because I didn't believe in God but because I didn't have the energy to pretend, I was okay.

A Reluctant Decision

I had recently given my life to the Lord, and since then, my mother and I rarely missed a church service. Sunday mornings, sometimes Sunday nights, and even Wednesday evenings became our routine, except for the occasional times when my mother decided we'd stay home. But that evening was different. I was exhausted, drained to my core, and I didn't have the energy to put on a mask and pretend like everything was okay.

Skipping church didn't seem like a big deal to me. There had been other nights we hadn't gone, and it was always at my mother's discretion. But this time, at eighteen when I decided not to go, she reacted differently. As I slipped out of my school uniform and stepped outside, she asked, "Aren't you going to church tonight?" "No, I'm not," I replied.

Time passed, but the question came again. "Aren't you getting ready for church?" Each time, I gave her the same answer: "I'm not going tonight." I wasn't trying to be defiant. I just didn't feel like going. Still, something shifted in the air between us, heavy and unspoken.

Tension Building

She checked yet again to see if I was getting ready for church, but I stayed quiet, hoping time would slip by until it was too late for me to go. My silence didn't deter her. She was relentless, clearly determined that I needed to go, whether I felt like it or not. In her eyes my feelings were irrelevant. I could feel she wasn't going to let it go but I kept hoping she would.

The air between us felt heavier with each passing moment. It was like standing in the moments right before a storm; still, thick and tense. The silence was taking charge, warning of what might come next.

A Forced Change in Direction

It started with an invitation from a young lady who lived nearby. She asked me to join her at a church called Pentecostal Tabernacle, which was just a short walk from where we lived. From the moment I stepped through its doors, I felt God's presence in a way I had never experienced before. I cried through Sunday school and the service, overwhelmed by His presence: so powerful, so real, that it moved me to tears.

When I returned home, I told my mother I wanted to get baptized at Pentecostal Tabernacle. But she didn't support my decision. Instead, she insisted that I attend her church. I was told we weren't going back to Pentecostal Tabernacle because of something my sister had done. I didn't know what it was, but I hadn't done anything wrong, yet I still had to face the consequences of her actions. It felt unfair, like I was being punished for something beyond my control. My heart ached, not just for the loss of the church community, but for the sense that I was being held accountable for someone else's mistake.

My mother had recently started going to a new church that was still in its early days. I wasn't drawn to it, but she left me with no choice. "Where I go, you go," she said. The truth was, I didn't see her as a Christian because her actions didn't reflect the faith she claimed. How could someone who treated me the way she did call herself a Christian?

The pastor of her church would sometimes visit our home, accompanied by a few members of the congregation. There was something different about the pastor, something I couldn't quite put into words. She had a light about her, a presence that was calming and genuine. Even so, my feelings about the church didn't change. In my mind, the others couldn't be much different from my mother. I believed the saying, birds of a feather flock together, and I wasn't eager to be a part of their group. But my mother wouldn't take no for an answer. So, I went. The church was small and attached to someone's house. I hated it. Everything about it felt uninviting. But the pastor was persistent. She sat me down, asked me questions, and talked to me about giving my life to the Lord. Eventually, I became the first person baptized at that church. It wasn't where I wanted to be, but over time, I began to feel a sense of belonging. Slowly, I let myself become a part of the congregation, even if it hadn't been my choice at first.

Living in the Tenement Yard

We lived in a tenement yard, sharing two connected rooms. My mother and her husband stayed in one, while my younger sister, brother, and I shared the other. My older brother had already moved out by then, leaving just the five of us. Two other tenants shared the yard. One was a Christian woman who lived with her daughter and grandchildren, and the other one was an older lady with two kids, and other family members do visit her occasionally and go. And there was an elderly woman who often passed through our yard to reach her own home.

Privacy was nonexistent. One neighbor and her family window looked directly in our front yard. and houses pressed in from every side. Some were separated by fences, others by the walls of neighboring homes. The yard was always alive with activity: children running, doors slamming. Despite the constant movement, it was fairly quiet in its own way. It wasn't noisy. The yard reflected the world outside intruding on my space, leaving nowhere to hide. The commotion outside mirrored the tensions brewing inside my home, a backdrop to my struggles that made everything feel more suffocating.

Reflection: Struggling for Peace and Belonging

Looking back on that time, I see how torn I was, caught between my seeking for a connection with God and the complicated, often painful relationship I had with my mother. Church, for me, was supposed to be a sanctuary, a place of refuge and strength. But my mother's insistence on taking me to her church felt more like an order than an invitation. I couldn't understand why she wouldn't support me in my spiritual choices, but at the same time, I wasn't ready to abandon my faith. Reconciling my longing for peace with the constant tension in our relationship felt impossible.

I often felt like an outsider, not just at home, but even in the church that was supposed to bring me closer to God. My mother's actions seemed less about faith and more about control. It was always her way or no way, and it wore me down. I started to question whether she truly lived her faith or if it was just another part of her routine. Her insistence on bringing me to her church didn't feel like guidance; it felt like another way to assert her authority over me. I didn't feel like a young woman growing into independence. I felt like a child being managed.

Over time, my faith became something deeply personal, something that belonged to me. It wasn't easy. It took time, patience, and painful self-reflection to understand that I didn't need to follow anyone else's spiritual path but my own. The tension, the disagreements, and the struggles with my mother didn't weaken my desire for a deeper connection with God. If anything, they strengthened it.

I learned that peace with God didn't always mean peace at home. That was a hard truth to accept, but it became a foundation for my spiritual growth as I got older.

The Conflict Begins: Shattered Expectations

The air was heavy with tension that night, thick and unrelenting, like the calm before a storm. What had started as an ordinary evening quickly unraveled into something far more intense. Something I couldn't have foreseen. I had decided not to go to church that night. The weight of everything I was carrying inside had left me drained, with nothing left to give.

When my mother confronted me about my decision, it felt like more than just a disagreement. It was as if an invisible line had been crossed, though I couldn't quite articulate why. How could something so small, something as routine as missing one church service, spiral into a conflict that would leave me shaken?

As the minutes stretched on and time passed, she stayed in the other room. There were no glances, no words. Just silence. I sat still, hoping she would realize it was getting too late to get ready and decide to let it go. Maybe, I thought, it would be over without a fight. But she didn't give up. I knew the drill: Sundays, Wednesdays, and sometimes Saturday evenings for choir practice. Church attendance wasn't required for everyone in the house. My younger sister, my little brother, and my stepfather didn't attend. But for me, it was expected.

Still, tonight was different. I couldn't explain it. I don't even remember if I was tired. I just didn't want to go. I thought it would end there, a brief standoff of wills. But my mother's reaction shattered that hope, turning a moment of disagreement into something far more painful.

The Storm of Words

When I refused to move from my spot on the bed, my mother's frustration erupted. She stormed into my room, and in a whirlwind of anger, began yanking my clothes off the hangers. For a moment, I sat frozen, paralyzed by the chaos unfolding in front of me. Her actions felt surreal, like she had lost all sense of control.

This wasn't just about church. This was about power, about her need to dominate. One by one, she threw my clothes outside, scattering them across the yard: part concrete, part dirt. I stared, stunned, as my belongings lay in disarray, exposed to the elements. The sight of my life reduced to a pile of crumpled clothes and dirt-covered memories was jarring.

The final blow came when she hurled my school folder onto the ground. It was the one thing that felt like a symbol of my effort and my identity. It wasn't just about the items being thrown out; it was about the message her actions carried. My choices didn't matter. I wasn't allowed the freedom to make decisions about my own life. In that moment, I felt discarded, stripped of autonomy, and left to wrestle with what it all meant.

The Final Straw

When I retrieved my folder and placed it back on the bed, I hoped, desperately, that it would end there. But my mother came back, her anger unabated, and threw it outside again. This time, the gesture felt final and irreversible. It wasn't just an act of rebellion against me; it was a silent message, as clear as any words. My presence wasn't welcome. My desires and my opinions didn't matter in the place that was supposed to be my sanctuary, my home.

At this point, I can't remember if she explicitly told me to get out of the room or house, but her actions spoke volumes. My chest tightened, a knot of hurt and disbelief pressing against me. Slowly, I stood, letting the reality settle in, and stepped outside. The night air hit me like a wall: cool, unfamiliar, and heavy with the weight of everything left unsaid. It was unmistakable. I no longer belonged here. In that moment, I wasn't her daughter. I was an intruder, unwanted and insignificant.

As I stood there, staring at the scattered remains of my belongings, the question I couldn't escape gnawed at me: Where was I supposed to go? The thought made my stomach churn. I was just a teenager, still in school, with no options, no safety net, and no place to turn. I felt utterly unmoored, as though the ground beneath me had disappeared.

A Recognized Conflict

The shouting and commotion didn't go unnoticed. One of the tenants in the yard caught sight of what was happening. I'm not sure if anyone else behind those walls heard it, but the noise was loud enough for someone to recognize the chaos that had taken over. Another neighbor, whose window faced our front yard, witnessed the way I was treated at my mother's house, perhaps feeling the weight of it as I did. It was the tenant next door who, one afternoon while I was outside washing clothes, glanced through her window and called me by name. She wasn't one to interfere openly, but her acknowledgment felt like a fleeting comfort. "Don't worry, you'll get big soon," she said, her voice tinged with a strange mixture of empathy and helplessness. Her words, simple and brief, carried the unspoken understanding of someone who could see the injustice of my situation but was powerless to change it.

Those words lingered with me. They weren't much, a small, seemingly encouraging remark, but they were a paradox. She had no real ability to stop what was happening, yet her empathy gave me a kind of validation I hadn't realized I craved. Someone was noticing my pain. And though it was a small comfort, it didn't erase the sting of humiliation from being trapped in such an emotional storm.

The idea that a neighbor (someone with no connection to our family) could see the weight of my suffering was both humbling and humiliating. I wanted to disappear from the world's gaze, to escape the scrutiny of others, but at the same time, it was oddly comforting to know I wasn't invisible.

Reflection

Looking back, I see that night as more than just a family conflict. It was a moment of profound emotional upheaval. What I felt wasn't confined to rejection and confusion in that single night; it was the culmination of years of feeling dismissed and controlled. My mother's actions that evening were extreme, but my reaction was born from the weight of a lifetime of emotional neglect.

The experience shook the foundations of my self-worth and left me grappling with questions I didn't know how to answer. Why was my voice so easily ignored? Why did my choices seem to matter so little? These questions lingered, haunting me. I couldn't shake the thought: Had there ever been a moment in my life when I truly felt seen, heard, and valued simply for being myself?

Over the years, I've come to see that this experience wasn't just personal. It mirrors the universal struggle of seeking validation and acceptance. Scriptures like Romans 8:31, "If God is for us, who can be against us?" now resonate deeply with me. They remind me that, while I felt abandoned by my mother, I was never abandoned by God. His love and validation were, and still are, the truest source of my worth.

From a spiritual perspective, I now recognize that the pain I endured that night wasn't only about familial rejection. It was a step toward discovering my inherent worth in the eyes of a loving, heavenly Father. My mother's rejection, painful as it was, drove me closer to understanding that true validation doesn't come from people. It comes from God, who values us for who we are, not for what others say or do.

The Physical Altercation

The yard seemed unnervingly still, but the air crackled with tension. Chaos had erupted to a level I never thought possible. My belongings, including clothes and personal items, had already been discarded. Their once-secure place inside the house was reduced to a scattered heap in the yard. I thought that was the worst of it, but then I saw my mother again, her movements sharp and deliberate as she picked up the pile. Without hesitation, she began marching toward the gate that led to the main road.

The sight froze me. My breath caught in my throat as I realized what she was about to do. The road wasn't just any street; it was a hub of activity. Bars, shops, and people filled the space, their conversations carrying in the evening air. Cars rumbled past, and although the school next door wasn't in session, it often held events that brought in groups. The idea of my belongings being dumped out there for everyone to see made my stomach churn.

I couldn't let it happen. Summoning every ounce of courage, I reacted on instinct. My legs moved before I had time to think, carrying me toward her with a speed I didn't know I possessed. She was already at the gate, her grip firm on my clothes, and I knew I only had seconds to act.

When I reached her, I didn't dare touch her. I wouldn't have. But I lunged for the pile of clothes in her arms. My fingers locked around the bundle, gripping so tightly that my muscles burned with the effort. My breath came in sharp bursts as I tried to pull them back toward me, every fiber of my being willing her to let go. I was determined to stop her, desperate to hold onto the last shred of dignity I had left. But my attempt to take control only enraged her further.

She spun around abruptly, her face contorted with fury. Her reaction was so swift, I had no time to brace myself. She let go of the clothes and seized me instead. Before I could process what was happening, I felt the sharp, searing pain of her teeth sinking into my back.

The first bite sent a jolt of shock through me. It burned like a hot iron pressed against my skin. Then came another. And another. Each one was deliberate, each bite carving into me like a weapon meant to wound. The pain was unlike anything I had ever experienced. It was raw, primal, and consuming. It wasn't just my skin she was trying to scar. It felt like she wanted to brand her anger onto my very soul. I twisted and thrashed, desperate to escape, but her grip was unrelenting. Her hands clamped onto me like iron. Her attacks were relentless. Each bite was a reminder of the power she wielded in that moment.

Through the chaos, I heard a voice. A sharp, urgent cry broke through the fog of my fear. A woman stood in her doorway; her silhouette frozen in horror as she shouted my mother's name. "Let her go! Let her go!" Her words cut through the nightmare like a lifeline, anchoring me in the moment. But they weren't enough to stop her. The biting continued. Each new wave of pain left me feeling more trapped, as though I were caught in a nightmare I couldn't wake from.

With a surge of adrenaline, I finally broke free. My chest heaved as I stumbled back, trembling, my body alive with pain. Every bite throbbed like a pulse, radiating heat and fury. In that moment, I stopped thinking about who she was to me. The word mother felt alien. Distant. All that remained was the pain. The searing, burning pain. And the anger that surged from somewhere deep inside me, hot and uncontrollable.

As I turned to run, I caught her gaze. Her eyes were blazing with fury. I couldn't take another bite. The searing pain in my back was unbearable, radiating through my body like a fire that wouldn't go out. Something inside me snapped. It wasn't calculated or premeditated. It wasn't even a conscious decision. It was pure instinct. A desperate reaction born from excruciating pain and years of unspoken anguish.

Before I realized what I was doing, I spun around. My fist connected with her face, the force of the action reverberating through me. The shock of what I had done hit me instantly. I had never raised a hand to her before, never imagined I would. But in that moment, the pain, the betrayal, and the overwhelming weight of injustice surged through me, unstoppable.

Somewhere in the background, the woman's voice, the neighbor who had tried to intervene, broke through the chaos: "I told you to let her go". They hovered there, too late, too soft. I was hurt. I was furious. And for the first time, I felt completely severed from my own mother. The pain wasn't just physical. It shattered something deep within me, something I wasn't sure could ever be repaired.

Time seemed to freeze. My hand remained clenched, trembling, my entire body shaking with the intensity of the moment. I stared at her, stunned by what I had done. This was my mother. The woman who had brought me into this world. The one who should have protected me. And now, I had struck her in anger. The weight of that realization hit me like a tidal wave, pulling me under with guilt and disbelief. I was eighteen years old, still in my final year of high school. How had it come to this? That question hung heavy in my mind, each word cutting like a blade. Anger. Pain. Betrayal. And beneath it all, a deep, unrelenting sadness that seemed to settle in my very bones.

Reflection

In the days and weeks that followed, I replayed that moment in my mind over and over again. Each time, it felt like a fresh wound tearing open, one I didn't know how to close. I struggled to reconcile the image of myself, a daughter striking her mother, with the person I believed I was. Yet I couldn't dismiss the pain that had led me to that breaking point. The physical wounds on my back healed quickly, but the emotional scars lingered, heavy and unrelenting. The bites, though painful, were fleeting. But the ache in my heart felt infinite, as though it had etched itself into my very being. I found myself wrestling with the same unanswerable questions: Was it my fault? Was it hers? Or was this the inevitable result of years of unspoken pain and unresolved conflict rising to the surface?

In my confusion, I turned to scripture, seeking the solace I had found many times before. Proverbs 15:1 spoke to me: A gentle answer turns away wrath, but a harsh word stirs up anger. But what happens when gentleness is met with fury? I had not answered harshly. I had not provoked. Yet anger still consumed the room, swallowing any chance for peace. Psalm 34:18 also became a lifeline: "The Lord is close to the brokenhearted and saves those who are crushed in spirit." In the depths of my pain, I clung to the promise that God saw me, even when I struggled to see myself clearly. I reminded myself that He understood my heartache, even when I couldn't make sense of it. Another verse that resonated deeply was Romans 12:21: "Do not be overcome by evil but overcome evil with good." Those words became my anchor, a beacon of hope that reminded me I had the power to rise above the darkness, no matter how overwhelming it felt. Looking back, I see that moment not just as a source of pain, but as a turning point; a catalyst that forced me to confront the fractures in my relationship with my mother and ultimately, with myself.

It was through that confrontation that I began to grasp the true weight of forgiveness, not just for others, but for myself as well. The journey has been anything but easy, and it's one I am still navigating. Yet, I've come to understand this: even in our darkest moments, there is always hope. Even when we feel broken, we are never beyond repair. And even when the people we love hurt us, there is a path to healing, one that begins with grace, understanding, and unshakable faith.

The Breaking Point
The scene had spiraled far beyond anything I could have imagined. My clothes were strewn across the yard, tossed out like garbage, my dignity crushed under a wave of

humiliation. The biting incident had already left me bruised, aching, and shaken. But it wasn't over. Not yet. Out of the corner of my eye, I saw my mother rush back into the house. Her steps were quick and deliberate, charged with purpose. It was the kind of movement that sends a chill down your spine. It signaled danger before your mind could fully catch up. I didn't know what she was about to do, but every instinct in me screamed to get ready. Seconds later, she reappeared, gripping a machete in her hand.

Panic surged through me: cold, raw, and more intense than anything I had ever felt. I bolted toward the neighbor's house, shoving her out of the doorway as I stumbled inside. She had been standing there, frozen, watching everything unfolds, unable or unwilling to step in. I slammed the door shut behind me and locked it, my hands shaking. But how much protection could a simple lock offer against her rage?

The image of her standing there, the machete glinting in the light, is burned into my memory. It wasn't just a weapon, it was her rage made manifest, aimed squarely at me. Her eyes were locked on the front door, scanning for an entry point. When she realized the door was locked, she turned her attention to the window. My heart pounded as I heard her raise the machete high before it crashed down against the aluminum panes. Clang. Clang. Each strike reverberated through the room like a death knell, relentless and unyielding. The window didn't shatter, but it buckled and twisted under the pressure. It couldn't hold much longer. Inside the small room, the air felt heavy and suffocating. My breath came in shallow, panicked gasps. Outside, her voice cut through the noise of metal against glass, rising in anger, laced with curses, her words curling into the night like smoke.

Then, in a moment so strange it felt unreal, she lifted her breasts to the sky and shouted: "Lord, you see these breasts that this child suck…" The sound of her words hit me like a dark chant, thick with malice and accusation. It was as if she was summoning something evil, something that wanted to crush me beneath its weight. I sat in a chair, feet dangling, knees pressed tight, hands trembling. My mind spun with questions that had no answers. What do I do? How does this end? I was eighteen, technically an adult, yet I had never felt so small or powerless. I just wanted it to stop. I wanted to be safe.

The Call for Help

That's when the idea struck me: call the police. The station was within walking distance. I knew that in Jamaica, a mother-daughter dispute rarely led to arrests, but I wasn't looking for anyone to be jailed. I just needed the chaos to stop, even if only for a moment. I hoped their presence would de-escalate the situation enough to let me leave the room unharmed. If nothing else, their arrival might buy me time to breathe and think clearly. With trembling hands, I made the call. My voice wavered as I spoke, carefully choosing my words.

I couldn't tell them exactly what was happening; I couldn't risk them dismissing it as just another family matter. Instead, I lied. "There's a war going on up the road," I said, my voice unsteady. It wasn't true, but I needed them to come. If I'd said, "My mother is beating me," I feared they wouldn't take it seriously enough to respond. I didn't need them to arrest her; I just needed their presence to help me get out of the tenant's house. As I waited, I could still hear her rage outside, her voice cutting through the walls like a blade. The neighbor who had watched earlier from her doorway remained a witness. She stayed there, still. She offered no comfort, no intervention. Then I heard footsteps. Relief coursed through me as I realized the police had arrived. They didn't approach with sirens blaring or guns drawn; instead, they moved with measured calm, as though they'd been called to scenes like this many times before. Slowly, I unlocked the door and stepped outside.

My mother met them first. she was already speaking by the time they reached her, her words pouring out in a rapid stream of justifications. She didn't pause for breath, her tone insistent, determined to make them see things her way. The officers listened intently, their expressions neutral. "She's stubborn," my mother interjected before I could answer. Every question they asked was met with the same refrain: I was stubborn. The officer closest to me leaned in slightly and issued a quiet warning: "Don't be stubborn." His voice was calm, almost measured, as if he were trying to walk a fine line. It wasn't the tone of someone accusing me. It felt more like an attempt to diffuse tension, to stop things from spiraling further. He didn't seem convinced I was at fault. From the way he carried himself and the careful neutrality in his words, it appeared he was trying to stop her from repeating the accusation, hoping to defuse the situation. I stayed silent. Anything I said would've been pointless. She had already constructed her version of the story, one that placed me as the villain. I could feel the futility of speaking up. My words would have fallen into the cracks of her narrative, unheard and unwelcome.

The officers weren't truly calming her; they were questioning her instead. I could tell they were trying to piece together the dynamic between us. Their questions, such as

"Why did she grow up with her grandmother?" hinted at what they might have been thinking. It was almost as if they sensed a trace of rejection from her toward me. Still, I was oddly relieved that their focus was on her and not me. At least the machete was no longer in her hands. At least, for now, she had stopped.

Breaking Free, But Not Quite

After the police left, fear still clung to me. I had told them I couldn't stay, but they insisted there was no other choice. Their departure left me with a hollow sense of security, empty and fleeting. They seemed to believe their presence would be enough to stop my mother from hurting me again. But deep down, I knew it wouldn't. Nothing had changed. Nothing ever would.

I stepped back into the house, my body still shaking, the weight of what had just happened pressing down on me like a heavy cloak. The anger and fear I had felt moments before began to twist into something else, guilt. I thought of what I had done. I needed to make it right.

I went to the kitchen, warmed some water, and gently anointed the spot where I had struck her. My words spilled out in a rush; each one laced with regret: "I'm sorry. I shouldn't have hit you. I was wrong. I'm so, so sorry." I kept repeating the words, trying to erase what I'd done, trying to mend something that felt irreparably broken.

And then, something I never expected happened. Her anger, so sharp and constant, cracked. It was as if a dam had burst, releasing something raw and unfiltered. But what came next wasn't peace or resolution. Instead, it was pain, her pain, pouring out in disjointed fragments, each one cutting through the air like jagged glass. "Someone once accused me of putting poison in soup," she said, her voice trembling with something between bitterness and sorrow.

Her words struck me like a slap, sudden and stinging. I couldn't help but remember the day she accused me of putting something in her tea. The memory resurfaced with startling clarity, sharp and raw, as though it had happened yesterday. Inside, I cried at the injustice of it. I had never done such a thing, and the accusation had cut deep, leaving a wound I wasn't sure would ever heal.

As she spoke now, her voice dipping into memories of her own past, I heard stories I hadn't fully grasped before. She told me about her poverty, how she had gone to job interviews without proper clothes to wear. For the first time, I saw how much those experiences had shaped her; and more disturbingly, how much she seemed to want me to endure the

84

same. It was as if she believed that only through suffering would I truly understand her pain. Or worse, she wanted me to become a reflection of it.

The realization settled over me like a heavy weight. It explained so much: the way she treated me, the way she justified her cruelty. My suffering, in her eyes, was not just inevitable; it was necessary, a continuation of her story. But even as I began to understand her truth, I felt the sharp sting of its unfairness. I didn't deserve this. I didn't deserve to be a mirror for her pain.

That moment felt like a wave crashing over me, leaving me gasping for air. I knew, with a certainty I had never felt before, that I couldn't keep living under her roof. I couldn't keep subjecting myself to the abuse, the accusations, the endless cycle of anger and hurt. Something had to change.

For the first time, I started to see the twisted pattern beneath everything; how the pain she had endured had hardened her and made her incapable of showing love the way I so desperately needed. The tension between us had been building for years, until finally it reached its breaking point. Years of emotional neglect, harsh words, and physical abuse had worn me down. Despite my deep longing for her love and approval, I had learned to expect only cruelty in return.

But this day, this moment, was different. It wasn't just another fight. It wasn't just another wound. It was the final straw, the one that would force me to make a life-altering decision.

Reactions That Revealed the Hidden Tensions

As the sting of what had just happened settled into both my skin and my heart, I became aware of the older neighbor who lived in the yard. I hadn't seen her during the altercation, but it was clear she knew what had happened. Either she had witnessed everything, or she heard about it afterward. That moment is a little faint in my mind. When the dust began to settle, she spoke, her voice sharp and cutting. "Serve her right," she said, a faint smirk tugging at the corners of her lips.

I froze. Was she… happy? I didn't know how to respond or even how to feel in that moment. Shame and anger churned inside me, twisting together in a way that left me unsteady. And yet, here she was, almost reveling in what had just happened. Her words lingered, replaying in my mind like an unwelcome echo. It made me wonder: how much of my mother's behavior had seeped into the lives of the people around us, affecting them in ways I had never noticed before? Were they witnesses to her cruelty, too? Were they cheering because they understood? Or because they didn't?

Later that day, when my stepfather came home and learned about the incident, his reaction was even more unsettling. I braced myself for scolding, for anger, for some kind of consequence. Instead, he surprised me. His voice carried an air of calm satisfaction. "Serve her right," he said, echoing the neighbor's words, as if my retaliation had been some form of overdue justice. I stared at him, stunned. Was this how he really felt? His response cracked open something I had long suspected but hadn't dared to confront. The dynamics of our household, the simmering tension, the silence, the unspoken alliances were more complicated than I could have imagined. The responses of both my neighbor and my stepfather left me deeply unsettled. On one hand, their reactions gave me an odd sense of validation, as if my mother's behavior had not gone unnoticed, as if someone, somewhere, understood what I had endured. But on the other hand, it only deepened the confusion and pain already swirling inside me. I didn't want anyone to cheer for what had happened. This wasn't justice. I didn't feel victorious. I felt broken.

The Incident at Church

Not long after the confrontation at home, my mother and I went to church. Her face was still swollen, the evidence of what had happened impossible to ignore. Sitting stiffly in the pews, I felt the weight of the incident pressing between us, heavy and unspoken. I tried to focus on the service, on the hymns and the prayers, but my thoughts kept circling back to what had happened.

After the service ended, the pastor approached my mother, her concern evident. "What happened to your face?" she asked gently. My mother's response was quick, almost rehearsed. "A ball hit me," she said brushing it off. For a fleeting moment, I thought that might be enough to end the conversation. But then she hesitated and before I could even prepare myself, she told the truth: "My daughter thumped me in the face."

The room seemed to exhale all at once, the air shifting as her words landed. It was as if the walls themselves absorbed her story, leaving me exposed. No one knew the full truth: the biting argument, the frustration that had been simmering for years, the impossible tension that had finally erupted. They only knew that a daughter had struck her mother, and to them, that was all that mattered.

I stood there, struggling to steady my breathing, my chest tight with a toxic mix of shame, frustration, and helplessness. I could feel the weight of their unspoken judgments settling on my shoulders. In that moment, I understood how a single act, torn from its context, could overshadow everything else.

It didn't matter what had led to this or what I had endured. All they saw was the swollen face of a mother and the silent figure of her daughter.

The pastor often visited our home, so it wasn't unusual for her to come by afterward. But this time, everything felt different. Knowing that others were now aware of what had happened, even though they only had a fragment of the truth, made the strained dynamics of our relationship even harder to bear.

The Final Decision

That same week, our pastor and a few church members came to visit. My mother put on her best performance, slipping into the role of the victim with practiced ease. I wasn't allowed to speak. I moved around the yard in silence, as she painted me as the aggressor.

The visitors looked at me with pity, their disappointment evident in their eyes. Once, that look would have crushed me. But now, I felt nothing. I had made up my mind. I couldn't live here any longer. The pastor eventually turned her attention to me, addressing my mother with a quiet concern. "What's her plan? Where is she going?" she asked, her expression soft but searching.

My mother's tone changed instantly, becoming sweet and measured for their benefit. "I don't know where she's going," she said, shaking her head with feigned innocence. Her voice carried just the right mix of worry and resignation; a performance meant to shield her from blame. But as soon as their backs were turned, her mask slipped. Her face hardened, and her words came cold and clipped: "You better come out," she said. That moment solidified everything for me. Her tone was the final confirmation. The door to my childhood, and everything it represented, had closed for good. I had no choice but to leave.

Police Incident and Leaving at eighteen

Even after everything, when I apologized and tried to make peace, my mother never acknowledged her role in the abuse. She refused to take responsibility, choosing instead to deny the harm she had caused. Her silence, her refusal to own what she had done, cut deeper than any words could have.

Though my mother's abuse continued, I found an inner strength I hadn't known I possessed. I leaned on my church and the few supportive people in my life, including my Bible school principal, whose guidance became a lifeline. While I didn't have access to traditional therapy, the counsel I received during those moments of vulnerability gave me the clarity and resilience I needed to rebuild myself. Slowly but surely, I began to grow stronger, piece by piece.

Reflection

Reflecting on that moment, I now see the strength it took to apologize to my mother, even though she never acknowledged her role in the pain I endured. My apology wasn't about absolving her or dismissing the abuse. It was about freeing myself from the weight of resentment. Holding onto anger felt like carrying a burden I was never meant to bear.

As I walked away from that conversation, I found comfort in the words of Ephesians 4:31-32: "Let all bitterness and wrath and anger and clamor and slander be put away from you, along with all malice. Be kind to one another, tenderhearted, forgiving one another, as God in Christ forgave you." Forgiveness, I've learned, is not always about reconciliation or expecting change from others. It's about choosing peace for myself. In that moment, I wasn't seeking validation from my mother; I was seeking closure within my own heart. The experience also brought me back to Proverbs 4:23: "Above all else, guard your heart, for everything you do flows from it." By choosing to let go of bitterness, I was guarding my heart, protecting the future I was working so hard to build. It wasn't easy, but it was necessary. It was necessary for my healing and for my hope.

Faith, Truth, and Resilience

Looking back on this experience, I realize that truth has a way of grounding us, even when it feels like it's costing us everything. In moments when deception and favoritism made me feel unseen and unworthy, I held onto my faith as my guide. It wasn't easy. But now, I see how God placed people like my cadet officer in my life. They were small reminders that I wasn't alone. His simple act of kindness became a light in a moment of despair.

To anyone reading this who has felt the sting of injustice or the burden of always doing what's right while others seem to escape accountability, I want you to know this: your truth matters. It may not be recognized immediately. It may even invite criticism. But it is the foundation of your strength.

Faith, honesty, and perseverance have a way of shining light into the darkest situations. Hold onto them. They'll guide you through moments when you feel betrayed, overlooked, or unseen. Even when the odds seem stacked against you, trust that every step forward, rooted in truth and resilience, is building a brighter future.

Your journey matters. Your strength can inspire others to find their own.

CHAPTER 4

Leaving Home and the Silence That Followed

When I left my mother's house at eighteen, I carried more than just a bag of clothes and a small bundle of dreams. I carried an unspoken expectation: a fragile hope that my siblings and I would hold onto our bond. Despite the chaos that marked our shared childhood, there had been moments, rare but powerful, that felt like anchors in a world that often spun out of control. I believed those moments would ground us and keep us connected, even when life inevitably pulled us in separate directions.

At home, I had two younger siblings: a brother and a sister who still lived under my mother's roof. Then there was my older brother, who had left home years before I did. He was my half-brother, like me, and together we shared an unspoken connection as the "outside children," the ones born outside my mother's marriage. That connection felt special to me. It was something I longed to nurture, but the years and circumstances had created a distance between us that I struggled to bridge. As I stepped out into the world on my own, I hoped my siblings and I would find ways to keep in touch. Yet, the silence from all three of them was deafening.

At first, I tried to rationalize it, telling myself they were giving me the space to adjust to my new life. In time, I thought, they'll call or at least check in to say hello. But days turned into weeks, weeks turned into months, and the calls never came. It didn't take long for me to realize that the responsibility of keeping our bond alive rested squarely on my shoulders. If I wanted to maintain the connection, I had to be the one to act. I got their phone numbers, often through mutual acquaintances or by sheer chance, and I made the effort to call. When we spoke, I would ask how they were doing. I kept the conversations light and warm, deliberately avoiding topics that could stir tension or make them withdraw further. Despite my efforts, though, the interactions always felt one-sided. I reached out, but they never reached back.

I began to wonder if my mother had played a role in shaping this dynamic. She had always maintained a close connection with my siblings, especially those born of her marriage. Her bond with them seemed effortless, natural even, but it often left me feeling like an outsider. Had she said something to influence the distance between my siblings and me? I couldn't be sure, but the thought lingered, a quiet undercurrent in my mind.

Despite my frustrations, I couldn't bring myself to feel anger or resentment toward my siblings. I loved them deeply.

We had never experienced any major conflicts or fallings-out that could justify the distance between us. When I thought back to our childhood, I recalled the small but meaningful moments that defined our bond. My younger brother and I would sit together watching TV, laughing at silly movies. We'd play games, teasing each other and finding joy in the simplest things. My sister and I weren't as close, but there had always been a quiet respect and understanding between us. I held tightly to those memories as proof that what we shared had been real, even if it hadn't lasted into adulthood.

One day, I ran into my sister at a pizza shop where she worked. It was an unexpected encounter, one of the rare occasions when our paths crossed. She greeted me warmly, her kindness washing over me like a brief but comforting embrace. She even insisted on making me a pizza before I left. It was a small gesture, but it spoke volumes. In that moment, I was reminded that there was no animosity between us, no hidden grudges or unresolved conflicts. And yet, even after that meeting, she didn't pick up the phone to call me.

I thought about my older brother often. I missed him dearly and yearned to reconnect with him. But my mother never encouraged that bond. She had his contact information, but she didn't share it with me. I remember an incident shortly before I left home, during the turbulent time when my mother and I had our falling-out. My brother had planned to visit her, but she intercepted him in Kingston. She gave him her version of the story, painting me as the aggressor without acknowledging her role in our conflict.

Later, she told me his response: "Don't let me come and see her there." She used those words to justify keeping us apart. I couldn't help but wonder if her actions had planted a seed of division between us. Regardless of her motives, I was left with the sense that she had made little effort to bring us together. What hurt the most was that my brother never considered whether I had the means to leave, if I even had somewhere to go, or even tried to hear my side of the story. That hurt deeply, though I had no choice but to forgive him.

Over time, my efforts to maintain contact with my siblings grew less frequent. Each unanswered call or unreciprocated gesture chipped away at my resolve. It wasn't that I didn't care. I cared deeply. But it began to feel like I was shouting into a void, pouring my heart into connections that weren't being returned.

Eventually, I stopped trying. It wasn't out of spite or bitterness, but out of self-preservation. I couldn't keep carrying the weight of one-sided relationships. I told myself that if they wanted to reach out, they would. Still, the silence stung in ways I couldn't fully articulate.

To this day, I don't know why my siblings chose not to stay in touch. Perhaps their loyalty to my mother played a part, or maybe they simply didn't feel the same sense of obligation to our bond that I did. Whatever the reason, the unspoken distance between us remains. It is a quiet ache that continues to shape my understanding of family and connection.

The Unspoken Rift with My Brother

Growing up, my older half-brother and I shared a relationship that, while not perfect, was easy and comfortable. We got along well, and I often admired his quiet strength and independence. He seemed steady, someone I could look up to even when things around us felt uncertain. I remember washing his clothes for him when he lived at home. He would pay me for the effort, and at the time, it made me feel both useful and appreciated. Those were small moments of validation that meant more to me than he might have realized.

We rarely had disagreements, but there was one incident that stayed with me for years. My brother had finished using his Principles of Accounts book for school, and it was passed down to me. I was excited to have it and immediately began using it for my studies. But one day, my mother complained to him about something I had done. Or, more accurately, something she said I had done. I remember the confrontation vividly. My brother, standing beside my mother, turned to me with sharp disapproval in his voice. He threatened to take back the book. Hurt and feeling cornered, I handed it over without a word. I never used it again.

Despite that moment, I poured myself into the subject, determined to succeed without the book. When the time came, I graduated with distinction in Principles of Accounts. It was a quiet triumph, one that meant the world to me. A personal victory that spoke to my resilience and resolve.

Other than that incident, our relationship was free of major conflict. In fact, I can still recall a moment from our childhood that now feels almost funny in hindsight. My brother owned a stylish denim cap, a prized possession at the time. One day, I borrowed it to wear to school. To my dismay, the cap was stolen. When he came home and questioned us about who had taken it, I denied being the one, just like my other siblings. Years later, I finally confessed to him that I was the one who had borrowed the cap. To my relief, he laughed it off as an insignificant memory. But for me, the guilt lingered far longer than the cap itself ever did.

When he eventually left home, the closeness we had shared began to fade. At first, his absence didn't feel permanent. I assumed we would stay in touch. But as time passed, it became clear that he had chosen to disconnect. I searched for him on Facebook, hoping to bridge the gap, but my search only led to a frustrating interaction with someone else who shared his name.

Even though my mother and I attended the same church during that time, she never offered to help me reconnect with him. She could have easily given me his contact information, but she didn't. His absence left an unspoken void in my life. He was my brother, my family, yet he felt like a stranger. I often wondered what I had done wrong or if there was something I could have done differently to preserve our bond. Over time, I came to accept that the distance between us might never close, but the desire for connection never truly faded.

Years later, I learned that my brother had moved to St. Thomas, a parish not far from where I was living. After he'd settled in, I decided to take the first step toward reconciliation. I found out where he lived and started visiting him. Each visit brought a mix of emotions: relief at seeing him again, but also a lingering sadness for the years we had lost. I never told him about the conflicts I had with our mother or the reasons I left home. I didn't want to burden him with my pain or risk reopening old wounds. Instead, I focused on rebuilding our relationship in the present.

By then, he was living with his children's mother, and I respected his new life while trying to carve out a small space for myself in it. One memorable day, there was a family gathering, and for the first time ever my mother offered to pick me up as she was passing close by my house. I would ride with her and whoever else was in her vehicle to my brother's house. From there we would all ride together in my brother's vehicle to the event destination. It was a rare occasion when we were all in the same space, and I hoped it would bring us closer. However, during the ride when we were all together in my brother's vehicle, my mother made a pointed remark about me being stubborn or feisty. By then, I had learned to handle such comments with grace. I replied lightly, "Well, if I'm feisty, I must have gotten it from either my mother or my father." The tension dissolved with a chuckle, but the moment stayed with me as a reminder of how fragile family dynamics can be. Why would she say that well into my adult life is beyond me.

On another occasion, when I was preparing to attend university, I reached out to my brother for help with my tuition fees. He initially agreed to assist me, and I was grateful for his support. But when the time came, he stopped answering my calls. I was disappointed, but I didn't hold it against him. By then, I had grown accustomed to handling life's challenges on my own.

Reflecting on his absence and our limited interactions, I realize that his presence or lack thereof has shaped my understanding of family and connection. His withdrawal often felt like an unspoken rejection, but I've come to see it as more complex than that. Perhaps he was dealing with his own struggles, ones he couldn't share with me. Or perhaps he simply didn't know how to bridge the gap between us after so many years apart. What I do know is that I've always valued our bond, even when it felt one-sided. Rebuilding our relationship has been a slow and ongoing process, but each visit, each conversation, is a step forward. His absence taught me the importance of persistence and forgiveness, not just toward him, but also toward myself. Family ties are rarely perfect, but they are worth fighting for, even when the fight feels lonely.

One-Sided Connections: My Role in the Relationship

Relationships, I've come to realize, are often shaped by the effort we're willing to invest in them. For me, the effort wasn't a choice; it was a necessity, especially within my family. I was always the one initiating contact, the one trying to

101

mend the cracks, the one holding on to the belief that, no matter how strained or distant, family was worth the work. But over time, a disheartening pattern began to emerge: the effort was one-sided. I was always the one reaching, while the other side remained static.

My brother's absence was particularly painful. The distance between us after he left home wasn't just physical; it was emotional, a gap that seemed impossible to close. I yearned to maintain our bond, but I lacked the means to do so. I didn't have his phone number, his address, or even a reliable way to contact him. All I knew was that he had moved to another parish, a fact I learned not from him but through fragmented accounts from others. Unable to call or write, I turned to social media, specifically Facebook, as my last resort. Night after night, I would search for his name, scrolling through endless profiles and studying photographs with an almost desperate hope that one might lead me to him. Each attempt ended in frustration. The sheer number of dead ends was overwhelming, and with each fruitless search, I was left to confront a painful truth: I was searching for someone who wasn't searching for me.

This pattern extended beyond my brother to others in my family. Time and again, I found myself being the one to reach out, asking how they were, making the effort to keep our relationships intact. Yet their responses were often brief and impersonal, as if keeping in touch was a chore rather than a desire. Rarely, if ever, did anyone take the initiative to reach out to me first.

The emotional toll of this imbalance was undeniable. It forced me to question my place within the family and the worth of the connections I was working so hard to maintain. Was it worth the struggle if the effort wasn't mutual? Did my role as the initiator mean I cared more than they did? These questions weighed heavily on me, leaving me feeling overlooked and unimportant.

At times, the lack of reciprocity felt like a quiet form of rejection. It was as if my attempts to connect were met with indifference, a painful reminder that my efforts might mean more to me than they did to anyone else. That realization cut deep. But rather than give in to the pain, it strengthened my resolve. If they wouldn't reach out, I would. If they wouldn't bridge the divide, I would build the bridge myself.

Looking back, I've come to understand that my persistence wasn't just about them; it was about me. It was about my need to feel connected, to feel like I had a place where I truly belonged. The effort I put into these relationships, even when it felt like I was carrying the weight alone, was a reflection of my values and my belief in the enduring importance of family.

When I think back to my brother, I often wonder how he perceived our relationship. Did he see my efforts as overbearing, something unnecessary? Or did he believe that our bond was unshakable, capable of withstanding the silence without effort? I may never know the answers to these questions, but they linger, quietly shaping how I view family and my role within it.

In many ways, navigating the one-sided nature of these relationships taught me resilience. I learned to keep pushing forward, even in the face of rejection or indifference. It forced me to hold tightly to my values, even when they weren't acknowledged or mirrored. But just as importantly, these experiences taught me about boundaries: how to recognize when my constant efforts were depleting me instead of nourishing me, and when I needed to step back for my own emotional well-being.

Still, despite the heartache and imbalance, I have no regrets about the energy I invested in these relationships. Every phone call I initiated, every search I conducted, every attempt I made to bridge the divide was a testament to the love I had for my family and my unwavering desire to stay connected. The outcomes weren't always what I had hoped for, but there was meaning in the effort itself. Even when it felt futile, the effort was my way of expressing what mattered most to me: family.

Bittersweet Encounters

Reconnecting with my siblings, even briefly, always felt tenuous, like holding onto something delicate that could slip away at any moment. The time I ran into my sister at the pizza shop was one such fleeting moment, filled with emotions I didn't know how to fully process. She greeted me with a warmth that seemed genuine, her smile lighting up her face as soon as she saw me. It had been years since we'd last spoken, and the distance between us felt like a chasm. But for a brief moment, I sensed the faint echo of our old bond, the connection forged by years of shared memories.

She made me a pizza. It was such a small act, yet it carried a significance that would have seemed invisible to anyone else. As she handed it to me, it felt as though the weight of all those years of silence, separation, and unspoken words had been momentarily lifted.

We exchanged pleasantries, engaged in a quick, casual conversation. On the surface, it was a pleasant surprise to see her again. I was genuinely happy in that moment. But when

I reflected on it later, I couldn't help but question what lay beneath the encounter. Was her warmth a gesture of affection, or was it born from an unspoken sense of obligation, a quiet acknowledgment that, despite the years of distance, we were still family?

As I replayed our interaction in my mind, I realized that, despite the smiles and kind words, it lacked depth. It was polite, cordial, and kind, but it danced carefully around the years that had separated us. There was no acknowledgment of the silence that stretched between us, no mention of the unspoken pain of those lost years. It was as though the past had been erased in favor of this brief, surface-level connection. And just as quickly as the moment came, it was gone. After that chance meeting, we didn't see each other again for years, and the silence between us returned, unbroken.

This pattern of brief, almost coincidental reunions with my siblings repeated itself over the years. Each time, I found myself left with the same bittersweet aftertaste. The moments were warm, yes, but fleeting, never enough to bridge the gap that time and distance had carved between us. I often wondered if the distance we felt was a reflection of how much we'd changed as individuals or simply a consequence of all the years that had passed. In many ways, it felt as though we were strangers bound by shared history, thrown together by circumstances but never truly finding a way to reconnect in any meaningful sense.

I also ran into my younger brother at the passport office once. Like my sister, our exchange was brief and casual, almost superficial. It was as if we had agreed, without words, to avoid touching on anything too deep. We spoke as though time hadn't passed, but the unspoken truths lingered between us, heavy and undeniable. There was so much I wanted to say, so much I knew he wanted to express too, but the words simply wouldn't come. Instead, we skirted around what mattered, settling for neutral topics that felt inconsequential in the larger scheme of our lives. The polite small talk masked the reality of our strained relationship, and as we parted, I found myself feeling mix of emotions. I was happy to see my brother after so long, but there was also a lingering sense of longing, knowing that our time together was brief. The conversation was light, but beneath it, I wished for something deeper: more time, more connection.

As I walked away, I carried both the joy of seeing him and the weight of how fleeting it was. These interactions seemed to underline a growing distance, one that I didn't know how to bridge. Despite everything, I kept telling myself they were still my family, still my blood. But each encounter reminded me that our connection was slipping further away. I yearned for more than pleasantries. I wanted to understand the truth of what had fractured us, to talk about the past, to untangle the years of silence, and to rediscover the bond we had once shared. Yet, those opportunities never came, and I was left with the ache of longing for a connection that refused to surface.

These brief meetings left me ruminating on the nature of family, the complexities of relationships, and the emotional weight of maintaining them. Why was it so hard to break through the barriers that had formed? Was it because I hadn't tried hard enough, or was it the years of unspoken pain that had solidified into an unyielding wall? I often questioned if I was the only one who felt this way, if I was the only one still haunted by the ties that had once bound us. Did they, too, feel the sting of our fractured connection? These encounters were bittersweet, tinged with the warmth of familirity and the sting of estrangement. They reminded me of what we had been, of what we could have been if things had turned out differently.

There was affection between us, but it was cloaked in a politeness that acted as a shield, keeping us from digging deeper. Despite our shared history, we had become strangers in many ways, bound only by blood and the occasional chance meeting. Reflecting on these moments made me realize how deeply they shaped my sense of belonging or my lack of it. I desperately wanted to feel connected to my family, to know that I mattered to them. But each passing silence and each unresolved moment chipped away at that hope, leaving me questioning my place in their lives. Was I merely an afterthought? Someone they remembered only when circumstance threw us together?

These fleeting encounters didn't bring me the answers I craved. Instead, they magnified the ambiguity and the ache of lost connection. The love I felt for them and the faint glimmers of affection they showed were overshadowed by the weight of what remained unspoken. In the end, I was left grappling with the paradox of family: a bond that endured in theory but was fractured in practice, a connection maintained by blood yet stretched thin by years of silence and missed chances.

The Ache of Absence

There are moments in life when the absence of something carries a weight far heavier than its presence. This was undeniably true of the silence that lingered between me and my family, a silence so profound it felt almost physical. It settled in the pit of my stomach, an ache that seemed to expand during times when family should have gathered, times when love and togetherness should have filled the air.

Christmas was always the hardest.

While others gathered around their tables, sharing laughter and joy, I sat alone. The emptiness felt sharper on those nights, the contrast between my solitude and the warmth I imagined in other homes making the silence feel unbearable. A few kind-hearted friends, aware of my isolation, occasionally invited me into their celebrations. Their gestures offered temporary relief, like a balm for a wound, but the comfort never lasted long. Even surrounded by well-meaning people, I couldn't escape the hollow space inside me, the space carved out by the absence of my own family. The disconnect from my own flesh and blood remained, an ever-present shadow that grew heavier with time. No matter how much kindness I encountered, the pain of being estranged from the people who were supposed to know me best was unshakable.

Holidays in Solitude

Holidays like New Year's Day were no better. The world seemed to hum with togetherness, every celebration an echo of unity I couldn't feel. I spent those days in solitude, reflecting on the gaping hole where my family's presence should have been. At times, the loneliness felt as though it had seeped into my very bones, and I couldn't help but wonder if my own sense of worth was tied to this absence of connection. In those moments, depression loomed, hovering in the shadows, ready to take hold.

But somehow, my faith in God, paired with the quiet reassurance that I wasn't truly alone in this vast world, helped me through. I reminded myself that my journey was different, unique in its struggles and lessons. While others gathered with their families, and though it hurt, I understood that my path was entirely my own.

Lessons in Giving

I made it my responsibility to visit my mother occasionally during Christmas. One particular year stands out in my memory: I had saved my Christmas bonus for something I needed, something important. But instead, I gave it all to her, hoping it would express my love and appreciation. I gave her the money because I thought it was the right thing to do. I just wanted to show love, as I felt a sense of obligation to express my gratitude.

The gesture, while meaningful, left a mark. It taught me something I didn't fully understand at the time: I couldn't keep giving away what I needed to survive. Sacrificing my own well-being wasn't sustainable, and over the years, I learned to use what I had to take care of myself. Still, even as I made those changes, the rare invitations from my mother during the holidays didn't fully mend the ache of the quiet that lingered the rest of the time. My family remained emotionally scattered, distant in ways that even a shared holiday couldn't fix. The chasm between us was still there, ever present and unyielding.

Fleeting Moments of Connection

Those rare invitations to my mother's house were always bittersweet. Stepping into the family gathering sparked a brief flicker of connection, a fleeting sense of belonging. I'd sit in the living room, engage in light conversation, and soak in the energy of family. In those moments, I truly felt good. I felt like I was part of something, like I belonged. It felt like home. But the feeling never lasted.

Years of silence and distance had built a barrier too deep to be broken by a single meal or a few shared hours in the same room. For a time, I could lose myself in the warmth. But once the gathering ended, the illusion would fade. The lack of consistency, the absence of real connection, made it clear. As comforting as those moments were, they couldn't sustain the kind of home I longed for. The absence of consistency, of genuine connection, made these gatherings feel like a fragile illusion of family rather than the real thing. As much as I cherished those small windows of togetherness, they couldn't erase the deeper ache of what was missing.

112

The Longing for Family

Even though the silence weighed heavily on my heart, it didn't stop me from seeking connections with others. The absence of family didn't close me off to the possibility of finding belonging elsewhere. Still, it left me with questions I couldn't quite shake about my place in the world, my worth, and my value.

As much as I tried to build relationships beyond the bounds of blood, there was always a lingering sense of incompleteness. It felt as if a vital piece of my life was missing, a gap that no amount of connection could entirely fill. Even in the presence of love and friendship, the void created by the lack of a stable family remained.

Finding Strength in Silence

Over time, I learned to navigate this emotional landscape. I looked for family in unexpected places. These included friendships, shared moments, and the kindness of others. Each new relationship brought its own set of challenges. While I found solace in these bonds, there was always an ache for the family I had once hoped to rebuild. I had to reconcile that, though I could create a chosen family, the absence of my own flesh and blood would remain a silent, ever-present part of my story. The silence from my siblings lingered like a quiet ache, one I carried with me through every holiday, milestone, and moment when the presence of family would have meant everything. Though I found comfort in the love of friends and those who became like family, the void was undeniable. Still, I learned to live with it and accept it as part of my journey. I realized that as much as I longed for connection, I had to become my own source of strength and my own pillar of support. Looking back, I came to understand that the weight of silence wasn't just about the absence of others it was also about the absence I felt within myself. That silence forced me to look inward, to ask the questions I had avoided for so long: Who am I? What do I mean to others?

It was during this time of introspection that I discovered the depth of my resilience. I came to see the quiet strength that allowed me to carry on, even when loneliness threatened to overwhelm me. In the end, the silence that once felt unbearable became something I could live with. It was never easy. The holidays still felt incomplete, but I came to understand that my identity didn't need to hinge on the presence or absence of others. My journey, shaped by solitude and introspection, taught me to find family in the most unexpected places and to embrace the person I had become along the way.

Finding Family in Unexpected Places: The Church as a Lifeline

At every stage of my journey, the church stood as a steady source of community and comfort. It wasn't just a place for worship; it became a refuge where I found a sense of belonging that I had long been missing. Within its walls, I met friends who bridged the gaps left by the absence of my family.

These friendships often extended far beyond Sunday services. Some friends invited me into their homes, where we shared meals and celebrated milestones together. Their kindness and companionship filled spaces in my heart that I thought would remain empty forever. Through them, I learned that family could exist in forms I hadn't expected, and that love wasn't always bound by blood.

University Connections

When I started university, I formed a handful of meaningful friendships that brought a new sense of richness to my life. I had never been someone who needed a large circle of close friends, but the few I had meant everything to me. One friend in particular, stood out. We shared a deep connection, often visiting each other's homes and supporting one another through life's inevitable ups and downs.

These gestures, though simple, reminded me that family isn't solely defined by blood. Family can also be found in those who choose to stand by you, offering love and support without obligation.

Church Friendships Beyond the Pews

Friendships from church remained a vital part of my life, offering a sense of connection that I deeply cherished. Both the male and female friends I met there became trusted, long-term companions. Together, we shared outings, meaningful conversations, and occasional visits to one another's homes.

These moments of connection felt like brief yet profound glimpses of the familial bonds I had always longed for. They created spaces filled with warmth and acceptance, places where I felt truly seen and valued.

A Mentor's Kindness

One of the most impactful relationships I formed was with my Bible school principal. She often invited me into her home for sleepovers, where I helped her organize books, worked on her computer and taught her how to navigate different apps and programs. Sometimes I simply spent time keeping her company. Her kindness and generosity in sharing her time and space gave me a sense of belonging that I had long been missing. She became more than just a mentor;

she felt like family.

Redefining Family

These friendships weren't just casual; they were life-lines. In the absence of the closeness I longed for from my biological family, these relationships became vital reminders that love, support, and understanding could come from unexpected places. Each one taught me that family isn't defined solely by shared bloodlines; it's built on shared experiences, mutual care, and the willingness to open one's heart and home to another.

Healing and Acceptance: Reflection on What I Have Learned

In the quiet space between absence and connection, I discovered some of my most profound lessons. The distance I once felt from my family forced me to confront my own emotional needs and the void they left behind. I came to understand that healing isn't always about seeking others to fill that emptiness; sometimes, it's about finding peace within yourself. By accepting the silence instead of resisting it, I uncovered a strength I didn't know I possessed. I realized that my identity wasn't solely rooted in my family or my past; it was shaped by the choices I made to move forward and redefine myself.

Forgiveness and Understanding in My Journey

Forgiveness became a vital part of my healing journey. There were moments when I resented the distance, the silence, and the lack of communication. But with time, I realized that forgiveness wasn't about excusing the hurt; it was about freeing myself from the weight of carrying that pain. Recognizing my family's limitations allowed me to accept that each of us had our own battles to face. In doing so, I was able to release the anger that had taken root in my heart. I came to understand that forgiving doesn't mean forgetting; it means choosing peace over pain and embracing healing instead of holding on to resentment.

Building My Own Life Outside of These Relationships

As I embraced healing and forgiveness, I began to focus on building a life beyond the fractured dynamics of my family. I shifted my attention to my own growth, the friendships I had nurtured, and the opportunities that shaped the person I aspired to become. It became a process of reclaiming my sense of worth, not through the approval or recognition of others, but through my own belief in myself. I created a life rooted in faith, meaningful connections, and self-respect. Over time, I came to understand that the most important relationships I could cultivate were the ones I had with God and with myself.

Encouragement for Others

To anyone who has experienced the ache of disconnection, I want you to know this: you are not alone. I understand the void left by the absence of familiar bonds, but I also want to assure you that healing is possible. It's not a quick fix or an easy road; it's a journey that begins with acceptance and unfolds over time. The path to healing may feel long and difficult, but take heart: growth often emerges from adversity, and the strength to overcome already lies within you.

As the Bible reminds us in Isaiah 41:10, "So do not fear, for I am with you; do not be dismayed, for I am your God. I will strengthen you and help you; I will uphold you with my righteous right hand."

CHAPTER 5

Breaking Free

Redefining myself and my future: Trusting My Path

As I stepped into adulthood, I found myself navigating the complexities of a life shaped by fractured relationships, particularly my mother. From an early age, I learned to lean on my faith in God, trusting that He was guiding my steps, even when the path ahead felt uncertain. I wasn't consumed with meeting my mother's expectation or trying to prove my worth to someone who has never given me the indication that she saw my potential. Instead, I drew strength from the belief that my purpose was far greater than the challenges I faced. This faith empowered me to rise above my circumstances, shifting my focus away from the limited view she held of me and towards fulfilling the unique calling I felt God had placed on my life. My journey became one of walking in alignment with the destiny I believed He had prepared for me, firmly anchored in faith and trust.

Faith Over Fear

There was never a moment when I feared failure. I did not see challenges as roadblocks but as stepping stones for growth and transformation. My faith in the promises of God was steady. I trusted that He would guide my steps and make a way for me. I kept my eyes fixed on the truth I carried deep within: God had a purpose for my life. My role was to walk in faith and obedience to fulfill it. As I moved through life, I came to realize that success was not measured by worldly standards, but by aligning my actions with my values, my faith, and the vision God had placed in my heart. This perspective brought me a profound sense of clarity and freedom. That same faith that steadied me in hardship began to shift how I viewed success itself.

Redefining Success

Over time, I began to see that success was not a one-size-fits-all concept. It was not about chasing accolades, titles, or external recognition, but about living a life that truly reflected my faith and values. I came to understand that success was not about comparison. It was not about trying to prove that I would make it in life by someone else's standards. It was about staying true to what I believed and finding peace in a purpose that honored God. Embracing this understanding was far from easy. There were moments of doubt when I questioned my choices, and times of difficulty when the path forward seemed unclear. Yet, I learned to trust the unique path God had set before me. This path came with its own challenges, but it was mine. I found peace in knowing that walking in alignment with His will was the truest and most meaningful measure of success.

Embracing Internal Fulfillment

Through this process, I discovered that true fulfillment came from within. It was not something that could be found in the approval or validation of others, but something I had to cultivate through faith and self-reflection. I stopped seeking acceptance in places where it could never be found and began to rest in the knowledge that I was already known and loved by God. My worth was not determined by others' opinions, but by the unchanging truth of His love and purpose for my life. This realization was liberating. No longer driven by external pressures, I was able to focus on becoming the person God had called me to be. With this newfound freedom, I embraced my ambitions with peace and confidence, knowing they were aligned with His plan for my life.

Resilience Through Faith

These challenges taught me to trust God on a deeper level, to lean on His strength rather than my own limited understanding. Each obstacle became a testament to His steady faithfulness and a reminder that no matter how insurmountable the odds seemed, I had the capacity to rise above them. I came to understand that failure was not something to be feared. To me, it was an opportunity. A chance to grow stronger in both faith and resilience. With God's guidance, setbacks were not signs of inadequacy but moments of refinement that helped prepare me for what was ahead.

Freedom in Purpose

Redefining success allowed me to release the need for external approval and instead embrace a life anchored in faith. This shift brought a profound peace and confidence, knowing that each step I took was guided by God. My ambitions became expressions of my values and calling rather than a pursuit of recognition. Living fully aligned with God's plan was the ultimate freedom and the truest measure of success for me.

With that assurance, I could step into each moment with confidence, trusting that every step I took was guided by the Lord. My ambition was no longer tied to recognition or validation, but deeply rooted in honoring the purpose and potential God had placed within me.

Struggling to Define My Own Identity: Living in the Shadow of Rejection

For years, I lived in the shadow of someone else's rejection. My mother's rejection was not merely an action. It felt like a message, one that echoed relentlessly in my mind. You are not enough. That sentiment was not always spoken, but it was lived. She was not there at my high school graduation.

It was a parent whose children lived next door to my grandmother, and whose daughter was graduating the same year, who took my photograph that day. Not because I asked, but perhaps because they saw I had no one else. They gave the photo to me afterward. It was not my mother behind the camera. She was not there. And she was not there for any of the events that marked my achievements. No cadet meetings. No award ceremonies. No proud moments shared. The only time I remember her coming to my high school was because my sister had asked her to come, if my memory serves me right. Her absence was not a single moment. It was a pattern. A silence that shaped how I saw myself. I did not just feel rejected. I felt invisible. My sense of self-worth became tangled in the belief that I had to earn love, prove my value, and justify my existence through achievement.

Outwardly, I carried myself with confidence. But inwardly, my identity was fragile, chipped away by her absence and shaped by her silence. It was not until I left my mother's home that I began to untangle myself from that shadow and truly search for who I was meant to be. I do not recall my mother ever encouraging me to aspire toward anything in life. She never offered words of support or affirmation about my potential. I will never forget a particular conversation, one that cut deeply and stayed with me. She said,

Your sister is going to be able to navigate life better than you. Looking back, I do not believe a mother should ever say something like that to her child. I have come to understand that we all have different personalities and strengths. And just because my personality did not mirror someone else's did not make me less capable of thriving.

I always tried to walk in obedience to God, even when it meant letting go of certain opportunities. My sister's path was different, guided by different choices and values. But I realized I did not have to compete or measure myself by any–one else's journey. God's purpose for my life was unique, and that was enough. One child might be more outgoing and expressive, while another is quieter and introspective. But that does not mean one is destined for success while the other is doomed to fail. People navigate life in different ways, and no path is inherently superior to another.

Her words left me with a lingering sense of inadequacy, reinforcing the belief that I was not enough. But as I ventured further into adulthood, I began to understand a liberating truth: my worth was not defined by her doubts, her silence, or even her rejection. My value was intrinsic, rooted in something far greater than anyone's opinion of me.

Breaking Free from External Expectations

As I ventured further into adulthood, I began to recognize how much I had allowed my mother's opinions to shape my identity. There were times when it was difficult to see myself through God's eyes, as His creation, beautifully and wonderfully made, because the lingering shadow of rejection distorted that truth. Yet even in the midst of those struggles, I felt a quiet but persistent reminder: my worth was not contingent on anyone else's approval or acceptance. That reminder became the foundation of my journey to self-dis–covery. It was a path that required both courage and faith.

The Lens of Rejection

Breaking free from the image my mother had imposed on me wasn't easy. My mother's rejection wasn't just a personal wound. It was a lens through which I viewed the world. I internalized the idea that if I wasn't good enough for her, how could I ever be good enough for anyone else? That belief shaped how I related to others and how I moved through life, often playing it safe, making choices that felt less vulnerable to rejection. But in time, I came to see that her view didn't define me. I wasn't not a reflection of her rejection; I was a reflection of God's grace.

Embracing Imperfection

This understanding didn't arrive all at once. It unfolded gradually, often shadowed by doubt and hesitation. For every step I took toward reclaiming my identity, it seemed as though I would stumble two steps back whenever memories of rejection surfaced. Yet each step, whether forward or backward, played its part in strengthening me. Slowly, I began to view my imperfections not as defects to conceal but as evidence of a life fully lived, filled with lessons that had shaped me. I came to understand that not having all the answers was okay. Flaws didn't diminish my worth; they were a reminder of my humanity.

A Shift in Perspective

Embracing imperfection became a turning point in my journey. For years, I had chased an unattainable ideal, convinced that perfection was the pathway to acceptance. But as I reflected on my life, I began to recognize how God had worked through my flaws, transforming them into tools for resilience, patience, and compassion. My imperfections were not failures; they were stepping stones for growth and vivid reminders of God's grace.

Finding Freedom in Authenticity

The more I leaned into this truth, the more freedom I discovered. I didn't need to be perfect to be loved. I didn't need to conform to anyone else's expectations to feel worthy. This realization freed me from the relentless need to prove myself and opened the door to a life rooted in authenticity. My identity was not something to be earned or validated by others; it was a gift to be embraced and lived boldly.

Redefining Success and Identity

Living under the weight of rejection for so long had shown me that I could survive without anyone's approval. But mere survival wasn't enough; I wanted to thrive. I longed to build a life that reflected my true self: a person loved by God, brimming with potential and purpose. Gradually, I began to see myself not through the lens of rejection, but through the lens of redemption.

Moments of Reflection

This journey of self-discovery wasn't just about rede–fining how I saw myself; it was about breaking free from the weight of expectations placed on me. It meant learning to quiet the voices that told me I wasn't enough and replacing them with the truth: I was already complete in Christ. It was about finding peace in the certainty that my worth wasn't tied to what I accomplished, but to who I was in Him.

My Serious Demeanor

During this time, I was frequently told that I seemed overly serious. One day, during a meeting, my manager looked at me and asked, "Why are you always so serious? Smile." Caught off guard, I managed a small smile. She paused, then told me I had a beautiful smile and encouraged me to show it more often.

Unwelcome Calls at Work

Reflecting on those days at work, it wasn't just my boss's well-meaning suggestions to smile more that weighed on me, but it was the constant interruptions from my mother. After I moved out of her house and began living on my own, I quickly realized that leaving her home didn't mean leaving behind the challenges of our relationship. She often called me at work not for casual check-ins, but to bring up painful or humiliating topics. These interruptions always seemed timed to derail my day, chipping away at my sense of peace.

Even when I tried to explain how disruptive these calls were, she persisted. Each conversation left me emotionally drained, struggling to regain my focus and energy.

Finding Refuge in Church

During that difficult time, church became my sanctuary, a place where I could share my struggles with friends who offered understanding and encouragement. Yet even in that sacred space, solace came with complications. Somehow, word would reach my mother, igniting her anger and leading to more confrontational calls that disrupted my workday and drained my spirit.

A Kindness That Changed Everything

One day, the emotional toll became unbearable. At work, I broke down in tears, unable to hold it all inside. My boss noticed and informed the personnel manager, who responded with an unexpected act of kindness. Even though I wasn't part of her department, she invited me to join a departmental trip, covering my expenses and ensuring I had the food and care I needed. That trip became a brief but meaningful reprieve, a moment of peace in the midst of chaos.

Enduring with Honor

Despite the relentless nature of her calls, I never spoke harshly to my mother. If I truly were the feisty child, she often claimed I was, living on my own would have given me every opportunity to assert myself. It would have been easy to ignore her calls, let them go unanswered, or even tell her plainly, "Don't call me at work; I'll call you later." But I didn't.

Instead, I felt an unshakable sense of obligation to answer, no matter how disruptive or distressing the timing. Even into adulthood, long after I had left her home, I still picked up the phone, not out of fear or weakness, but out of humility. Despite the sting of her words, I held onto the belief that honoring her was the right thing to do. Each time I answered, I chose to endure, leaning on my faith and holding tightly to the quiet hope that grace would see me through.

At work, a friend once jokingly called me antisocial. Her words were meant in jest, but they struck a chord within me. I wasn't antisocial. I was reserved, shy, and perhaps socially anxious, a reflection of all I had been through. I thought back to my early years, even in basic school, when I would sit alone while the other children played. I often wondered if this stemmed from being given away to my grandmother as a baby. Perhaps I had missed that critical connection to my mother that every child craves. These reflections brought me clarity: my past had shaped my personality in ways I was only beginning to understand.

Healing Through Acceptance

Looking back, I can see how much I've grown. The journey to define my identity wasn't easy, but it was essential. It taught me to embrace who I am, imperfections and all, and to find strength in my vulnerability. I learned that rejection doesn't have to define you, but it can refine you. Most importantly, I discovered that true freedom comes when you stop striving to meet someone else's expectations and start living out your God-given purpose.

The Struggle to Find My Own Path

As I began releasing the weight of external pressures, I discovered a new sense of clarity. For the first time, I understood that only I held the power to define my worth and choose my path in life. The more I embraced this realization, the more liberated I felt. My journey was no longer about molding myself to fit someone else's vision of who I should be.

Instead, it became about listening to the quiet truths of my own heart, truths rooted in the faith and strength I had come to rely on within myself. Success and fulfillment, I realized, were not measured by the fleeting approval of others, but by staying aligned with my values and following the path that felt most authentic to me. It was about living for what resonated with my soul, not what others had envisioned for me.

Aspirations Beyond Expectations

When I was in high school, I had the chance to take the Army proficiency test as part of the cadet program. It was known for being a tough challenge. Many had to retake it multiple times, but I passed on my first attempt, if my memory serves me right. That achievement felt monumental at the time, signaling what I believed was the start of a future in the Army, a career I had envisioned for myself. But that dream came to an abrupt halt, not because of my abilities, but because of the church I attended with my mother.

The church's rules prohibited women from wearing pants, a restriction that created an impossible barrier to pursuing a military career. Despite earning my place through hard work and determination, I had to abandon this path. The church's expectations left no room for my personal ambitions unless they conformed to its rigid boundaries.

Missed Opportunities

During high school, I was also honored to be selected for the air proficiency program, which offered a select few cadets the rare opportunity to learn how to fly planes. It was a thrilling opportunity, one that many of my peers could only dream of. But like so many other moments in my life, this dream was cut short. Due to the challenges, I faced at home, which I've shared in earlier chapters, I didn't meet the academic requirements to qualify.

Even so, my cadet leaders believed in me. They saw my potential and encouraged me to continue pursuing the air proficiency course. Their faith in me was both uplifting and bittersweet. Without the required number of subjects, however, I couldn't move forward.

These missed opportunities felt like more than just personal failures. They became painful reminders that the path I longed to follow was so often blocked by circumstances beyond my control.

Breaking Through Boundaries

In the cadet program, I had an experience that stood out. Although I was naturally quiet and reserved, one of my cadet officers recognized leadership potential in me and made the unexpected decision to promote me directly to the rank of sergeant. This decision bypassed the usual progression through private, lance corporal, and corporal. I was the only cadet to achieve such a promotion, and while it was a remarkable accomplishment, it wasn't something I had actively pursued.

I had simply focused on doing my best, staying true to who I was and committing myself to hard work. If I remember correctly, they had me wear the ranks of Lance Corporal and Corporal for about a week or two, not because it was required, but to create the appearance of following protocol. Normally, ranks weren't meant to be skipped or held for such a short time, but the real intention was always to promote me quickly to Sergeant.

My officer's decision to elevate me so quickly was both surprising and humbling. It served as a reminder of my capabilities, even when I hadn't fully realized them myself. Taking on the responsibilities and trust that came with being a sergeant was both an honor and a challenge. It wasn't a role I had expected, but it was one I carried with pride.

The Struggle to Define My Identity

Looking back on these experiences, I now recognize how deeply they were shaped by the external voices and expectations I had let guide my life. The ambitions I chased, the dreams I nurtured, many of them weren't entirely my own. They were tangled with what others wanted for me, their hopes and visions woven into my decisions.

With time, and as I moved further into adulthood, I began to see the boundaries I had once accepted for myself. Slowly, I started to push against them. I discovered that while I could appreciate the opportunities handed to me, I didn't have to be defined by them. I realized I had the power to step outside the role's others had imagined for me. My identity didn't belong to the labels imposed on me, nor did I need to follow the neatly drawn paths dictated by society or my upbringing. I learned to redefine who I was, not out of rebellion, but in recognition of my own strength and potential.

The Journey Toward Self Determination

Embracing this newfound clarity wasn't easy. It required deep reflection and the courage to let go of the fear of disappointing others. For so long, I had allowed the voices around me to shape my choices, but I began to realize that those voices didn't hold the power to determine my future. Slowly, I came to understand that I could create my own path, one guided by my faith, shaped by my experiences, and aligned with my values.

No longer was it about living up to others' expectations or conforming to predefined molds. It became about building a life that truly reflected who I was, rather than who others thought I should be.

The influence of external voices had been undeniable, but as I turned inward, I discovered a guiding voice that was uniquely mine. By accepting this truth, I began to live with a sense of freedom, a life defined not by the limitation others had placed on me, but by the strength and clarity I had found within myself.

Building a Foundation of Self-Worth

The journey of reclaiming my self-worth was neither quick nor easy, but it was necessary. For years, I believed my value depended on my mother's approval. The pain of endlessly seeking her validation shaped my emotional world, embedding in me the belief that my worth was conditional, always fluctuating with her expectations, which often felt impossible to meet.

I convinced myself that if I could somehow prove I was enough, I would finally feel the love and acceptance I craved. But over time, through countless moments of disappointment and heartache, I began to understand a painful truth: no matter how much I tried, I could never reach the elusive standard that would make me "enough" in her eyes.

This pursuit, far from bringing me closer to the love I so desperately sought, left me feeling hollow. Instead of finding fulfillment, I was trapped in a cycle of striving and falling short, over and over again.

Realizing True Worth Comes from Within

Over time, I came to understand that true worth isn't something external, nor is it dependent on the approval or validation of others. It is a truth that originates deep within, a quiet strength cultivated through self-acceptance and a genuine connection with my own identity.

I began to see that my value wasn't determined by how others perceived me or by meeting their ever-shifting expectations. Instead, it was grounded in the unshakable truth that I am loved and valued by God, unchanged by circumstances or human judgment. This realization transformed my perspective, freeing me from the relentless pressure of seeking approval. I learned to embrace myself fully, trusting that I was enough just as I was, flaws and all. My worth was no longer tethered to anything external. It was intrinsic, steady, enduring, and wholly my own.

The Pain of Rejection and the Beginning of Healing

This shift didn't erase the pain of rejection, nor did it instantly heal the wounds that had formed over the years. The hurt of feeling unseen, misunderstood, and unworthy lingered. But for the first time, I could begin to heal. Slowly, I started to process the deep feelings of abandonment and neglect that I had carried for so long.

Instead of exhausting myself by trying to prove my worth to those who failed to see me for who I truly was, I turned my attention inward. I realized that the validation I had sought from others provided only fleeting relief, like a balm that quickly wore off. In contrast, self-acceptance became the solid, enduring foundation I needed, one upon which I could finally rebuild my sense of self.

Embracing Boundaries and Growth

As I ventured deeper into this process, I began to grasp the importance of boundaries. Reclaiming my self-worth required me to recognize when it was necessary to step back from relationships that were harmful or failed to honor the person I was becoming. It wasn't about severing ties entirely but about protecting the space I needed to grow into my authentic self.

For so many years, I had lived in reaction to the expectations of others, constantly contorting myself into a version of someone I was not. Now, I was learning to stand firm in my truth, embracing my flaws, my individuality, and my humanity.

Freedom in Self-Acceptance

This new way of thinking was liberating. For the first time in years, I could breathe freely, unburdened by the constant pressure to meet others' demands. The freedom I gained felt like the chains around my heart and mind had finally fallen away. I was no longer a prisoner to the belief that my worth depended on someone else's perception of me.

This realization didn't come overnight, nor did it erase the pain of rejection. Yet, with each passing day, I felt myself growing closer to a version of myself that was whole, a self no longer tethered to the need for external validation.

Reclaiming Worth through Faith

The journey of healing wasn't without its difficulties, but every step was worth it. I began to build a foundation of self-worth, a cornerstone upon which the rest of my life could stand. The road wasn't easy, but it was necessary for my growth.

For so much of my life, I had searched for something outside of myself, convinced that I could only feel whole if others saw me as enough. But as I reclaimed my worth, I came to a profound realization: I had always been enough. I was deserving of love and respect, not because of what I could do or who I could be for others, but simply because of who I was at my core.

The strength of reclaiming self-worth

The journey to reclaim my self-worth was both difficult and transformative. Over time, the process of emotional and inner healing opened the door to a more genuine version of myself. I began to see my imperfections not as flaws to hide but as unique facets of who I am. No longer striving for perfection, I found freedom in accepting my humanity, in stumbling, learning from my missteps, and growing through every moment.

The weight I had carried for so many years began to lift as I surrendered my need to control how others perceived me. I came to understand that my steps were ordered by the Lord and that He had already equipped me with everything I needed. I didn't have to prove myself to anyone; He had already declared me worthy.

Embracing Imperfection and Moving Forward

The process was anything but straightforward, and there were moments when I faltered. Yet, every time I fell, I found the strength to rise again, holding on to the truth that I was still deserving of love, still valuable, and still enough. My worth was not defined by my accomplishments or setbacks, nor by the standards of others. It was an intrinsic part of me, unchanging and untouchable.

The Cornerstone of Self-Worth

In the end, the foundation of self-worth I had created became an enduring source of strength. It gave me the resilience to confront life's challenges with the certainty that, no matter what unfolded, I was enough. This shift in mindset was profound, a transformation that paved the way for my future and gave me the courage to stand firmly in my truth. I had finally realized that my value wasn't something to strive for or prove; it had always been there, waiting for me to claim it.

Creating My Own Path Forward

By the time I reached my twenties, I had come to understand that my past did not have to dictate my future. I no longer needed to carry the burden of rejection and failure with me indefinitely. I started to explore new paths, embrace new opportunities, and build relationships that nurtured the growth of the person I had always aspired to become. It wasn't an easy journey. There were moments of doubt, times when old wounds resurfaced, but I learned to face those challenges with resilience. I knew that I had the power to shape my own story, and no one, not even my mother, could take that away from me.

Hope in the Midst of Struggle

Despite the pain I had endured, I discovered hope within the struggle. There were days when the weight of rejection and disappointment felt unbearable, as though it might crush me entirely. In those moments, it was difficult to imagine a future where the hurt wouldn't define me. But over time, I came to see that rejection wasn't the end of the road; it was a redirection toward something better, something greater. Each setback, every instance of feeling unworthy or unloved, held the possibility for growth. I had faced so much, but I wasn't broken. In truth, I was stronger than ever before. And with that newfound strength, I carved out a path that was completely and uniquely mine.

Finding Hope Through Faith

In the darkest moments of rejection and loneliness, I found solace and hope in the Word of God. His promises became my lifeline. When the world turned its back on me, God's love remained steadfast. I clung to scriptures that reminded me of His unchanging nature and His promise to never leave or forsake me. In my weakest moments, I sought refuge in the Bible, immersing myself in the stories of people who endured tremendous struggles yet emerged victorious.

David, rejected by his own family but chosen by God, became a beacon of hope for me. His story revealed how God used his pain and rejection to mold him into a mighty king. That understanding gave me the strength to persevere, knowing that even in my own struggles, God could create something meaningful and beautiful out of them.

Joseph's story resonated just as deeply. Betrayed and rejected by his brothers, sold into slavery, and wrongfully imprisoned, Joseph's journey was marked by unimaginable pain and isolation. Yet, despite every hardship, Joseph held fast to his faith. In the end, God transformed his suffering into a purpose far greater than anything he could have envisioned. His story reminded me that even when others turned away, God still had a plan for me, just as He had for Joseph.

The stories of those who endured great trials became a powerful source of strength for me. Through their lives, I saw how God's love could take even the most painful experiences and transform them into purpose. Their journeys inspired me to believe that my own struggles would one day lead to something greater in His perfect timing.

The Power of Church and Community

In addition to the Word of God, the messages and sermons I heard at church became a vital part of my journey. I remember sitting in the pews, listening to words that seemed to pierce through my pain, speaking directly to the depths of my heart. These messages reminded me that God had a purpose for my life, even if I couldn't understand it at the time.

The church community also became a source of strength, offering me support and encouragement when I needed it most. Their kindness, prayers, and unwavering belief in me lifted my spirits and reassured me that I wasn't alone. Through this spiritual foundation, I began to look beyond my immediate circumstances and trust in God's plan for my life, a plan that was unfolding even when I couldn't see the full picture.

Setbacks as Opportunities for Growth

As I reflected on my journey, I began to view setbacks not as obstacles, but as opportunities for growth. Each time I was knocked down, I found the strength to rise again. The pain of rejection became a catalyst for self-reflection, pushing me to confront my weaknesses and identify areas where I could grow. It wasn't always easy; there were moments when I wanted to give up, but each setback revealed something valuable about myself. I learned the power of resilience, of choosing to rise no matter how many times life tried to push me down. With every challenge, I grew stronger, developing the emotional and mental fortitude to face whatever lay ahead.

Building Resilience Through Struggle

The struggles I endured became the foundation of my resilience, a strength that would carry me through life. I didn't become immune to pain, but I learned how to face it. Struggle, in its own way, became a teacher, showing me that pain didn't have to define who I was. I could learn from it, grow through it, and emerge stronger on the other side. It was in these difficult moments that I came to understand my own strength. I realized I was far from fragile. I could withstand the storms life threw at me, and each challenge prepared me to face what lay ahead with grace and perseverance.

Forging a Unique Path with Confidence

With each lesson acquired, I began to carve a new path, one that was entirely my own. No longer held back by the limitations of my past or the voices that had once defined me, I embraced my individuality. I understood that my experiences had shaped me into the person I was becoming. I wasn't the person others had expected me to be; I was becoming the person I was always meant to be. In that realization, I found the confidence to move forward with purpose. Though my past was filled with pain and rejection, it became the solid foundation upon which I began to build my future. I learned that even in the darkest moments, there was always the potential for growth, and that growth held the key to unlocking my true potential.

A New Sense of Purpose

As I embraced this new path, a renewed sense of purpose filled me. I was no longer searching for validation from others or striving to meet their expectations. My focus shifted to my own journey, grounded in the belief that God had a plan for me and that I was capable of fulfilling it. The hope I discovered amid struggle gave me the courage to move forward, even when the path ahead seemed unclear. With each step I took, I knew I was drawing closer to the person I was always meant to be. The struggle had not defeated me; it had transformed me. And now, I was ready to face the future with hope, confidence, and determination.

New Beginnings: Pursuing Education and Career

As I moved through the healing process, I began to understand that my future was not shaped by my past. Years of pain and rejection had marked my journey, but I knew they did not have the power to define the course of my life. I made a deliberate choice to focus on building a future that would allow me to live the life I had always envisioned. One of the most significant steps in this new chapter was pursuing an education.

A Commitment to Growth

It became clear that breaking free from the limitations of my past meant investing in my education. For years, I had postponed furthering my studies due to financial constraints, but I knew it was time to take control of my future. This decision wasn't just a practical step; it was a commitment to myself, a promise that I would no longer let my past dictate the course of my life. Education became the key to unlocking opportunities I once thought were beyond my reach.

I started with a certificate in Computer Studies at a government institution, followed by a diploma in Biblical Studies at an apostolic institution. I also earned a certificate in Early Childhood Education. I remember being asked to write a reflection on where I saw myself in five years. I confidently wrote that I planned to attend university and continue my studies. Though it didn't happen within that timeframe, the seed had been planted, and I was determined to make it a reality. Starting

Starting University by Faith

When I began my journey toward a degree in Early Childhood Education, I had no money to cover my tuition. I stepped into this chapter of my life with nothing but faith, trusting that God would make a way. During that first week of classes, several students, including myself, were pulled out of the classroom for not having paid the required fees. It was disheartening, but I refused to let that stop me. I remained focused, prayed continuously, and clung to the belief that a path would unfold.

As time went on, provision came in ways I hadn't anticipated. From payday loans to small, yet impactful, acts of kindness, and an unyielding resolve, I managed to cover my tuition. Despite the constant worry that I might be asked to leave at any moment, I pressed on, relying on both God's faithfulness and my own determination. Each semester was a test of endurance, but I never missed an exam, and I never gave up.

Financing the Dream

During my university years, I grappled with intense financial hardships. I recall one particular day when, on my way to class, I stopped at a patty shop and unexpectedly encountered my mother and stepfather. Seizing the moment, I asked my mother if she could help with my tuition fees. Her response was disheartening; she told me she couldn't help. But before I left, she bought me a patty. Though it wasn't the financial support I desperately needed, that small gesture held its own significance. I held on to that bit of warmth and continued my journey to school.

While my parents couldn't provide financial support, others around me stepped in during critical moments. There was a time when I was so overwhelmed that I nearly decided not to return to school. The constant worry about how I'd find tuition fees weighed heavily on me. Just when I thought I couldn't go on, a close friend called, offering words of encouragement. Despite her own struggles, she gave me some money to help. Her selflessness reignited my resolve, and I returned to school with a renewed sense of purpose.

Another pivotal moment came when I posted on Facebook, asking for help with my tuition. One of my cousins responded generously, offering to assist. But this act of kindness triggered unexpected tension within the family. Some cousins, whom I had only recently met, began questioning my need for help. They pointed out my distant connection to a well-known singer and my brother, who was also in the music industry, assuming that those connections meant I didn't need financial assistance. The assumption that I was somehow well-off because of family ties added a layer of emotional complexity to my struggle.

Social Tensions and Support Challenges

The situation quickly escalated into a public argument on Facebook. Despite my attempts to clarify that I wasn't close to my singer cousin or my brother, the narrative had already taken on a life of its own. While I was in class with my phone turned off, I had no idea what was unfolding online. When I finally checked, I found that the post had spiraled out of control. The cousins who initially wanted to help were now clashing with those who opposed offering me assistance, and some began expressing their frustration at me for not stepping in sooner.

In the end, I received no help from that situation. The misunderstanding created so much conflict that any chance of support was lost. Although deeply disheartened, I made the decision to rise above the chaos. I reminded myself that my journey was never dependent on anyone else's approval or assistance. With God's guidance, I would find a way forward, as I always had.

Even though financial support from my parents never came, my grandmother, the woman who raised me and instilled in me the strength to endure, recognized my struggles. Despite no longer working, she found a way to help. She saved the small amounts of money she received from others and entrusted her niece to hold it until the end of the year. She then instructed her niece to give me the money to assist with my education.

When I learned about her quiet sacrifice, I was deeply moved by her determination to see me succeed. I didn't use the money for tuition; instead, I applied for a visa to the United States. By God's grace, I was granted the visa. When I arrived in America, I knew I had to find a way to pay my outstanding school fees. Though I was on a visitor's visa and not allowed to work, preaching engagements began opening up. Each time I received an honorarium for speaking, I sent it back home to help pay for my university fees. It was a humbling yet empowering journey. I was taking full responsibility for my education while relying on faith to guide me.

Academic Achievements

During my time at university, I discovered many opportunities to showcase both my abilities and resilience. One of the most significant highlights of my academic journey was a research article I wrote titled "Using Reflections to Explore Self-Study as an Early Childhood Mathematics Learner and an Emergent Teacher." This article was published in the Mico-University Journal of Education, Volume 4, in November 2011. Being among the few students whose work was selected for publication was a deeply validating moment. It served as a powerful reminder of how far I had come, especially in light of the numerous challenges I had faced along the way.

Beyond academics, I also found avenues to express my creativity. One of my most cherished projects was an art book that showcased a variety of artistic genres. It featured a wide array of works, from intricately crafted placemats to vibrant paintings and other creative pieces. I felt an immense sense of pride as I put the book together. Initially, I intended to keep it for myself, but my teacher recognized its uniqueness and asked to display it at the university. This recognition was deeply meaningful, offering yet another confirmation that my hard work and passion had not gone unnoticed.

A class on Personal Development also became a pivotal part of my growth. The course provided a safe space for me to confront the lingering pain of my past, release the heavy burden of unforgiveness, and embrace a journey toward healing. As part of this transformative process, I wrote a poem on forgiveness. This poem not only captured the essence of my personal growth but also symbolized my ability to let go of the pain others had caused me.

The Power of Forgiveness

The poem I wrote for the Personal Development class became a powerful declaration of my healing journey. It was more than just words; it was a reflection of the profound work God was doing in my heart. The poem, titled *"Get Past Your Past,"* reads:

You can get past your past no matter what it costs.
Your situation is not unsurpassed.
The devil is a liar; he wants you to die,
But lift up your head, for the limit is the sky.

Life presents struggles; at times, you have to fight,
But at the end of the tunnel, there will be a shining light.
Don't be disgruntled because of your plight.
To complement the day, there must be night.
What you've been through will work for your best,
If you view the disappointments each as a test.
The struggles you've endured will build your character.
Each and every one is a unique factor.

Life experiences teach the greatest lessons.
Disguised in the circumstances are the greatest blessings.
Your family and loved ones can hurt and cause you much
pain,
But if you refuse to forgive, your health will surely drain.

Stand up like a man and make the decision to forgive,
Because your purpose in life is not to die but to live.
Forgiveness is a process that takes place overtime,
but with great effort and determination you will be just fine.

This poem marked a significant moment in my journey of forgiveness. It wasn't the first time I had forgiven my mother. I had always tried to forgive her immediately, knowing that unforgiveness had no place in my desire to make heaven. But this poem reinforced that forgiveness in a deeper way, bringing a sense of peace and freedom that allowed me to fully embrace the life God intended for me.

Teaching Practice Triumph
Another significant moment in my journey occurred during my teaching practice. The head of the Early Childhood Department, a seasoned professional known for her high standards, was responsible for my evaluation. I was anxious but leaned on prayer, trusting God to guide me through the process. As the evaluation began, something remarkable unfolded: she became so absorbed in my lesson that she momentarily forgot she was there to assess me. The experience

left a lasting impression, and I was awarded an A+, which reflected my dedication and passion for teaching.

Defying the Odds

Through determination, faith, and hard work, I graduated with an upper second-class honors degree in Early Childhood Education. Every step of the journey was a testament to the resilience God had cultivated within me. I had overcome significant financial and emotional barriers, emerging stronger and more confident than ever before.

Education became more than just a means to an end; it became a symbol of my perseverance, a reflection of my ability to overcome challenges, dream boldly, and achieve what once seemed impossible. It reminded me that my past did not define me, and that my future rested securely in the hands of the Lord.

Personal Growth Through Work and Service

My personal growth during this time extended beyond academic achievements and was deeply influenced by the service I provided to children and my community. As part of my university journey, I taught early childhood students, which not only allowed me to contribute to their education but also helped me cultivate patience, creativity, and communication skills. Additionally, I organized career talks, inviting professionals like dentists and police officers to engage with the students. These experiences illuminated the value of service and the profound impact of sharing knowledge with others.

Coordinating these events instilled a strong sense of responsibility and reinforced my belief in the importance of community engagement. Through these opportunities to serve and lead, I not only enriched the lives of those around me but also deepened my understanding of my own capabilities and purpose.

Forgiveness: A Lifelong Journey

Forgiveness is not just an act; it is a process, a lifelong journey that demands patience, grace, and, most of all, an open heart. For much of my life, I carried the weight of unresolved pain, especially in my relationship with my mother. The hurt and rejection I felt left deep scars that I once believed were impossible to heal. But, over time, I began to understand that forgiveness was far more complex than a singular decision. It was an ongoing process, requiring me to confront my pain, acknowledge the wrongs, and ultimately choose to let go.

Forgiving my mother was one of the most transformative experiences of my life. I had to accept that her actions, though deeply hurtful, did not define who I was. Forgiveness didn't mean excusing her behavior or pretending the pain didn't exist. Instead, it meant freeing myself from the burden I had carried for so long.

Releasing the silent weight of pain and unanswered questions that held me captive allowed me to take steps forward in my life. It wasn't immediate. It took time, prayer, and a willingness to surrender my need for justice. I had to believe that true freedom lies in forgiveness.

Equally important in my journey was learning to forgive myself. As I reflect on those years, I now see that self-forgiveness was just as essential as forgiving others. It meant accepting my humanity, acknowledging my mistakes, and embracing my imperfections. Only when I extended grace to myself did I find lasting peace. In those moments, I understood the profound and transformative power of grace in my life.

What I've come to learn is that forgiveness rarely comes easily, nor is it a decision made just once. It's a choice we make over and over again. In that continual choice, I discovered freedom. It was a freedom from the weight of shame, silence and the need for answers. Forgiveness allowed me to heal, not only from the wounds caused by others but also from the ones I had inflicted upon myself.

This realization changed me. I began to see that forgiveness is not solely for the benefit of the person being forgiven. It is also for the one doing the forgiving. It is a gift we give ourselves. A gift that unlocks the door to peace, joy, and healing. By forgiving, I gave myself permission to move forward, to pursue my purpose unhindered by the past.

As I continue along this journey of forgiveness, I am reminded that it is not a destination but an evolving process. Each day brings new opportunities to forgive, to heal, to release old hurts, and to embrace the future with an open heart. Though the road may be long, the peace that comes from forgiveness is worth every step.

Building Resilience Through Faith

Life is full of challenges, and though we cannot avoid them, faith gives us the resilience to persevere. For me, faith has been the cornerstone of my strength, a foundation I leaned on during moments of profound pain, overwhelming hardship, and the internal struggle to forgive.

The Word of God has been more than a source of comfort. It has been my guiding light. In times of uncertainty, it reminded me that hope is not lost and that resilience is possible, even in the darkest moments. Through faith, I found not only the strength to endure but also the courage to believe in healing and renewal.

Strength Through Christ

One of the scriptures that has sustained me through life's challenges is Philippians 4:13: "I can do all things through Christ who strengthens me." This verse became the cornerstone of my resilience, a reminder that no obstacle was too great to face with God's strength.

Whether I was grappling with personal struggles within my family or the heavy burden of unforgiveness, I clung to the belief that Christ's power within me would see me through. At times, the challenges felt insurmountable. There were moments when the weight of it all seemed too much to bear, but I reminded myself that by leaning on God's strength, I could always find a way forward.

Trusting God's Plan: Romans 8:28

Another powerful scripture that gave me hope during my hardest moments is Romans 8:28: "And we know that all things work together for good to them that love God, to them who are the called according to his purpose." This verse reminded me that even in the midst of painful and confusing circumstances, God was working behind the scenes, aligning everything for my ultimate good.

I came to understand that while not all things are inherently good, they can work together for good when I place my trust in God. This truth became a source of courage, helping me endure difficult seasons with faith. It reassured me that God was using every struggle, every moment of pain, and even my journey of forgiveness to shape me into the person He had called me to be.

Forgiveness Through Faith

Forgiveness tested me in ways I didn't expect. The pain inflicted by others, especially my mother, often felt overwhelming, almost too heavy to carry. Yet, the Word of God reminded me that forgiveness is not just a command; it is a path to freedom.

Ephesians 4:32 says, "Be kind and compassionate to one another, forgiving each other, just as in Christ God forgave you." This scripture became my anchor, helping me find the strength to forgive, not because the other person deserved it, but because I had come to understand the magnitude of God's forgiveness toward me.

Through faith, I learned to release the anger I didn't always recognize. The kind that surfaced in irritability or sharpness when I felt provoked. Forgiveness became a deliberate choice, not driven by feelings but by surrender. In doing so, I discovered that forgiveness wasn't just about letting go of the pain others caused. It was about setting myself free from the chains of bitterness.

Trusting God's Timing

Building resilience through faith also means trusting in God's timing and His sovereignty. Isaiah 55:8–9 says, "For my thoughts are not your thoughts, neither are your ways my ways," declares the Lord. "As the heavens are higher than the earth, so are my ways higher than your ways and my thoughts than your thoughts."

There were moments when I wanted to rush the healing process or force circumstances to align with my own plans. But over time, I learned that true resilience isn't about hurrying through the storm; it's about standing firm in faith, even when the path forward isn't clear. Trusting in God's perfect timing taught me that He is always at work behind the scenes, orchestrating something far greater than I could imagine.

The Unseen Strength of Faith

The process of forgiveness and the strength to navigate life's challenges were made possible through my faith in God's promises. Hebrews 11:1 says, "Faith is the substance of things hoped for, the evidence of things not seen." It was in the unseen. In trusting God's promises and his unchanging character, I found the resilience to persevere.

Each time I faced a setback or felt overwhelmed by life's difficulties; I was reminded that faith in God's Word would sustain me. With every victory, no matter how small, my faith deepened, and my resilience grew stronger.

Conclusion: Resilience in Christ

Through faith, I found the courage to face life's struggles, to forgive, and to move forward, secure in the knowledge that I was never alone. The Word of God gave me the strength to persevere, the wisdom to forgive, and the hope to keep pressing on.

Resilience through faith is not merely about enduring hardship; it is about thriving in the midst of it. It is about embracing the assurance that, with God's help, no challenge is insurmountable.

Reflection: A Journey of Growth

As I look back on my journey, I am amazed by the growth and transformation I've experienced. There were moments when I felt completely overwhelmed by my circumstances, unsure of how I would make it through. Yet, with every challenge, I discovered strength, resilience, and hope. Who I am today is a testament to my faith, the lessons

I've learned, and the grace I've received along the way.

When I reflect on the hardships I endured, including the struggles with my family, the pain of separation, and the moments of self-doubt, I am reminded that every step, no matter how difficult, was essential to my growth. Those moments shaped me, taught me invaluable lessons, and drew me closer to understanding the purpose behind my journey. Looking back, I see how each trial became an opportunity for God to refine me and build my character.

One of the most significant lessons I've learned is the power of forgiveness. Forgiveness wasn't always easy, and there were times when holding on to pain felt more natural than letting go. But through faith, I came to understand that forgiveness is not just a gift for others; it is a gift to myself. It brought healing, freed me from the chains of resentment, and allowed me to move forward with peace in my heart.

Reflecting on my academic and personal achievements, such as publishing my research and receiving recognition for my art, reminds me of the importance of believing in my potential. Despite the obstacles I faced, I refused to let my circumstances define me. I pursued my education, worked diligently, and placed my trust in the plan God had for my life. It was a plan far greater than anything I could have imagined.

Encouragement to Others: You Are Not Alone

If there's one message, I hope readers take away from my story, it's this: no matter how overwhelming life may feel, you are never truly alone. I understand what it's like to face obstacles that seem insurmountable, to wrestle with feelings of inadequacy, and to wonder if things will ever improve. But I also know the power of resilience, the strength that faith provides, and the peace that comes from forgiveness.

To anyone struggling with family issues, loneliness, or the weight of unforgiveness, I want you to know that healing is possible. It may not happen overnight, and setbacks may test your resolve, but every step you take toward forgiveness and healing is a step toward freedom. You don't have to carry the burden of resentment any longer. Release it and give yourself the space to heal.

I encourage you to trust the process, even when the path ahead feels unclear. Believe that your challenges are not the conclusion of your story, but a vital part of the journey shaping you into the person you are meant to become. Hold on to your faith, trust in God's timing, and remember you are stronger than you think.

If you are pursuing something meaningful, whether it's education, a career, or personal growth, don't give up. I know how difficult the journey can be, but I also know that perseverance, hard work, and faith can lead to incredible victories. I've walked that path, and I am living proof that resilience, when fueled by faith, leads to triumph.

Final Words: A Life of Purpose

As I close this chapter of my life, I am reminded that my journey is far from over. Each day brings a new opportunity to grow, to learn, and to step closer to becoming the person God created me to be. I want to encourage you to keep pressing forward, no matter what obstacles you encounter. Remember, your story is still being written, and you have the power to shape it through your faith, your actions, and your resilience.

You are not defined by your past or your struggles. You are defined by your faith, your courage, and your ability to rise above life's challenges. Keep moving forward, trust in the process, and hold on to the belief that the best is yet to come.

CHAPTER 6

Navigating the Complex Ties of Family and Forgiveness

The Challenge of Family Expectations

When my mother asked me to give her my National Housing Trust (NHT) points, I felt a deep and familiar conflict rising within me. On the surface, it seemed like a simple request: just one family member helping another. But beneath that request were layers of expectations and assumptions. It also carried an unspoken dismissal of my own needs and aspirations. Those points were more than just numbers. They represented my opportunity to invest in my future, to create a home of my own. Yet here I was, being asked to give them up for her benefit, leaving myself empty-handed and vulnerable.

By this time, I had been living on my own, paying rent, and navigating the challenges of adulthood. My mother and sister had already made plans to move into a new house together, plans that did not include me. Yet, despite my exclusion, I was being asked to contribute though not in a way that acknowledged or supported my own goals.

The request wasn't for a joint effort, where pooling our resources would benefit all of us. Instead, she wanted me to sign over my points entirely, permanently surrendering a resource I might one day need. The weight of the decision pressed heavily on me. Refusing my mother was not something I took lightly. I had grown up being taught to respect her wishes, often at the expense of my own needs.

But this time it felt different. I could feel the tension between honoring her request and prioritizing my own needs. If I gave in, I would be sacrificing the dream I had worked so hard to achieve. It was the dream of purchasing my own home and establishing my independence.

When I gently but firmly told her no, her response stung. She asked, "So, you're going to buy house?" Her tone carried a sharp disbelief, as if the very idea of me owning a home was absurd. In that moment, I realized she didn't see me as someone capable of achieving such a milestone. Her question wasn't just an expression of surprise. It was a reflection of how little she believed in my potential. "Yes," I replied, holding my ground. I knew what I was capable of, even if she couldn't see it.

At the time, I hadn't yet obtained a visa or made significant strides toward my dream, but I was working diligently toward a better future. I had faith in my ability to succeed, and I wasn't about to let someone else's doubt dictate my path. Still, her reaction left me questioning my place in her life. It wasn't just about the points; it was about what the request symbolized. To me, it felt like another instance where my contributions and sacrifices were taken for granted. I was being asked to pour out what little I had, without any acknowledgment of my own struggles or aspirations. It wasn't the first time I had felt this way, and I knew it wouldn't be the last. As I reflected on the situation, I couldn't ignore the unequal dynamics that so often defined our family interactions.

My sister, who was living with my mother at the time, wasn't asked to make a similar sacrifice. Instead, they moved into the new house together, deepening their bond while I was left on the outskirts. Once again, I was confronted with the disparity I had grown up with, the persistent feeling that my needs and desires were always secondary.

This time, however, I chose to prioritize myself. Refusing my mother's request wasn't an act of rebellion or selfishness; it was an act of survival. I realized I couldn't continue to pour from an empty cup. Setting boundaries wasn't about shutting others out; it was about creating space to honor my own goals and dreams.

Saying no, in that moment, was my way of affirming that my life and aspirations held value, even if others failed to acknowledge them. That decision, though empowering, wasn't without its challenges. There were moments of doubt and guilt, but I found solace and clarity through prayer and reflection. I came to understand that my choice wasn't about rejecting my mother's needs. It was about protecting my ability to build a stable foundation for my own life. The Bible reminded me of the importance of stewardship and thoughtful planning for the future. As Proverbs 21:5 teaches, "The plans of the diligent lead surely to abundance, but everyone who is hasty comes only to poverty." That verse became an anchor for me, a reminder that safeguarding my goals was a step toward the abundance God had in store for me.

Looking back, I recognize that moment as a turning point in my life. It wasn't just about holding onto my NHT points; it was about something much deeper. It was about learning to advocate for myself and recognizing my worth in a way I hadn't before.

Setting boundaries wasn't an act of disrespect; it was an essential declaration of self-respect. The decision to stand firm shaped the course of my life in profound ways. It wasn't easy to assert myself, especially when it came to my mother, who always expected compliance. But prioritizing my future allowed me to take a significant step toward building the life I envisioned for myself. In doing so, I discovered a reservoir of strength within me that I hadn't fully acknowledged. Through this experience, I learned an important truth: sometimes, the people we love may not understand the vision God has placed in our hearts. But that doesn't mean we should abandon it. Our purpose and potential don't depend on others' approval or understanding. They come from God, who equips us with everything we need to succeed.

By trusting in His plan and staying true to myself, I was able to navigate that season of my life with both grace and determination. While it was painful at times, it ultimately brought me closer to the person I was meant to become.

The Moment of Confrontation: Seeking Answers.

After resolving the issue with my National Housing Trust points, I felt a deeper need to confront another chapter of my past, one I had forgiven but never fully understood. While I had made peace in my heart with much of the pain I endured, lingering questions remained. I decided it was time to address them, not out of anger or bitterness, but to seek closure. This time, it was about the man my mother had once claimed was my father. A man who had written me letters filled with unsettling and inappropriate words.

These letters weren't just words on paper they were evidence of manipulation and betrayal. This man had tried to convince me he was my father, when in reality, he was a predator. The content of those letters was a dark reminder of the emotional turmoil I had endured as a child. My decision to confront my mother wasn't driven by anger or resentment; I had long since forgiven her. Instead, I needed to understand why she allowed this falsehood to take root in my life. Why had she let this man's lie define a part of my identity?

When I finally decided to bring the letters to her, I approached cautiously but firmly. I handed them over, explaining exactly what they were: the manipulative words of a man who had preyed on my innocence. Then I asked the question that had haunted me for years: "Why did you tell me he was my father?" I needed to know how she could have allowed such a damaging untruth to shape my life.

Her response, while calm, offered no clarity. "He asked me to tell you that," she said, as though that explanation could undo the years of confusion and hurt I had carried. There was no apology, no acknowledgment of the emotional weight of her decision. I wanted more. I needed more. But her words left me feeling a deep sense of disappointment. This was her opportunity to provide truth, perhaps even to apologize, but instead, I was left with even more questions.

171

I then asked gently, choosing my words carefully to avoid conflict: How could you, as a Christian, allow a man who isn't even a Christian to convince you to tell me something that would affect me so deeply. As my mother, she was supposed to be my protector, the one person I could depend on for truth. Instead, she had allowed someone else's narrative to dictate a significant part of my life.

In that same conversation, I found the courage to ask another question I had carried for years: "Why did you abuse me?" My voice was steady, but beneath it was a quiet aching hope for honesty. Her response was immediate: a sharp denial. It was brief, cutting, and dismissive, as if the physical and emotional pain I remembered so vividly had never happened. She refused to acknowledge it, as though her denial could erase the scars.

Even though I didn't receive the answers I hoped for, the act of confronting her was powerful. This moment wasn't about changing her perspective or forcing her to admit her mistakes. It was about reclaiming my voice and standing in my truth. For years, I had carried those questions in silence. Finally voicing them was an act of liberation, a declaration that my experiences mattered, even if she couldn't validate them.

When I walked away from that conversation, my emotions were mixed. Disappointment lingered, along with a sense of incompleteness. I had forgiven her long ago, but I now understood she wouldn't offer the closure I wanted. And yet, there was a quiet strength in knowing I had done what I needed to do for myself. Closure, I realized, doesn't always come from someone else. Sometimes, it is found in the act of confronting the past and choosing to let go of the pain it holds.

Denying the Truth: A Mother's Denial

As I walked away from that conversation with my mother, a heavy feeling of incompleteness followed me. I had hoped for closure, but instead, I was left with more questions than answers. The questions I asked about the man who falsely claimed to be my father, and the abuse I endured under her roof, were met with evasions and denials. I had forgiven her long ago, but part of me still longed for something deeper, an acknowledgment of my pain. It was that universal longing to be seen, to be heard, especially by the one person who was supposed to love and protect me unconditionally.

When I confronted her, this time about the emotional and physical abuse I had suffered as a child. I knew my truth; I had lived it. Yet her refusal to acknowledge it cut deeply. In her eyes, I wasn't a victim of neglect or mistreatment; I was simply "feisty" and "stubborn." She dismissed my reality entirely, reducing years of pain, frustration, and sorrow to a matter of attitude. To her, I wasn't a child who had needed care, love, and protection. Instead, I was a "problem" to be managed, a child who could simply be disciplined into submission.

When I tried to make her see my pain, it felt like speaking to a wall. She either couldn't or wouldn't hear me. The years of broken trust, the countless nights I cried myself to sleep, the quiet moments when I sat in silence hoping for a word of comfort, seemed invisible to her. I had hoped for an apology, an acknowledgment that her words, actions, and neglect had hurt me. But instead, I was met with accusations of being "difficult," as though my suffering was a product of my own shortcomings and not the result of years of mistreatment.

I had forgiven her. I truly had. But forgiveness doesn't erase the yearning for validation. No matter how much I told myself I had moved on, there was still this deep, aching desire for her to finally see me, not as the "stubborn" or "difficult" daughter she remembered, but as a person who had been deeply hurt. To her, my pain was an inconvenience. Acknowledging it would mean admitting that she had failed me, that she had hurt me in ways that left lasting scars. Denial was easier for her. Denying my truth was easier than confronting the weight of her choices and their consequences.

Despite everything, I couldn't shake the yearning for her validation. I needed to know I wasn't crazy, that the pain I endured wasn't imagined. Every person, regardless of their history, craves that connection with their mother, their acknowledgment, their understanding, their love. Even though I had forgiven her and worked hard to release the hurt, the absence of her recognition still felt like an unfinished chapter in my story. It lingered like a book left open to a page that I could never turn. In the silence that followed our conversation, I came to a difficult realization: I could no longer depend on her to give me the validation I sought. I had to accept that I might never receive it. Her inability to acknowledge her role in my pain wasn't just about me; it reflected her own struggles, her own guilt, and her refusal to confront the truth of her past. While that truth was painful, I also knew I had the power to shape my own healing.

I didn't need her acknowledgment to heal. Closure, I realized, would have to come from within me. But that understanding didn't make the process any easier. Her denial became a burden I could no longer carry. Her refusal to confront the truth about the abuse I endured was a reflection of her, not of me. It wasn't just my story. It was hers too, and I couldn't force her to face what she wasn't ready to see. And while forgiveness had freed me from bitterness, I also realized that forgiveness didn't require me to accept her version of events. The truth I carried was mine alone, not as a weight but as a reflection of my resilience and strength.

The Gifts that Stung: Feeling Undervalued

During that same period, another moment occurred that deepened my sense of neglect and worthlessness. It came unexpectedly, in the form of a simple gesture. One that carried far more weight than it should have. My mother handed me a pair of shoes. At first glance, they seemed ordinary: a little worn, slightly scuffed, but still serviceable. It wasn't the shoes themselves that struck me. It was the way they were presented, the context in which they were given, and, most importantly, the way they made me feel.

"They were your sister's," she said, explaining that my sister was about to throw them away. It was as if the fact that they were salvaged from the garbage should make me grateful to receive them. The implication behind her words hit me harder than the gesture itself: Here, take this. It's better than nothing. In that moment, I couldn't shake the feeling that I was being handed something no one else wanted, that I was somehow less deserving of anything new or untouched. It wasn't about the shoes themselves it was the underlying message they carried. Once again, I was made to feel like a second thought, expected to accept whatever was left over, as though that's all I was worth. I had worked so hard in my life, fought so fiercely to prove my worth, to create a better future for myself.

Yet, in that moment, it felt as though none of it mattered. Instead of being recognized for how far I had come, I was being handed someone else's cast-offs, a clear reminder that my needs and desires were still seen as secondary. The shoes weren't the problem. What hurt was the unspoken message: that I wasn't worthy of anything more than the scraps others didn't want.

As I stood there holding the shoes, I couldn't help but reflect on how that moment seemed to encapsulate my relationship with my mother. For years, I had tried to prove that I was capable of more, that I was worthy of more than just the leftovers. Yet here I was, once again being handed something discarded as unimportant. It felt as though she had forgotten everything I had overcome, the sacrifices I had made, and the dreams I had worked so hard to achieve. To her, I was still the child expected to make do with what was left. Still the person who should be satisfied with whatever was offered, regardless of how little thought or care went into it.

The shoes, I realized, weren't just an object. They were a symbol of how I had been treated for so long, a reminder that I was always an afterthought, always expected to accept what others didn't want. Even now, after all these years, it felt as though my mother still saw me as someone unworthy of effort, someone who didn't deserve to have her needs met in the same way others did. No matter how far I had come, no matter how hard I had worked to create a life of my own, I was still being made to feel as though I didn't deserve the new, the valuable, the things that were given with love and intention. It wasn't the shoes themselves. It was what they represented. They made me feel like I was still that child, overlooked and undervalued, still being asked to take what others had cast aside.

That moment forced me to confront an undeniable truth: no matter how much I had forgiven, no matter how much I had worked to let go of the past, these old wounds still had the power to cut deep. It wasn't about the shoes. It was about the implication behind them that I wasn't worth more, that my worth was measured by what others had deemed unworthy. I had spent my life fighting to prove that I was more than what had been handed to me, yet here I was, once again feeling like I was being judged by the same dismissive standard.

It wasn't just the act of receiving something rejected by someone else. It was the lingering feeling that I didn't deserve better that my dreams, my desires, and my hopes for a better future were somehow irrelevant. The shoes were a tangible reminder of all the times I had been made to feel invisible, all the times my needs had been ignored or dismissed. They weren't just old shoes. They were a symbol of what I had been given and more painfully, of what I had been denied.

And yet, as I held those shoes in my hands, a quiet realization began to take shape. I was worth more than that. I had always been worth more than that. My worth wasn't defined by what others were willing to give me or by how they treated me. It wasn't determined by their ability or inability, to see me. I had built something greater for myself, and I would continue to do so. But in that small, painful moment, I was reminded once again of the ways I had been undervalued, unseen, and overlooked. It was as if, no matter how far I had come, I was still haunted by the feeling that I wasn't enough.

The shoes were merely a symbol of something deeper: the message they carried. A message I had received countless times throughout my life. A message that told me I was still the child who had to accept whatever others didn't want, the one expected to make do with what was left. And in that moment, I understood something I hadn't fully grasped before: no matter how much I had grown, no matter how much I had forgiven, those old feelings of inadequacy would linger until I truly claimed the worth, I knew I had. My healing wouldn't come from her acknowledgment; it had to come from me.

The Weight of Expectations: Less Than and Yet More

During one of my rare visits to my mother's home, I learned that my sister was in America. I carried with me a quiet hope. Perhaps, just perhaps, things might begin to improve between us. I yearned for a normal relationship, one where the past didn't hang over us like a shadow. She had never apologized for what she had done, but I had chosen to let it go. I decided to focus on the future, trying to build something meaningful from the little we still shared.

I remember one particular moment when she asked me about a personal matter, and I explained everything though not in full detail. But enough to give her an understanding of what had transpired. I took responsibility, even though I knew that if I had gone into specifics, she would have realized I wasn't entirely at fault. In that moment, I approached the conversation as though we were simply a mother and daughter sharing a meaningful exchange. I allowed myself to be vulnerable, thinking and hoping that my openness might encourage her to see that I was ready for something better between us. Maybe she would meet me halfway. Maybe this was the beginning of the connection I had always wanted. I didn't realize then that this moment of vulnerability would later be shared with my brother to paint me in a negative light.

On one of those visits, I found myself sitting in her living room. The air, for once, felt lighter, and my younger brother and sister were there too. We laughed, talked, and even took family pictures together. It felt like a moment of connection, like the gap that had always existed between us was finally beginning to close.

For the first time in years, I let myself believe that this could be the start of something different, something better. The warmth I felt was fleeting, but for that brief moment, I held onto it tightly. I wanted to believe that the years of pain and distance were behind us, that we were finally turning a corner. But that fleeting warmth didn't last. Later, when I asked my mother for a simple favor, the fragile hope I had been holding onto began to crack. Her unexpected refusal wasn't just disappointing, it was revealing. I had thought that maybe we were beginning to understand each other, that our bond was growing stronger, but her response brought me back to reality. The warmth I had felt before wasn't grounded in anything real. It was an illusion, a fragile facade that dissolved as quickly as it had appeared. Once again, I was left to confront the depth of our disconnection.

In that moment, I understood something I hadn't been ready to see before: despite the surface-level interactions and occasional moments of apparent closeness, there was no true foundation between us. I had hoped for change, for a shift in our relationship that would allow us to heal, to move forward together. But the truth was that my hope had been built on a fragile assumption that her actions would one day match her words, that the image of a loving mother I carried in my heart could somehow become real. Instead, what I found was the unrelenting weight of expectation. The expectation that I would always be the one to bend, to give, to forgive. As much as I wanted to believe in the moments that felt like steps toward healing, I realized they were just moments, brief flashes that couldn't sustain a deeper connection. Beneath them, nothing had really changed. I was still left navigating our relationship on my own, still carrying the weight of feelings I didn't know how to set down: inadequacy, frustration, the quiet ache of never quite measuring up to whatever unspoken standard she had for me.

No matter how much I tried, I couldn't shake the feeling that I was always being judged, always being measured against a yardstick I could never reach. And as much as I had hoped for things to improve, I realized that I could no longer keep trying to measure my worth by her standards. I had learned to survive without her validation, to find strength within myself. But the weight of those expectations still lingered, like a ghost that refused to let me go.

Though I had forgiven her, the pain of feeling undervalued and unseen remained. And with each passing interaction, the hope I once had for a deeper connection with her felt increasingly out of reach.

Forgiveness: A Choice, Not an Obligation

Forgiveness was never an easy choice, but it was one I was determined to make. The Scripture declares, "If you forgive not men their trespasses, neither will your Heavenly Father forgive you," and I knew that unforgiveness could hinder my journey to heaven, a place I deeply longed to be. Yet, forgiveness wasn't something I offered lightly, nor was it something I owed her. I had been hurt in ways far beyond what words could express, but even so, I decided that forgiveness was possible.

I chose to forgive her not because she deserved it, but because I needed it. Resentment and bitterness were poisons I refused to entertain. I came to understand that those feelings would have bound me to the past, weighing me down and keeping me from living fully.

Despite the pain she caused (the neglect, the emotional and physical abuse), I realized forgiveness wasn't about her; it was about me. It was a choice I had to make for my own peace, my own healing, and my own future.

Healing and moving forward required me to release every weight of unforgiveness. Forgiveness, I learned, wasn't about excusing her actions or erasing the past but it was about finding freedom. It was about choosing peace over pain and reclaiming my life from the grip of the past.

It took time to come to that conclusion. There were moments when it felt easier to hold on to my anger, to stay bitter because it felt justified. My mother had let me down in so many ways, and she hadn't apologized for it. She hadn't even acknowledged the depth of the pain she caused. But forgiveness was never about waiting for an apology that might never come, nor was it about her changing. Forgiveness was about me finding the strength to let go of the power her actions had over me.

The emotional weight of forgiveness was heavy, but with every decision to forgive, my heart grew lighter. It wasn't a one-time choice but an ongoing process. Each time the past resurfaced, I had to decide again to forgive. Some days, I felt like I had made progress; other days, it felt like I was back at square one, dragged into the pain all over again. Forgiveness wasn't linear, it ebbed and flowed. But through the setbacks, I kept choosing to forgive. I kept choosing to release the hold anger had on me.

In forgiving her, I wasn't saying that what happened was okay. It wasn't okay. It wasn't okay that I was mistreated, neglected, or that I suffered emotionally and physically in a place that should have been safe and loving. Forgiveness didn't excuse or justify her actions. It was about acknowledging that I could no longer let her actions define my life. I couldn't control her behavior, but I could control how I responded to it. I had the power to release the bitterness and hurt, and I chose to use that power for my healing. Forgiveness didn't change the past. It didn't erase the years of pain or make everything right. It didn't mean I forgot what had happened or that I was willing to expose myself to further harm. But forgiveness freed me from the chains of resentment. I didn't have to carry the weight of the past with me anymore. I could move forward not with a heart full of bitterness, but with a heart full of peace.

I came to understand that forgiveness wasn't a single decision; it was a lifelong process. There would always be moments when the past tried to creep back in, when memories of what I endured threatened to overwhelm me. But each time, I could choose to forgive again. Each time, I had the opportunity to choose freedom over bondage and peace over pain. Forgiving my mother didn't mean that what happened was acceptable, nor did it mean our relationship was suddenly healed. It didn't mean forgetting or pretending that nothing had ever happened. What it did mean was that I was no longer allowing her actions to control my future. I refused to let the past define me anymore. Instead, I chose to move forward, to heal, and to live a life that was no longer held captive by anger and resentment.

Forgiveness, I realized, wasn't a gift I was giving her, it was a gift I was giving myself. It was the key that unlocked the door to my healing and the path to a future where I could live with peace, even if that peace didn't come from reconciliation. I wasn't waiting for her to change or apologize. I had already made the choice to let go of the past and create a life free from the chains of resentment.

Moving Toward Closure

When I confronted my mother with the truth of my past, I was met with a painful realization: closure might never come from her. Despite all my efforts, all the years I spent hoping for acknowledgment, I finally understood that she wasn't ready to face the reality of what had happened. She wasn't prepared to admit the pain she caused, and that was something I had to accept.

This moment was pivotal. It marked a turning point in my emotional journey, where I realized that closure wasn't something she could give me. It had to come from within myself.

For years, I had longed for her acknowledgement, for an apology that never came. I thought that if I could make her see the truth, if I could just get her to understand the depth of the hurt, then maybe things would be different. I believed that her understanding would somehow allow us to heal together, but I had to let go of that dream.

The more I held onto the hope that she would provide me with the closure I so desperately craved, the more it kept me tied to the pain of the past. I realized that the closure I sought wasn't hers to give. It was mine to claim. Letting go of my need for closure from her was one of the hardest yet most liberating steps in my healing journey.

For years, I had tried to repair a relationship that was fractured beyond repair. I had waited for her to acknowledge the things I had endured, for her to offer some form of apology or recognition that might validate my experiences. But each attempt was met with resistance and denial. The weight of those unmet expectations grew heavier and heavier until I finally understood that the only way forward was to release my attachment to her approval, her understanding, and her validation.

It wasn't an easy process. Letting go felt like losing a part of myself that I had carried for so long. The need for validation, the desire to hear the words I had always longed for, was a deep ache that had shaped much of my emotional life. But over time, I began to see that I didn't need her acknowledgment to be worthy of love, healing, or peace. My worth wasn't tied to her recognition or apology. I was worthy simply because I was, regardless of whether she ever understood my pain or took responsibility for what had happened. Releasing my need for closure was a profound act of freedom.

No longer did I have to hold my breath, hoping she would change or suddenly see the truth. I let go of the emotional weight tied to the hope of reconciliation, and in doing so, I found the freedom I had been searching for. I stopped looking for her to fix me or to make it right. I finally understood that healing had to come from within not from her, but from me. This wasn't just about forgiving her; it was also about forgiving myself. I had to forgive myself for holding onto expectations that were never going to be met. I had to release the emotional burden I had carried for years, the burden of hoping for a version of our relationship that was never going to exist. I realized I had spent so much time yearning for something that wasn't real, and I had to make the conscious choice to stop. I forgave myself for hoping, for waiting, and for believing that my healing was tied to her actions. It wasn't.

Letting go of my need for closure allowed me to finally find peace within myself. My healing no longer depended on whether or not she came to terms with the past. I began to see that I had been healing all along, even without her acknowledgment. My journey wasn't hers to control but it was my own. And once I truly understood that, everything changed.

I discovered that I could move forward without the weight of the past holding me back. I didn't need her to understand in order to heal. I could love myself in spite of her inability to acknowledge the hurt. I could live with joy and peace, knowing I had reclaimed my own power and taken control of my healing. Letting go of my need for closure didn't mean forgetting what happened or pretending the past didn't matter. It meant choosing not to let the past define me.

I refused to let it control my emotions, my thoughts, or my future. I also understood that healing would never be a straight line. There would still be moments when the past resurfaced, when the pain felt fresh again. But I had made the decision to release the emotional grip the past had on me. And each time those memories crept back in; I chose to forgive again. I chose to move forward. The closure I had once longed for wasn't going to come from her, it had to come from me. And once I realized that I embraced a renewed sense of freedom.

In the end, closure wasn't something I could wait for someone else to give me. It was something I had to give myself. It was about accepting that some things would never be resolved and finding peace in the fact that I could heal without answers. I didn't need her acknowledgment to move on. I was free to write my own story, to define my healing, and to live a life no longer constrained by the past.

The Road to Self-Worth: Reclaiming My Value

Reclaiming my sense of self-worth was a journey, a slow, deliberate process filled with effort, pain, and setbacks. It didn't happen overnight. It required learning to see myself for who I truly was, beyond the scars and the voices that once tried to define me. For so long, I had looked at myself through the lens of my past wounds: my mother's harshness, the mistreatment I endured, and the shame that had taken root in my heart. But as I began to step more deeply into my faith, I discovered a life-changing truth: I was not what I had suffered, nor was I defined by what others had said about me. I was far more than the sum of my past experiences. I was a child of God, made in His image, worthy of love, respect, and peace.

The first steps in reclaiming my worth were rooted in my faith. While I had always known that God was with me, even during my darkest moments, it wasn't until I leaned fully into that faith that I began to see myself differently. I stopped seeing myself as a victim of circumstances. My identity wasn't shaped by the mistakes of others or by the unhealed wounds they had left behind. Instead, I began to draw strength from the truth of God's unwavering love for me. The Bible reminds us: "I am fearfully and wonderfully made" (Psalm 139:14). I began to claim this truth for myself, letting it take root in my soul and shift how I saw my reflection.

The pull of the past was strong, and there were moments when I questioned my worth. Transitioning out of the pain wasn't easy, but through prayer, reflection, and reading the Word, I began to uncover a new version of myself. I saw someone who was strong, capable, and filled with potential. God's love, unconditional and steady, became the foundation upon which I rebuilt my life. Each time I affirmed my worth, I let go of the lies that had weighed me down for so long. I released the shame, guilt, and resentment that had clung to me, replacing them with the truth that I was loved by a higher power, with a purpose uniquely designed for me.

Part of reclaiming my worth was learning to build boundaries, a critical step in my healing. For years, I allowed others, particularly my mother, to define my value. Her words and actions shaped how I saw myself, leaving me feeling unworthy of love, respect, or kindness. But as I grew in faith and began to understand my inherent value, I realized that I needed to protect myself from further harm. Building boundaries wasn't about shutting people out, it was about honoring my needs, my emotional well-being, and my sense of self. I learned that it was okay to say no, to step back, and to distance myself from relationships that no longer served me or respected my worth. Creating boundaries didn't mean I stopped loving others, it meant I started loving myself enough to stop tolerating toxicity.

Another key realization was that I had to stop seeking validation from others. For years, I longed for acknowledgment, for my mother's love and approval, and for some external recognition of my pain. But I came to see that validation from others was fleeting. True worth came from within.

Once I began to affirm my value through my relationship with God, I no longer needed external approval to feel whole. I discovered peace in knowing that I was enough just as I was, and I no longer sought to mold myself to fit anyone else's expectations.

There were moments when memories of the past would resurface, moments that threatened to pull me back into the feelings of smallness and inadequacy. But I reminded myself that those memories no longer defined me. I wasn't the girl who had been abandoned, neglected, or mistreated. I was a woman with purpose, dreams, and a future. I had faced my pain, confronted my past, and made the choice to live the life that God had prepared for me.

One of the most liberating parts of this journey was letting go of the need for others, especially my mother to understand or acknowledge my pain. I didn't need her validation, apology, or acknowledgment to heal. Forgiveness became an act of self-liberation. I forgave her, not for her sake, but for mine. I chose to release the emotional weight that had tethered me to the past, understanding that my healing didn't depend on her actions, it depended on my decision to let go. By giving up the need for external closure, I found freedom. I no longer waited for her acknowledgment or her apology. I didn't need her permission to move forward. My healing wasn't tied to her. It was mine to own.

Embracing My Worth and Moving Forward

Standing in the freedom of this reclaimed self-worth, I saw myself clearly for the first time. I wasn't the broken girl who had been discarded or forgotten. I wasn't defined by the neglect or mistreatment of my past. I was a woman of strength, faith, and purpose. I was deserving of love, respect, and all the good things life had to offer. My past no longer held power over me. Instead, my faith, my choices, and my self-love became the foundation for the life I was building. Reclaiming my worth gave me the confidence to step boldly into the future. I was no longer afraid to create new relationships, pursue my dreams, or believe in my right to happiness and success. My life was no longer shadowed by the pain of my past, but illuminated by the hope, strength, and love I had cultivated within myself. I realized that my worth wasn't just about who I had been, it was about who I was becoming. And as I moved forward, I carried with me the understanding that I was enough. Not because of what anyone said or did, but because I had chosen to believe it for myself.

CHAPTER 7

An Invitation to My Father's House

Living on my own became a pivotal chapter in my life, one that demanded resilience, adaptability, and an unshakable faith. When I left the shelter of my mother's house, I wasn't entirely prepared for the challenges ahead, but I knew that survival meant finding a way to make it work. I was young and still learning to navigate the demands of adulthood while striving to achieve my goals. Initially, I took on various jobs to make ends meet. None of them paid much, but each role served as a stepping stone, teaching me invaluable lessons about myself and the world around me. I managed to pay my rent, handle my bills, and build a semblance of a life for myself, even as the weight of new responsibilities and uncertainties surfaced.

Before I found my footing in teaching, I worked a string of different jobs, each one shaping me in some way. I worked as a secretary, telephone operator, customer service representative, and even as a sales agent. Each position came with its own set of challenges and responsibilities. While these roles weren't part of the life I had envisioned for myself, they taught me perseverance and adaptability. From learning to communicate effectively with people to managing tasks

195

under pressure and navigating the unpredictable world of sales, I grew in ways I hadn't anticipated.

During that time, I also gained a deeper understanding of what it meant to be truly independent. Living on my own meant there was no one to rely on but God and myself. That realization was a double-edged sword: it empowered me to see my own strength but overwhelmed me with the weight of knowing that every decision, every misstep, was mine alone. I learned to stretch my resources, budgeting every dollar carefully to cover necessities like rent, food, utility bills, and transportation. It wasn't easy, but it instilled in me a resourcefulness I hadn't known I possessed and underscored the importance of planning ahead.

Even with the financial struggles, I made it a priority to stay connected to my faith. Going to church became a lifeline, a place where I could find strength when I felt utterly drained. Prayer and the sense of community I found in church reminded me that I wasn't truly alone, even when the weight of the world felt like it rested entirely on my shoulders.

Eventually, my path took an unexpected turn, leading me to a teaching position, a role I hadn't actively pursued but one that seemed to find me. I was offered a position at an early childhood institution, a private school that, while not a government-run facility, provided me with an opportunity. The pay wasn't much, but it was a start. Looking back, I firmly believe that God opened that door for a reason. That job gave me stability, not necessarily financial stability, but a sense of purpose.

The institution was small, and the demands were immense. Working with young children required endless patience, creativity, and emotional strength. It wasn't easy, especially knowing my salary barely covered my basic needs, let alone allowed me to save. Yet, the bright, innocent smiles of the children I taught reminded me daily that my work carried meaning. For over nine years, I poured my heart into that role, finding fulfillment not in a paycheck but in the impact I had on their lives.

Summers, however, were a different challenge. Private institutions didn't provide work during the summer months, which meant no income. Those summers were a constant struggle. I relied on the small savings I managed to scrape together throughout the year, counting every penny and stretching every dollar. At times, the school's principal extended a small financial contribution to help me through those difficult months. Despite the struggles, I always found a way to make it work, until one summer, when my life took an unexpected and heartbreaking turn.

That summer, my younger sister passed away. Her death was sudden and devastating, plunging my father's side of the family into grief and a season of uncertainty. It was during that time, in the midst of mourning and trying to process my own emotions, that my father extended an invitation that would alter the course of my journey. The offer came out of nowhere, and while our relationship hadn't been particularly strong, there was something in his voice that gave me pause.

My Father's Call After My Sister's Passing

When my younger sister passed away, it was sudden and devastating. She had recently experienced stomach issues, but it wasn't considered serious or life-threatening. No one anticipated that her discomfort would escalate into a tragedy. The pain became severe enough to warrant a trip to the hospital. The doctors performed surgery, but despite their efforts, she passed away shortly afterward. The news hit us like a lightning bolt, unforeseen and utterly disorienting. It was as if time had collapsed between the moment she was admitted and the moment we lost her. The grief that followed was overwhelming. I found myself grappling with a swirl of emotions: profound sadness, shock, and disbelief over a life taken far too soon.

In the days following her death, it was customary for friends and family to visit my father and his family's home, offering condolences and support. Though my relationship with my father was distant, I felt it was important to be there, not only to honor my sister but also to stand with the rest of the family during this difficult time. Visiting my father's house during those days felt unfamiliar but I made myself comfortable. I was present to provide support in the midst of loss, even as the emotional distance between us lingered quietly in the background.

Each night, family members, friends, and neighbors came together to mourn and share stories about my sister. These evenings were heavy with sorrow, but they were also brightened by the warm memories of her life. It was during those moments that I caught glimpses of a father quietly wrestling with his own grief. He was silent, stoic, and perhaps reflective in ways I hadn't witnessed before.

Amidst the grief and the quiet weight of these gatherings, my father made an unexpected gesture. He invited me to move into his house, specifically offering me the room upstairs that had once belonged to my sister. His words caught me off guard, and I was left uncertain about how to respond. We had never been close, and this offer felt uncharacteristic of the man I had come to know. I couldn't help but wonder if my sister's passing had stirred something within him. Perhaps it was regret. Perhaps it was a desire to mend what had long been broken.

Was this his way of reaching out to me? Or was he simply trying to fill the sudden void in his home? The invitation carried weight and meaning, but it left me conflicted. While part of me wanted to believe in his intentions, my history with him made me cautious.

The house itself carried a story of its own. It was a two-story structure, although it hadn't always been that way. When my father and stepmother first bought it, it had been a modest single-story home. Over time, they rented out the downstairs while working on building the upper floor. Most of the renovations were funded by my stepmother, who frequently traveled to America and sent money back to support the project.

Her sacrifices were visible in every detail of the upstairs section. Small touches reflected her vision for a family home. But those sacrifices also added to the complexity of our household dynamic. The house, like our family, was a mixture of effort, ambition, and unspoken tension.

Tensions With My Stepmother

Living in my father's house, though far from perfect, initially felt like an opportunity for stability. After the loss of my younger sister, he had invited me to stay, assuring me that I wouldn't have to worry about bills. His words brought a sense of relief, a reprieve from the constant pressure of financial survival that had weighed on me for so long. For the first time in years, I felt I could breathe, even if only temporarily.

I was deeply grateful for this gesture, particularly because my father had never been a consistent presence in my life. It felt like he was attempting to make up for lost time, offering the kind of support he hadn't provided before. Yet beneath the surface of his invitation, I sensed an unspoken tension that I couldn't ignore. Not long after moving in, I learned about a conversation that would change how I viewed my time there. A family member, possibly my aunt or grandmother, had spoken negatively about my living arrangement. They questioned my work ethic, insinuating that I didn't like to work, and criticized my father for allowing me to stay. When my father shared these comments with me, I was devastated. The person who said these things didn't understand the complexities of my situation, and their words cut deeply. I had always been transparent with my family about my struggles, whether it was being between jobs or facing financial challenges. I wasn't proud of those moments, but I never hid them either.

What hurt most was the betrayal. The person who made these comments had known me since childhood, yet they had chosen to judge me without knowing the full story. They didn't see the sleepless nights, the constant uncertainty, or the quiet resilience I needed to make it through each day. None of them had ever stepped in to offer financial help or emotional support when I was struggling, and I wasn't expecting them to.

But hearing these words from someone so close felt like a personal attack, as though they were undermining all the effort I had put into surviving and staying afloat. The fact that my father told me about these comments complicated things further. On the one hand, I understood that he was simply passing along what had been said.

On the other, it felt like a violation of my privacy. Those words, spoken behind my back, had now infiltrated my life, creating an invisible wedge in what was already a fragile situation. When I mentioned the situation to my grandmother, she only responded with a rhetorical question: "Who would have said such a thing?" As the days went on, the atmosphere in the house became increasingly strained. What had initially felt like a refuge now felt like a battleground, filled with unspoken judgments and hidden grievances.

The house offered me shelter, but it lacked the emotional safety I desperately needed. I had hoped for more than just a roof over my head and a break from bills. I wanted connection, understanding, and a chance to rebuild a relationship with my father that had been strained for years. Adding to the tension was my stepmother, who had been cold toward me from the beginning. Her behavior made it clear that she didn't want me there. What hurt most were her constant comparisons between me and my younger sister, who had passed away. She would talk about how my sister had been a companion to my older sister and how they had shared activities that I didn't partake in. These activities, including outings to places that clashed with my Christian values, weren't things I could participate in with a clear conscience.

As a born-again Christian, I couldn't compromise my beliefs to fit into her world. Yet her repeated comments felt like thinly veiled criticisms, subtle reminders that I didn't belong. Her words were more than casual remarks; they were dismissive and isolating. It didn't take long for me to realize she was using these differences to justify her discomfort with my presence. Every time she brought up how my younger sister had fit into their lives; it was as though she was reinforcing the idea that I didn't. Her demeanor, combined with her subtle jabs, made it increasingly clear that I wasn't welcome.

The emotional strain of living under the same roof with someone who didn't want me there began to take its toll. I tried to stay quiet to keep out of the way, but the tension was impossible to ignore. Every interaction, every cold glance, was a reminder that I didn't belong. One day, the tension boiled over, and I couldn't keep pretending everything was fine. I decided to speak up to my father, something I had never done before. I needed him to know how uncomfortable I felt, how unwelcome I was in the house.

When I finally voiced my concerns, my father listened. He seemed to understand, but I hadn't expected the reaction from my stepmother. She became defensive. Her response was far more intense than I anticipated. In a moment of anger, she even made a shocking threat: "I will take this Bible and hit you," she said. Her words stunned me, both for their absurdity and their hostility. My father stepped in immediately, telling her, "It's not your child; you can't hit her."

While his intervention diffused the immediate situation, it didn't solve the underlying problem. Her anger and hostility were symptomatic of a larger issue; one I could no longer ignore. Standing in that room, I realized this wasn't a place where I could stay. It wasn't just about her threat; it was about the deeper realization that I was unwanted in their home. My stepmother's actions, her words, and even her silence all pointed to one undeniable truth: I didn't belong there.

When my father wasn't home, I often overheard conversations between my stepmother and others. Though they didn't directly mention me, the undertones of their discussions made it clear that my presence in the house was an issue.

These moments left me feeling more isolated than ever, as though I had become entangled in a dynamic I didn't want to be part of. I didn't have the energy to navigate their unspoken conflicts or to fight for a place in a household where I clearly wasn't wanted. Eventually, I made the difficult decision to leave my father's house. I wasn't ungrateful for his offer.

I truly appreciated it, but the emotional cost of staying was too high. I needed peace, and I knew I wouldn't find it there. As I packed my belongings, I felt a mixture of sadness and relief. Leaving wasn't just about finding a new place to live. It was about reclaiming my life and my sense of self-worth. I was taking control of my narrative, choosing to define my own path rather than letting anyone else dictate who I was or what I deserved.

A Deliberate Choice for Independence

Leaving my father's house, after he had extended the invitation for me to stay, was an act of self-preservation, one of the most pivotal decisions I had made in years. While I had already lived independently before moving in with him, leaving this time carried a deeper meaning. It symbolized my determination to reclaim my independence, not just physically, but emotionally as well. It was about creating space where I could prioritize my well-being and rebuild my sense of self without the weight of constant tension and judgment.

The more I thought about my circumstances, the clearer it became that leaving was my best option. Living in that house had begun to feel stifling, like every action I took was being scrutinized and every word I spoke was being misinterpreted. It was exhausting. I wasn't a dependent child anymore, relying on my parents for guidance or approval. I was an adult, a woman who had experienced enough challenges to know that sometimes, the only way to protect your peace is to remove yourself from toxic environments, even if those environments are tied to family. With that understanding, I made the difficult choice to leave.

It wasn't a decision I made lightly. Leaving brought with it its own challenges, uncertainty about what came next, the sting of disappointment that things hadn't worked out, and the lingering sadness of walking away from the hope of reconciliation with my father. But deep down, I knew it was the right thing to do. Staying in a home where I didn't feel welcome, where every day brought more tension than peace, was not sustainable. By choosing to leave, I chose to prioritize my emotional health, to protect my own sense of self-worth, and to reclaim control over my life.

There was a part of me that wished things could have been different. I would have preferred to stay and find a way to make it work, perhaps even repair the broken relationship with my father. But I had learned that sometimes, prioritizing your own well-being means letting go of what you want and choosing what you need. Living in that house might have offered temporary stability, but it came at the cost of my peace. I couldn't afford that trade-off anymore. In leaving, I solidified an important lesson about boundaries. It wasn't just about walking away; it was about recognizing that I had the right to protect my emotional space. It was about understanding that my self-worth wasn't tied to anyone else's approval, nor was it something I was willing to sacrifice to avoid conflict. Leaving my father's house wasn't just a step toward reclaiming my independence; it was a declaration of my commitment to my own growth, peace, and resilience.

Shifts in My Mother's Behavior

Reflecting on the period when I moved in with my father, I noticed a marked change in my mother's behavior. Before, our interactions were fleeting brief exchanges centered around necessities and logistics.

But after my relocation, something shifted. She began calling me every morning, asking how I was doing and making plans to spend time together. She'd invite me over for small, seemingly intimate gestures, like doing her hair.

At first, I welcomed these calls with open arms. They felt like a long-awaited bridge to a relationship I had quietly longed for. Her attention gave me hope, a glimmer of something I hadn't realized I was missing. I interpreted her gestures as love: the daily calls, her sudden eagerness to spend time with me, and the closeness I thought was budding between us. The timing felt right, and I let myself believe that this was the start of something meaningful.

Yet now, as I reflect, I see the possibility of other motives. Had my moving in with my father triggered something in her? Was she worried that our relationship might slip away, or that I might grow closer to him than to her? Perhaps it was guilt, competition, or even fear that spurred her sudden interest in reconnecting. At the time, though, I didn't allow myself to question her intentions. I was too busy basking in the glow of her newfound presence in my life. Looking back, I wonder if she feared I'd tell my father about the abuse I endured living with her.

I think I wanted to believe her love was finally showing itself the way I had always hoped it would. I didn't stop to wonder if her motives might be more about her than about me. But now, with the benefit of hindsight, I can see there was more complexity beneath the surface than I realized back then.

This time in my life brought an unexpected mix of emotions. The joy of hearing her voice every morning was real; I won't diminish that. But so, too, was the undercurrent of confusion I didn't fully acknowledge at the time. Was this warmth genuine, or was it driven by something she couldn't admit to herself? These questions didn't form until much later, when I had the distance to unpack what really happened. In hindsight, I see this period as a poignant reminder of how fragile familiar relationships can be. They are shaped not just by love but by fear, insecurity, and unspoken needs.

Her increased communication was a double-edged sword: it gave me a sense of connection but also raised questions about authenticity that I wasn't prepared to face then. For anyone experiencing similar shifts in family dynamics, I've learned how important it is to take a step back and reflect. When someone's behavior changes suddenly, especially in relationships as layered as those between parent and child, it's worth asking why. Honest conversations though difficult can shed light on those motivations, helping you navigate the emotions that arise. Ultimately, my mother's sudden increase in communication during the time I lived with my father was both joyful and complex. While it brought a sense of reconnection and hope, it also prompted deep reflection on our relationship and the underlying factors that shaped it. This experience ultimately became a turning point in my personal growth, deepening my understanding of the complexities of familiar bonds.

The Turning Point: The Calls That Stopped Coming

This daily communication had given me hope that our relationship was finally strengthening, fostering a closeness I had longed for. However, when I relocated, the daily calls stopped abruptly. Days turned into weeks without hearing from her. At first, I tried to rationalize her silence, convincing myself that she might be giving me space to adjust to my new environment. But as time passed, a deep sense of abandonment and confusion set in. The stark contrast between her earlier eagerness to connect and her current silence left me bewildered.

When she eventually called, her tone was sharp and accusatory. "So, you can't call me?" she asked, as though maintaining our relationship was entirely my responsibility. Her words felt like a reprimand, disregarding the fact that communication is a two-way effort. I reminded her of the daily calls she'd made when I was staying at my father's house and questioned why that effort had disappeared. "Calls go both ways," I replied, trying to express that building a relationship requires equal commitment.

This conversation became a turning point for me. It forced me to confront the reality of our relationship dynamics and recognize a troubling pattern: her increased communication during my time with my father wasn't about genuine concern for me. Instead, it seemed driven by her desire to assert her presence, perhaps out of fear or control. Once I was no longer in that environment, her motivation to maintain consistent contact faded.

Coming to terms with this realization was both painful and liberating. It illuminated the conditional nature of her attention and affection, compelling me to reevaluate my expectations and the emotional energy I invested in our relationship. I began to understand that my sense of self-worth could not depend on her unpredictable involvement in my life.

At first, her silence felt like a profound loss. But in hindsight, it was an opportunity, a chance to break free from unhealthy dynamics and take a bold step toward emotional independence. This journey wasn't without its challenges, but it was a necessary process. I began to assert my individuality and build a life grounded in self-respect, autonomy, and genuine connections.

Embracing emotional independence transformed every aspect of my life. I learned to prioritize my emotional health, seek relationships that were mutually fulfilling, and stand firm in my journey toward self-discovery. By stepping away from conditional love, I created space for authentic relationships that nurtured my growth and happiness. I started to dismantle limiting beliefs I had carried for years and replace them with a healthier self-image rooted in self-acceptance and self-love. For the first time, I focused on nurturing my well-being, pursuing personal interests, and building reciprocal, supportive relationships.

In closing, I want to share that while therapy can be a valuable tool for many, I found my strength through my unwavering Christian faith. Although I didn't have access to therapy, God's Word became my guide and comfort during the darkest moments of my life. I leaned on His promises, trusting that He would never leave me nor forsake me. Through prayer, reflection, and His guidance, I found the strength to heal and overcome struggles that once seemed insurmountable.

If you're reading this and carrying burdens of your own, know that you don't have to face them alone. Seek help in any way that is available to you. Whether through therapy, a trusted friend, or by turning to God. Healing is possible, and you can rise above your challenges. Take that first step toward healing. With faith, perseverance, and God by your side, you are capable of overcoming anything. You are stronger than you realize.

The Realization: No More Games

For many years, I longed for closure, a deep internal peace that I believed would come from the kind of support and validation I thought only a parent could provide. I searched for someone to tell me that I mattered, that I was worthy, and that my struggles were not in vain. The absence of that support, especially from my mother, left me feeling

213

incomplete, like a puzzle missing a crucial piece.

Yet, in my search for answers and healing, I came to a profound realization. I didn't need closure from anyone else. The turning point came when I realized that my worth was never tied to someone else's acknowledgment or approval. The closure I had been seeking had to come from within me.

For so long, I felt incomplete, believing that only a certain conversation or moment of understanding with my mother could fill that void. But as I grew in my relationship with God and began to see myself through His eyes, I understood something life-changing: I had always been enough. My worth was not defined by others' actions or their ability to meet my expectations. I had to learn to see my own value, regardless of how others treated me or the validation I once craved.

This realization empowered me in ways I hadn't anticipated. I stopped waiting for someone else to provide the answers, the comfort, or the acknowledgment I thought I needed. I let go of trying to prove I was worthy of love or care. I realized God had already given me everything I needed to thrive, His love, His Word, and the strength He had instilled within me. I began to embrace my journey and my healing, not because of external circumstances but because I chose to take control of my story.

With this newfound sense of agency, I began to build my life around my faith and values. No longer did I see myself as a victim of my circumstances or someone incomplete because others failed to meet my expectations. Instead, I embraced the truth that I was a work in progress. Each step I took toward personal growth became an act of empowerment. I learned to set boundaries, make decisions aligned with my values, and trust that I was capable of creating a life that honored who I was.

This empowerment wasn't about rejecting others; it was about embracing my own power and worth. I no longer depended on others to define me. I had always held the power to shape my life, and this realization gave me the courage to move forward in a way that honored myself and my faith. I wasn't waiting for someone to complete me anymore. I was whole, just as I was, and my journey was about embracing that truth.

In this new chapter of my life, I stopped allowing the past to define my future.

For years, I carried the weight of old wounds, believing I couldn't move forward without an apology or acknowledgment from others. But the true release came when I realized my healing wasn't dependent on anyone else. It was within me. I could choose to forgive, let go, and move forward, regardless of others' actions or inactions. That was the ultimate empowerment: the freedom to choose peace, healing, and a path that aligned with who I was becoming. Healing, I've learned, is a process. It doesn't happen overnight. It requires facing pain, acknowledging the hurt, and making the conscious choice to move forward with faith and determination.

There were still moments when I felt the sting of past wounds, but I no longer let them consume me. Instead, I faced them with a sense of control and understanding. My past no longer defined me unless I allowed it. And I chose not to. As I embraced this newfound strength, I began to build relationships founded on mutual respect, trust, and authenticity. I no longer felt the need to prove myself or seek validation from those who couldn't give it. I could simply be myself fully and unapologetically and that was enough.

The relationships I built were stronger because they were grounded in self-respect and honesty, not the need for approval. By taking control of my narrative and recognizing my own worth, I discovered a purpose and direction I had never felt before. I was no longer a passive participant in my life. I was in control, and the choices I made reflected the person I was becoming. Freed from the burden of seeking closure from others, I found peace in creating a life grounded in faith, self-worth, and inner strength. In the end, the most powerful form of closure came from within. It was not about waiting for someone else to fix what was broken. It was about taking ownership of my own healing, my own journey, and my own life. I can now stand tall, knowing I've overcome obstacles that once seemed overwhelming. I have the power to continue building a life that honors who I am. And in that, I found the freedom I had been searching for all along.

CHAPTER 8

Introduction to the Visa and the Need for a Safe Haven

I had dreamed of a life beyond the confines of my reality for as long as I could remember, but the opportunity to go to the United States always felt like a distant hope, something I barely dared to imagine. When the chance finally came, I had no money saved, no concrete plan, and no clear direction. What I did have was faith, and that faith had always been my source of strength. I trusted that God's plan for me would unfold in His time. But this moment felt different, urgent, monumental and impossible to ignore.

The day before my interview at the U.S. Embassy, my emotions were a whirlwind of excitement and anxiety. I trusted God to guide me, but I couldn't shake the enormity of the step I was about to take. That night, I prayed with everything I had, asking God to show me whether this was truly His will. As a prophetess, I knew the Lord often spoke to me through visions, and that night, He gave me one. In the vision, I was at the U.S. Embassy, and my visa was approved. While the finer details of the vision have faded over time, the clarity I felt in that moment remains vivid. I knew without a doubt that I would receive the visa. The next morning, as I stood in line at the embassy, anticipation weighed on me like a heavy cloak. The people around me exuded nervous energy. Some walked out of the building with defeated expressions, their slumped shoulders telling stories of rejection. Watching them stirred the fear that lingered quietly in my mind, but I refused to let it take hold. I clung to the vision God had given me and the peace that had settled in my heart. I reminded myself that God had a plan, and that this moment was part of it. I shifted my focus away from the anxiety surrounding me and chose instead to trust that He would make a way.

When my turn came, the experience felt almost surreal. The officer barely asked me any questions. She glanced at my documents, exchanged a few brief words with me, and then handed me the visa. I had braced myself for a challenging, even grueling, interview, but the process was smooth and effortless. In that moment, I could feel God's grace covering me. His provision and faithfulness left me in awe. My joy didn't end there. At the time, I had been preaching regularly on an overseas prayer line, and during one of those sessions, I received an invitation to attend a conference abroad. To my amazement, they even offered to pay for my travel expenses. It felt like divine confirmation of everything I had been preparing for. For years I had been receiving prophecies about traveling overseas. One prophecy in particular had stayed with me: it said that after I graduated from university, I should prepare to leave my home country. Those words had resonated deeply, and now they were beginning to materialize in ways that felt both miraculous and humbling. I didn't know exactly how it would all come together, but I trusted God completely.

As I prepared for this next chapter of my life, I began to give away my belongings. I didn't want to be burdened by unnecessary expenses back home, especially since I only had a visitor's visa, which limited my stay in the U.S. to six months. I was determined to save every bit of money I could for the journey ahead. Paying rent simply wasn't an option, so I made the decision to part with most of my possessions, keeping only a few essentials. This act of letting go, while practical, also felt symbolic. It was a step of faith, an acknowledgment that I was ready to leave behind the familiar and step into the unknown. For a time, I stayed with a male friend while I waited for everything to fall into place. However, the arrangement quickly made me uncomfortable.

As a Christian, I firmly believed in the scripture that calls us to "abstain from all appearance of evil." I knew that staying with a male friend, no matter how innocent the circumstances, didn't align with my faith. It weighed on my conscience, and I felt convicted to find another place to stay. That's when I decided to ask my mother if I could stay with her until I left for the U.S. Asking her was not a simple decision. My relationship with my mother had always been complicated, and I knew this request could reopen old wounds. But I also knew I couldn't let fear dictate my choices. I placed my trust in God, praying fervently before approaching her. I believed that if it was His will, my mother would agree. And so, with a mix of hope and trepidation, I prepared to ask for her support.

The Conversation with My Mother

A few days after I received my visa, I went to my mother's house to share the news with her. I didn't feel the need to make a grand announcement; instead, I simply told her that I had received the visa. It was a significant step for my future, but my excitement was tempered with the weight of what lay ahead.

This marked the beginning of a new chapter, one that I trusted God had prepared for me. I believed this was part of His plan, a step closer to the opportunities He had opened for me. Even as I felt anticipation for what was to come, there was also a quiet humility, a readiness to step into the unknown, trusting in His guidance. When I arrived, I sat down with her and said, "Mom, I got my visa." I tried to contain the excitement bubbling inside me. She looked at me, her expression unreadable, before asking, "So, who are you going to stay with abroad?"

Her question caught me slightly off guard. I had assumed I could stay with family, but I didn't have a concrete answer. "I don't know," I admitted honestly. Then, in a hopeful tone, I added, "Maybe I can stay with your sister. I know she lives abroad, and I thought that could be a good place to start." Her response was swift, almost dismissive. "It's only her who works," she said matter-of-factly. "It wouldn't be possible for you to stay with her. Whenever I travel to visit her, I have to save up my own money."

The weight of her words settled heavily in the room, and disappointment washed over me. I had hoped for a sense of encouragement, for her to understand how important this opportunity was for me. Instead, her response felt like a closed door. I tried not to let the hurt show on my face, but inside, I wrestled with the sting of rejection and the uncertainty of what would come next. Even as I processed my emotions, I reminded myself of my faith in God's plan. I believed that He would make a way forward.

He wouldn't have opened the door for me to receive the visa without providing a path for what lay ahead. Quietly, I reassured myself that although my mother's response wasn't what I had hoped for, I could still trust in God's provision. If it was His will for me to go abroad, He would make the way clear, just as He had brought me to this first step.

Prayer and Trust in God's Will

Before I approached my mother, I took a moment to pray. It was a quiet, deeply personal prayer, seeking God's guidance amid the uncertainty of my situation. I had already taken a leap of faith by trusting Him to open the door for me to receive the visa, and now I needed to lean on Him once more for the next step. In that moment, I felt a profound sense of reliance on His will, trusting that if this was part of His plan, He would make a way forward.

I prayed earnestly, pouring my heart into every word. "Lord, if it's Your will for me to stay at my mother's house, let her say yes. But if it's not Your will, let her say no." It was a simple prayer, but it carried the weight of my hopes and fears. More than anything, I wanted to ensure that whatever happened, I was aligned with His greater purpose for my life. I wasn't asking for my desires to take precedence but for His will to unfold in the way that was best for me.

Though uncertainty loomed, I was overcome by a sense of peace that softened my anxiety. I didn't know what her response would be, but I believed that if God wanted me to stay with her, he would move her heart to say yes. If not, I resolved to accept it, trusting that He had already prepared an alternative path for me.

When the moment came to ask my mother if I could stay with her, I was filled with hope, yet the possibility of rejection weighed heavily on me. It was a vulnerable question, one that stirred a quiet storm of emotions. For someone who had been independent for so long, asking for help even from my own mother felt almost foreign. It wasn't just about finding a place to stay; it was about finding a refuge, a place to feel safe and supported as I prepared for the next chapter of my life.

I could feel the remnants of my prayer lingering in my heart as I spoke to her. "Mom," I said, summoning all the courage I could muster, "can I stay with you for a few weeks so I can save up money to travel?" My voice carried an unspoken plea for more than just a roof over my head. I was asking for emotional shelter, for a sense of connection as I faced the unknown.

When she said no, the words didn't cut as deeply as I thought they would. There was no sharp sting of rejection. Instead, I felt a quiet assurance, a knowing that God's plan was unfolding as it was meant to.

Her refusal wasn't a setback; it was a redirection. I realized in that moment that His will was already at work, paving the way for something I couldn't yet see. Rather than bitterness or hurt, I felt a calm understanding. This was His answer, and I trusted it. The path before me was still unfolding, and though it wasn't the one I had envisioned, I knew it was the one He had prepared for me. With quiet resolve, I released the question into His hands, ready to take the next step wherever He would lead me.

Her Refusal and the Emotional Impact

When My mother said no. My initial response wasn't anger or bitterness. It was a quiet understanding: that this was somehow part of God's plan. Spiritually, I was at peace. I had prayed, asking the Lord to let me stay with her if it was His will, and I trusted that His will was unfolding no matter the outcome.

Deep in my heart, I had faith that God would provide a way, even if that way wasn't through my mother's home. However, that peace didn't immediately erase the emotional weight of her refusal. As her daughter, it was impossible not to feel the sting of rejection. It wasn't just about being denied a place to stay. It was the painful realization that, despite having the space, she chose not to offer me the safe haven I had so desperately hoped for.

My emotions were conflicted. On one hand, I tried to rationalize her decision. Perhaps her refusal was influenced by practicalities or circumstances I couldn't fully understand. But on the other hand, as her child, I couldn't ignore the deep ache of wanting her to extend a gesture of kindness and compassion in my moment of vulnerability.

This wasn't merely about finding a roof over my head. It was about longing for her to create a space of safety, warmth, and understanding during a pivotal time in my life. Instead, I was left to face the uncertainty alone, when all I wanted was her support.

Deep down, her refusal felt personal. It left me silently questioning whether she truly cared about my well-being. I didn't want to dwell on that thought. It was too painful to confront fully, but it lingered in the back of my mind, shaping how I processed the moment.

The emotional conflict was heavy. I had built up an expectation, one rooted in the hope that a mother's love would naturally extend to me in my time of need. I had worked hard to reach this point in my life, completing my university degree, attending personal development classes, and striving for independence. Yet here I was, humbling myself to ask for a small act of kindness: a temporary place to stay while I prepared for the next major chapter of my life.

Her refusal wasn't just a denial of housing. It was a denial of the comforting, unspoken reassurance I had hoped for as her daughter. And while I understood that this wasn't necessarily a rejection of me as a person, the absence of that gesture still cut deeply.

The Path Forward: Seeking Help from a Friend

After my mother's refusal, I found myself grappling with the daunting task of figuring out my next step. While I held tightly to my faith that God would provide, the weight of the situation began to settle on me. I didn't have the resources to pay rent while also saving for my journey abroad, and I needed a temporary place to stay. It was a difficult position to be in, but as He always does, God made a way.

A dear friend from university, who had witnessed my character and values over our five years together, shared my situation with one of our former classmates. That classmate, now living in Canada, felt moved to help. Remembering the faith and integrity I had shown back in university, she contacted her brother in Jamaica, explained my circumstances, and asked if he could offer me a place to stay. She even vouched for me, telling him that I was a trustworthy person and someone deserving of their kindness.

Her brother, who lived with his wife and children, agreed to help. Despite their limited space, they made adjustments to accommodate me. In an extraordinary gesture of generosity, the wife moved their children into her and her husband's bedroom so I could use the children's room. It was a kindness I hadn't expected, and I was overwhelmed with gratitude for their willingness to disrupt their lives to support me.

During my stay, I was mindful of being a respectful and low maintenance guest. I knew my presence had altered their routine, but they treated me with warmth, patience, and grace. Often, I found myself reflecting on how God had orchestrated this outcome through people who barely knew me. It was a poignant reminder that even after my mother's refusal, I was never truly alone. God was working behind the scenes, through the hands and hearts of others, to provide for me in ways I could never have anticipated. This experience also underscored the importance of character and the lasting impressions we leave on others. My friend's willingness to vouch for me, and her brother's decision to open his home, were testaments to the relationships I had nurtured and the values I had lived by. They had seen me fasting, praying, and working diligently at university, and it made a difference when I needed help the most. While staying with them, I kept my focus on preparing for the next phase of my journey. Every dollar mattered, so I was careful with my spending, knowing how critical those savings would be when I arrived abroad.

The situation wasn't ideal, but I was determined not to impose more than necessary. It was a temporary solution, one that allowed me to continue moving forward. Looking back, I see how God used this experience to teach me about humility, gratitude, and the unexpected ways He provides. Sometimes, the help we need doesn't come from the people or places we expect, but it comes all the same.

Living with Strangers and Learning to Trust Again

Staying with strangers was an experience I never anticipated, and it brought a whirlwind of emotions. On one hand, I was profoundly grateful for their kindness. A family I had never met was willing to disrupt their own lives to provide me with a safe place to stay. I recognized the sacrifices they made and felt humbled by their generosity. On the other hand, I couldn't ignore the unease of living in someone else's space. I was acutely aware of my role as a guest and didn't want to overstep any boundaries or impose. Trusting people, I barely knew required a leap of faith, and while I leaned on God for strength, I also had to confront my own reservations.

The first few days were the hardest. Everything felt foreign: the layout of the house, the family's routines, even their way of communicating. I made it a point to stay out of the way, showing my gratitude in every small way I could. The wife, who had so generously given up her children's room for me, was kind but understandably protective of her space. I noticed the quiet sacrifices they were making, and it humbled me deeply. It reminded me that God often works through people, using them as instruments of His grace in ways we least expect.

As time passed, I began to adjust to the household rhythm. The little boy was lively and energetic, while the little girl came across as quieter and more well-mannered. He connected with me right away, ready to play, while she needed a bit more time to feel comfortable, but in the end, she did, bringing unexpected moments of joy. The little boy, in particular, would eagerly seek me out to play, his energy and enthusiasm a welcome reprieve from the heaviness of my thoughts. His older sister, more reserved at first, observed me quietly before gradually opening up. Their unique personalities helped me feel more connected and made the transition easier in ways I hadn't anticipated.

The husband remained polite and respectful, and as the wife saw how considerate I was, she too began to feel more at ease. I realized that trust isn't something immediate. It's built slowly through small moments of kindness and mutual understanding. This experience challenged me to let go of my pride and embrace vulnerability. Relying on others, especially people I had never met before was not easy. Growing up, I was taught to be fiercely independent, to work hard and carve out my own path. But here I was, in a position where I had to accept help. At first, it felt like a personal failure, as though needing others somehow made me weak.

Yet, as the days turned into weeks, my perspective began to shift. I realized that accepting help takes courage. It takes strength to admit you can't do it all on your own, and even more strength to trust that others won't let you down. Living with this family taught me resilience in ways I hadn't expected. I had to adapt to a new environment, adjust to their way of life, and respect their household dynamics, all while staying focused on my future. It wasn't easy, but it shaped me into a stronger, more adaptable person. I came to trust not only the people around me but also God's provision.

This experience reinforced my belief that He places people in our lives for a reason, even if only for a season. Most importantly, my time with this family reshaped my understanding of trust. Trust isn't about blind faith; it's about taking small, intentional steps forward, even when you're unsure of the outcome. It's about seeing the goodness in others and recognizing that we are all interconnected in some way. By the time I left, I realized I had gained more than just a temporary place to stay. I left with a deeper sense of gratitude and a renewed belief in the kindness of others, a reminder that even in moments of uncertainty, God's grace is always present.

Reflecting on God's Timing and Provision

Looking back on this chapter of my life, I can see clearly that God's timing and provision were perfect even when I couldn't fully grasp them in the moment. At first, my mother's refusal to let me stay in her home felt like a closed door.

While I leaned on my faith and trusted that her "no" was part of God's plan, it didn't completely erase the emotional sting. As her daughter, I had hoped for a small measure of support, a safe space to gather my thoughts and prepare for the next step in my journey. But God had other plans that would teach me about His faithfulness in ways I could never have foreseen.

One of the most powerful lessons I learned during that time was to trust in God's provision, even when it felt like there was no way forward. In Matthew 6:26, Jesus says,

"Look at the birds of the air; they do not sow or reap or store away in barns, and yet your heavenly Father feeds them. Are you not much more valuable than they?" This verse resonated deeply as I reflected on how He provided for me.

I didn't know where I would stay or how I would navigate this uncertain season, but I trusted that the God who cares for even the smallest sparrow would not abandon me. God's provision came through unexpected support. A college friend saw my need and stepped in to help, and her brother's family welcomed me into their home despite the disruption it brought to their lives. These acts of kindness reminded me that God's blessings often come through people. At first, I focused on what I didn't have, but over time, I began to see how God was working behind the scenes, orchestrating everything for my good.

This experience also taught me the value of waiting on God's timing. In Isaiah 40:31, we're reminded, "But those who wait on the Lord shall renew their strength; they shall mount up with wings like eagles, they shall run and not be weary, they shall walk and not faint." In my impatience, I wanted a solution to appear immediately, one that was comfortable and predictable. But God's ways are higher than ours, and His plans are always better. The delays and detours were part of a greater purpose, one that stretched my faith and strengthened my resilience.

The pain of rejection was real, but it was also necessary. It forced me to depend on God in ways I hadn't before. If my mother had said yes, I might have missed the profound lessons I learned about trusting Him completely. I might never have experienced the beauty of being helped by strangers or the humility that comes with accepting grace from others. Romans 8:28 became my anchor during this time: "And we know that in all things God works for the good of those who love him, who have been called according to his purpose."

Every closed door, every disappointment, and every moment of uncertainty was part of a greater plan. What felt like rejection was, in reality, redirection. God was aligning everything to lead me toward the future He had prepared for me.

Now, as I reflect on this season, I am filled with gratitude not just for God's provision but for the lessons of faith, patience, and trust. I've come to understand that His timing is always perfect, even when it doesn't align with my expectations. He sees the bigger picture, and if we trust Him, He will always guide us to exactly where we're meant to be.

Conclusion: Embracing Growth Through Faith

As I reflect on this chapter of my life, I can now see how every trial, every tear, and every unanswered question served a purpose in shaping who I am today. At the time, my mother's refusal to let me stay at her home felt like another closed door, a moment of deep disappointment in a life that had already seen its share of hardship. But in hindsight, her "no" wasn't a rejection; it was a redirection, a nudge toward the path God had prepared for me all along.

Through this experience, I learned to rely on God in ways I never had before. He became my refuge when I had no physical home to run to. During that season of uncertainty, the words of Psalm 46:1 resonated deeply with me: "God is our refuge and strength, a very present help in trouble." Each step I took, even in moments of fear and rejection, was guided by His steady hand. Living with strangers brought lessons I could never have learned otherwise. It reminded me that help often comes from the most unexpected places and people.

God's provision doesn't always arrive in the form we expect; sometimes, it comes through the kindness of strangers or the selflessness of a friend we least expect to step forward. These moments of provision taught me humility, gratitude, and the importance of looking for God's hand in every situation, even when the road ahead felt uncertain.

The challenges I faced during this time didn't just test my faith; they strengthened it. I came to understand that trusting God's timing requires patience and surrender, even when His plans don't align with my expectations. Proverbs 3:5-6 became my anchor: "Trust in the Lord with all your heart and lean not on your own understanding; in all your ways acknowledge Him, and He shall direct your paths." Though I couldn't see it at the time, every closed door was bringing me closer to the life He was preparing for me.

This season also reshaped my perspective on family and relationships. It taught me to extend grace, even when it isn't returned, and to find peace in letting go of what I cannot change. It reminded me that my worth is not tied to anyone's approval or acceptance but is instead rooted in God's love and His purpose for my life. As I prepared to leave for the United States, I carried these lessons with me. The pain of rejection had been transformed into resilience, and uncertainty into unshakable faith. I wasn't just stepping onto a plane, I was stepping into a future that God had orchestrated, trusting that He would continue to be my guide and provider.

This chapter of my life was about so much more than getting a visa or finding a place to stay. It was about learning to recognize God's hand in every detail, to trust Him in the midst of life's storms, and to embrace the growth that comes from walking through valleys. Even in moments of isolation, I came to understand that God was always with me, preparing the way forward. For that, I am eternally grateful.

CHAPTER 9

Crossroads of Faith and Destiny: Stepping into the Unknown

Leaving the home of the strangers who had kindly taken me in was a bittersweet and faith-filled moment. As I prepared to take the next step in my journey, an overwhelming mix of emotions filled my heart. I was deeply grateful for their generosity, yet I knew this chapter had come to a close. It was time to move forward, to embrace the unknown once again, and to trust in God's plan for my life.

I had no idea who I would stay with or what lay ahead as I prepared to travel to America. What I did know was that God had orchestrated every step of this journey, and I was determined to walk by faith and not by sight. Leaving Jamaica, I carried with me the prayers whispered during sleepless nights, the hope that had sustained me through uncertainty, and the quiet assurance that God was with me.

When I arrived in America, those first few moments felt surreal. The air was different, the sights and sounds unfamiliar, yet I was enveloped by a sense of calm, as if God was whispering, "I've got this." I didn't know where I would stay or how the details would unfold, but I trusted that He would provide, just as He had so many times before. A friend from Jamaica connected me to a woman who graciously opened her home to me.

Though she didn't know me personally, she welcomed me based on my friend's recommendation. Her kindness was a powerful reminder that God often works through others, placing the right people in our path when we need them most.

Her home became my refuge for five months. Although I didn't know what the future held, her generosity provided me with stability and peace during a time of transition. It was humbling to rely on a stranger's kindness, but it deepened my understanding of God's provision in ways I hadn't experienced before.

During my time in America, I remained active in ministry. I had initially been invited to attend a conference, and I made numerous connections along the way in the months that followed. I preached at various churches, sharing the message of God's faithfulness and grace.

These churches blessed me with honorariums, and those funds became a lifeline. They allowed me to send money back to Jamaica to pay my school fees, a tangible testament to how God continued to provide for me, even in unfamiliar territory.

In addition to preaching, I was actively involved with a Prayer Line Ministry before coming to America, and it was through this ministry that I received the invitation to attend the conference. While in America, I continued my work with the Prayer Line, preaching and praying regularly. Sometimes twice a week, I shared words of encouragement and hope with those who joined the calls. The Prayer Line became a vital connection where I could pour out the lessons God was teaching me and witness the power of intercession. Even after returning to Jamaica, I remained committed to the ministry, preaching and praying regularly for years. To this day, I still visit the church occasionally, maintaining the bond formed through this powerful ministry.

The five months I spent in America were deeply fulfilling but not without challenges. There were moments when the weight of uncertainty pressed heavily on me. Without a clear roadmap for what lay ahead, I chose to focus on what I could do in the present. Each sermon I preached, every prayer I lifted, and every connection I made felt like a step in a bigger plan that God was unfolding. Looking back, I can see how those months were a season of preparation.

They were filled with divine appointments and opportunities that shaped my journey. The honorariums I received were more than financial blessings; they were confirmations that God was using my ministry to touch lives. The Prayer Line wasn't just a platform; it was a space where I could witness God's power and faithfulness in answering prayers. As I transitioned into this new phase of my life, I began to understand that stepping into the unknown requires more than faith; it requires surrender.

Letting go of control and trusting God's timing wasn't easy, but it was necessary. Each sermon, each prayer, and every moment of uncertainty shaped me into the person God had called me to be. Stepping into the unknown was never simple, but it was always worth it. It taught me to lean not on my own understanding, but on God's wisdom and guidance. It reminded me that even when the path is unclear, He is always present, leading and providing in ways that exceed our expectations.

Unexpected Encounters and Faith in America

During my time in America, as I navigated the uncertainties of where I would live and how God would provide, I experienced a series of moments that tested my faith and discernment. One such moment occurred during a visit to Holy Land; a beautiful place dedicated to celebrating faith. It was there that a young man approached me. He seemed genuinely interested in me, and after exchanging phone numbers, we began talking. Over time, he expressed a desire to marry me.

On the surface, it seemed like a potential answer to my prayers: a chance for stability, companionship, and the opportunity to remain in America. But as our conversations deepened, I began to sense that something wasn't aligning. My faith has always been my compass, guiding my decisions and helping me discern God's will. I've learned to trust His still, small voice, especially in matters as important as this. I asked the young man questions to better understand his character and intentions, and as I listened to his answers, it became clear that he wasn't the one God had prepared for me. Though he was kind and appeared eager, his spiritual values and vision for the future did not align with mine. In my heart, I knew it wasn't God's will for my life.

Saying no wasn't easy. Turning away from what appeared to be an open door required a deep trust in God's plan, even though I couldn't see what lay ahead. After prayer and reflection, I let the young man know that I didn't believe our connection was God's will. Ending that relationship was an act of surrender, a choice to trust that God's timing and provision were perfect. Though no immediate answers followed, I held onto my faith, confident that my steps were ordered by the Lord. That season in America, however, wasn't defined solely by this decision.

It was also a time of growth, unexpected blessings, and witnessing God's provision in extraordinary ways. I had the opportunity to visit various churches, where I preached and shared the Word of God. Often, I received honorariums in return: not just financial gifts, but affirmations of the value of the message God had placed on my heart. Each invitation to speak felt like a confirmation that I was walking the path He had set before me, even in the midst of uncertainty.

The kindness of strangers during this period was yet another reminder of God's care and provision. People I had never met opened their hearts and homes to me, supporting me in ways I could never have imagined. The pastor who had invited me to America through her prayer line ministry made a lasting impression. Her generosity amazed me. She blessed me with two brand-new dresses and even gave me money, encouraging me to purchase another suit and a pair of shoes for church. These weren't just material gifts; they were expressions of God's love, proof that He was attentive to the smallest details of my needs. Each item was a reminder that God doesn't just provide. He provides with care and precision.

These moments humbled me deeply. As I traveled from church to church, meeting people and sharing God's Word, I saw how He uses His people to care for one another. Strangers became friends. Pastors became encouragers. Congregations became an extended family.

The love and generosity I experienced through them reflected the heart of Christ in ways that left me profoundly moved.

Amidst all this, I remained steadfast in my faith, trusting that God was working behind the scenes to make a way for me to stay in America. I didn't know how it would happen, but I believed He had a plan far greater than anything I could imagine. While marriage had seemed like one possible avenue, I chose to trust God to bring the right partner into my life in His perfect timing. In the meantime, I poured myself into the ministry He had called me to, preaching, praying, and encouraging others through His Word.

Looking back, that season taught me invaluable lessons about faith, discernment, and surrender. It showed me the importance of saying no when something doesn't align with God's purpose, even if it looks like the "right" opportunity. The young man at Holy Land was a part of my journey, but he wasn't my destination. God had something better in store for me, and through it all, He was guiding me step by step.

My time in America wasn't just about navigating relationships or finding a way to stay; it was a transformative period marked by both challenges and blessings. The honorariums, the kindness of strangers, and even the young man who crossed my path were all pieces of a greater story. Each moment, whether joyful or painful, was a step in the process of shaping me into the person God intended me to become. Through it all, I held onto one unshakable truth: God's plans are always good. Even when the path seemed uncertain or the answers didn't come immediately, I trusted that He was orchestrating every detail for His glory and my good. That faith sustained me, giving me the courage to keep moving forward and the confidence to embrace the unknown with hope.

The Ordination: God's Promises Fulfilled

Reconnecting with a friend from Jamaica brought unexpected blessings into my life during my time in America.

When the Prayer Line Ministry needed a speaker, he was the one who recommended me to preach, which became my first connection with them. Through his introduction, I stayed spiritually connected and was given the opportunity to minister and share God's Word with others. His support was a meaningful part of my journey during that season.

When I first arrived in America, I was warmly welcomed by everyone I met. My friend and his wife, both active members of their church, along with her mother and a few others, invited me to attend their services. That church quickly became a pivotal part of my journey. I began attending regularly, immersing myself in the vibrant community, sharing in fellowship, and growing spiritually. During those visits, the pastor and congregation began to notice the anointing God had placed on my life.

The pastor of the church, a humble yet visionary leader, saw something in me. After hearing me preach on a few occasions, he approached me with a decision that marked a significant milestone in my spiritual walk: the church wanted to ordain me as a pastor and evangelist. The news came as both a surprise and a confirmation. Though I had already been ordained as an evangelist in Jamaica, this ordination carried a deeper weight. It symbolized not only a new chapter in my ministry, but also the fulfillment of God's promises for my life.

As I prepared for the ordination, I reflected on the journey that had brought me to this point: the challenges, the sacrifices, and the faith that had sustained me. I thought about the prophecy spoken over my life years ago, one that declared I would preach the gospel to nations, with signs and wonders following. I also remembered my mother's words that had stung so deeply: "You're not going to become no evangelist." Her disbelief had lingered in my mind for years.

Yet, rather than letting it fester as bitterness, I used those words as fuel for my determination to fulfill God's calling. But God's promises are never bound by human doubts or limitations. Standing in that church on the day of my ordination, I felt overwhelmed by His faithfulness. Here I was, in a foreign land, far from the familiarity of Jamaica, being recognized and affirmed in my calling. It was a moment of validation, not just of my ministry, but of the faith I had placed in God's plan. He had guided me every step of the way, turning every trial into a stepping stone toward my destiny.

The ordination ceremony itself was a beautiful and unforgettable experience. Members of the congregation, including my Jamaican friend and his family, gathered to witness the occasion. As the pastor laid hands on me and prayed over my life and ministry, declaring God's blessings for the journey ahead, I was deeply moved. My friend's wife was also being ordained on the same day, which made the occasion even more meaningful. I remember feeling that the day was one filled with shared purpose and divine confirmation.

Tears welled in my eyes as I knelt at the altar, feeling the weight of the moment. It was the culmination of years of obedience and faith, a reminder of the scripture: "For the gifts and the calling of God are irrevocable" (Romans 11:29). As I stood before the congregation, now officially ordained as a pastor and evangelist, I couldn't help but reflect on the contrast between this moment and my mother's earlier words. Her disbelief in my calling had once been a source of pain, but God had taken that pain and turned it into purpose.

This moment wasn't about proving her wrong; it was about walking in the destiny God had ordained for me long before I was even aware of it. The ordination also served as a powerful reminder of God's perfect timing. There were still prophecies over my life that had yet to come to pass, but this moment was evidence that God's promises are always fulfilled in His time. As Jeremiah 29:11 declares: "For I know the plans I have for you, declares the Lord, plans for welfare and not for evil, to give you a future and a hope."

After the ceremony, the congregation celebrated with joy and love. My Jamaican friend and his family expressed their pride and excitement, rejoicing in how far God had brought me. The pastor shared words of encouragement, reminding me that this ordination was not just a title, but a sacred responsibility to walk in obedience and humility as I continued to serve God.

Looking back on that day, I am reminded of the significance of faith and perseverance. There were moments when discouragement tried to creep in, but God's voice was always louder. He reminded me that His promises are "yes and amen" (2 Corinthians 1:20). This ordination marked the fulfillment of one part of His plan for me, but it also signaled the beginning of a new chapter, one where I would walk in even greater faith and responsibility, trusting Him to lead me every step of the way. Even now, as I reflect on that moment, I am filled with gratitude. It wasn't about receiving a title; it was about stepping fully into the calling God had for me. It was a testimony to the truth that no matter who doubts you, when God has a plan for your life, nothing and no one can stop it.

God's Provision Through Filing

The decision for the church pastor to file for me to stay legally in the United States was a significant turning point in my journey. It was a moment when I could clearly see God's hand at work. Though the circumstances weren't ideal, and the marriage itself didn't work out, this opportunity became part of a much larger plan God was orchestrating in my life. It was evident that His provision was unfolding in ways only He could arrange.

The pastor, who had already shown immense kindness and faith in me, was willing to go a step further by filing for my legal status. However, time was not on our side. As my stay in the United States was nearing the four- to five-month mark, he explained that we needed more time to complete the process, without me overstaying my visa. He suggested that I temporarily return to Jamaica. This would reset the timeline and allow me to re-enter the United States legally, giving us the additional time required to finalize the filing process.

Initially, the idea of returning to Jamaica felt risky, even daunting. Having spent nearly five months in the U.S., I knew that leaving and attempting to re-enter could draw attention from immigration officials. The uncertainty of whether I would be allowed back into the country weighed heavily on my mind. But deep in my heart, I believed this was a moment to trust God completely. If this was truly His plan, He would make a way.

With that faith guiding me, I decided to return to Jamaica. My stay there was brief, just a few weeks, but it was filled with prayer and reflection as I prepared emotionally and spiritually for the journey ahead. It wasn't an easy decision, but I chose to lean on God's promises and remain obedient to His leading. My time in Jamaica became a season of seeking clarity and favor for what lay ahead.

In the days leading up to my departure from the United States, I had a conversation with a woman who approached me with what she presented as concerns about my plans. She suggested that I consider traveling to the Bahamas, first before heading to Jamaica and then returning to the U.S. She believed that taking an alternate route might reduce the chances of being flagged by immigration officials upon reentry. While her advice may have seemed practical on the surface, I found it unsettling, especially since I never shared my travel plans with her directly. However, I felt a deep conviction in my spirit to take the direct path instead. My faith was strong, and I trusted that if this journey was truly part of God's plan, He would pave the way, even through the challenges.

It was a difficult choice, but faith often calls us to step into the unknown without guarantees. Despite moments of doubt, I decided to travel back to the United States directly from Jamaica. There were times when I questioned my decision, wondering if it would lead to rejection or complications, but I chose to hold onto God's promises and let Him lead.

The journey back to the United States became a test of that faith. I faced obstacles that could have easily shaken my resolve, but each challenge reminded me of God's power and provision. While the specifics of my immigration encounter are a story for another section, I can confidently say that God proved Himself faithful once again. His hand was evident in every step of the process.

What stood out to me most during this time was how God worked through people to create opportunities I could never have orchestrated on my own. The pastor's willingness to go above and beyond for me was a testament to God's provision. He saw something in me, God's calling and purpose, and was moved to support my journey. For that, I am eternally grateful. It wasn't just about the filing process; it was about God using others to affirm His plans for my life.

This chapter of my life taught me that trusting God doesn't guarantee a smooth road or an easy path. Trusting Him means stepping forward, even when the odds seem stacked against you. It means believing that He is working behind the scenes, orchestrating every detail for your good and His glory.

Returning to Jamaica and coming back to the United States wasn't a step I took lightly. But looking back, I can see how that decision strengthened my faith and deepened my understanding of God's perfect timing. It reaffirmed my belief that when God opens a door, no one can shut it. His provision may not always look the way we expect, but it is always exactly what we need.

Although I did not marry the young man, the filing process became a key part of God's provision for my life. It wasn't the end of the story, but rather a stepping stone to the fulfillment of His promises. Sometimes, God uses unexpected means to bring about His plans, and in this case, the filing process was one of those means.

Through this experience, I learned to trust God in ways I never had before. I learned to rely on His wisdom instead of my own understanding and to take steps of faith even when the path seemed unclear. This was just one chapter in my journey, but it was a chapter that shaped me, prepared me, and reminded me of God's unwavering faithfulness.

Thoughtful Gestures: Returning to Jamaica with Love

My return to Jamaica after spending five months in the United States was more than just a homecoming. It was an opportunity for reflection and gratitude. This trip wasn't simply about going back; it was about returning with a heart full of thankfulness for all that God had done in my life during my time away. As I prepared for the journey, I wanted to show my family that, despite the challenges and distance that often defined our relationships, I hadn't forgotten them.

Before leaving the United States, I carefully selected gifts for my loved ones. I remember walking through the aisles of a store, picking out small but thoughtful items such as soaps, t-shirts, and other little treasures. Each choice reflected intentionality, a desire to extend love and care. These weren't extravagant gifts, but they were meaningful tokens, a way of saying, "I was thinking of you." Whether it was for my mother, my grandmother, my cousins, or my aunt, I wanted each gift to serve as a reminder of my connection to them. I also made sure to bring something for the children at the house where I had been staying before my travels. Showing gratitude for their warmth and kindness was just as important to me as honoring my family.

It wasn't about the monetary value of the gifts; it was about the gesture. These small offerings reflected my effort to embody the love of Christ, who teaches us to give generously, even in situations where kindness may not always have been reciprocated. For me, this act of giving was about extending grace, even when it required stepping outside of my comfort zone.

One moment from that trip stands out vividly, and it's tied to something as simple as a pair of slippers. Before leaving the United States, I had come across the most unique pair of slippers I'd ever seen. They were unlike anything I had ever owned, and something about them immediately captured my attention. I purchased the slippers from a swap shop in Fort Lauderdale. The moment I saw them, I knew I couldn't leave without them. These weren't just slippers to me; they were special, a small luxury that felt like a reward after months of trusting God and relying on His provision. They were comfortable, stylish, and undeniably unique. When I wore the slippers for the first time, they brought me an unexpected sense of joy. It may seem trivial to feel so attached to a pair of slippers, but for me, they represented more than just footwear.

They were a symbol of how far I had come, a treat I had allowed myself, a reminder of God's faithfulness and provision during a challenging season. Every time I slipped them on; I felt a quiet confidence and a sense of gratitude. After arriving in Jamaica, I eagerly shared the gifts I had brought with my family. I watched as they unwrapped the soaps, tried on the t-shirts, and smiled at these small but heartfelt gestures. It felt good to give, even in simple ways. When it came to my mother, our relationship had always been strained, but

I still wanted to extend kindness and love. I handed her the gift I had chosen for her, feeling at peace knowing I was doing my part to honor her, despite our complicated history.

Then came an unexpected moment that tested my willingness to give. My mother noticed the slippers I was wearing. She had no idea what my plans were or if I intended to go back to the US. But the moment she saw the slippers on my feet, her eyes lingered on them, and I could see the admiration in her expression. She didn't know how many other shoes I had, yet she still felt comfortable asking for the very ones I was wearing. In that moment, it became clear that my well-being wasn't her concern, only what she could get from me.

Finally, she asked, "Can I have those slippers?" For a moment, I froze. Her request caught me off guard. She had no way of knowing how much those slippers meant to me. She didn't know they were my little reward to myself after months of uncertainty and faith. And yet, she asked. It would have been easy to say no. After all, they were mine. I had every right to keep them.

But as I stood there, something stirred in my heart, a gentle reminder of the grace God had shown me time and time again. This was an opportunity to extend that same grace to her. Without hesitation, I took off the slippers and gave them to her. I still remember the look on her face as she accepted them. It was a mixture of surprise and gratitude, and perhaps even a hint of recognition of what the gesture meant.

For me, it wasn't just about giving her the slippers; it was about responding in love, even in the face of our complicated history. That moment taught me a profound lesson about sacrifice and kindness. Sometimes, God calls us to give in ways that challenge us; to release the things we cherish in order to show love to someone else. It wasn't about the slippers; it was about the act of giving, about putting her needs or desires above my own.

In hindsight, giving her those slippers felt symbolic, a step in my journey of healing. It was a reminder that I could choose love, even when it wasn't easy. While my mother may never have understood how much I loved those slippers, I knew that giving them to her was an act of obedience to God's call to love unconditionally.

The days I spent in Jamaica after returning were filled with moments like these, opportunities to give, to reconnect, and to reflect on how far God had brought me. Every gift I gave, every smile I shared, every act of kindness was a way of honoring my journey and expressing gratitude for God's provision. Each gesture was a way of saying thank you to Him, acknowledging that everything I had, even the slippers on my feet, ultimately belonged to Him.

Looking back, I realize the slippers were just one small part of a much larger story. They reminded me that the blessings we hold dear are often the ones we're called to share. And in sharing, we discover that God always provides for us, often in ways we least expect.

A Test of Faith at Immigration

Leaving Jamaica this time felt different. As I packed my bags, uncertainty weighed heavily on my heart. I wasn't sure when I would return. There was no clear timeline, just a quiet determination to step out in faith and trust that God's plan for my life would unfold as it was meant to in the United States. My decision to leave was not made lightly. Each item I placed in my suitcase (clothing, essentials, and a few keepsakes for comfort) seemed to hold more meaning this time. The journey ahead stretched out before me like an open road, undefined and unpredictable.

Boarding the plane brought a flood of emotions. Nervousness about the unknown intertwined with hope for what might lie ahead. Beneath it all was a deep surrender to God's will. Though I couldn't foresee what the future held, one thing was certain: I wasn't walking this path alone. God was guiding me, even as I wrestled with uncertainty.

When I landed in the United States, the transition was far from smooth. After navigating the immigration process, I discovered that my bag was missing. Standing by the carousel, scanning the endless rotation of luggage that wasn't mine, anxiety started to creep in. My mind raced with questions and scenarios. What if something had gone wrong? In the chaos of the moment, I closed my eyes and whispered a prayer, asking God to take control. Moments later, I was guided through a process where my belongings were searched and my documents checked. I was eventually allowed to continue my journey shortly after I started praying in tongues. Relief washed over me, replacing the fear and doubt. That moment reaffirmed my faith. Even in my panic, God's hand was present, steadying me. I had prayed, trusted, and believed, and He had carried me through as He always had.

As I stepped out of the airport into an unfamiliar world, a deep sense of purpose settled in my heart. The setbacks I had faced didn't feel like obstacles but rather pieces of a larger story God was writing for me. This was just the beginning of a new chapter, a chapter that would undoubtedly hold more uncertainty, growth, and joy. But through it all, I trusted in the unraveling truth that God's plans were greater than anything I could imagine. Step by step, He was leading me, and I was walking in faith toward the future He had prepared for me.

Back to America: A New Chapter of Independence

As I returned to America, it marked the beginning of a new chapter in my life, one where I began to embrace independence, stand firm in my own decisions, and detach myself from the lingering shadows of my past. Leaving Jamaica quietly, with only the bare essentials, felt symbolic of this new path. It was a decision to move forward, to be self-reliant, and to build a life no longer tethered to the crumbling relationships I had left behind.

Initially, I believed the filing process would be my way forward. The pastor had assured me, he would help me stay in the country legally, and I trusted his word. But as months passed with no progress, I began to feel disheartened. My repeated attempts to contact him were met with silence or vague responses. By the time I approached the six-month mark, I realized the filing process hadn't even begun. It was a painful, frustrating realization. I felt isolated and abandoned, as though the support I had relied on had evaporated. I had trusted that God would make a way through the pastor's help, but instead, I found myself back at square one, without legal status and feeling more alone than ever.

Despite this setback, I refused to give up. I clung to the prophecy I had received, one that instructed me to move to a specific state. It became clear to me that I needed to take action. With my legal status in the United States nearing its expiration, I packed my bags once again and left for that state. I still had a little time before the six-month window closed, but I knew the clock was ticking. Even in the uncertainty, I felt God's hand guiding me.

When I arrived, it didn't take long for the reality of my situation to sink in. Time was running out. As the expiration date approached, I reached out to the young man I had met at Holy Land. I had told him before that the Lord had revealed he wasn't the one for me, but in my vulnerable state, I found myself reconsidering. Uncertainty surrounded my future, and the thought of marriage seemed like a possible solution. When I reached out, he was eager to move forward, ready to buy a ring and fly to Texas to marry me.

That night, as I prayed for direction, the Lord gave me a clear and stern warning: He is not the one. The vision I received left no room for doubt. When I woke up the next morning, I couldn't wait to tell him. I explained, once again, that the Lord had made it clear he wasn't meant to be my husband. Naturally, he was confused. "Are you sure about this?" he asked, and while his question lingered in the air, I felt no uncertainty in my heart. I knew the answer. With my legal status set to expire soon after, I released the idea of marriage as a solution. It wasn't God's plan. During that time, I decided to reach out to my mother. I messaged her on Facebook a simple "hello, how are you doing?" Weeks passed with no response. Then, one day, I posted a picture of myself in Texas. I was standing inside a beautiful home, smiling confidently, with hope in my heart. I captioned it: "Smiling into my destiny." To my surprise, that post prompted a response from her.

My phone rang, and when I picked up, I heard her voice on the line. "So, you and I aren't going to get close, huh?" Her words lingered in the air, heavy with emotion.

My mind flashed back to the time I had asked to stay with her in Jamaica, a moment when I'd hoped we could reconnect. Her refusal had been firm, and now in light of this unexpected call the sting of that memory rose to the surface. As I listened to her voice on the phone, I responded gently but firmly. 'When I was in Jamaica not too long ago, I asked if I could stay at your house. That was an opportunity for us to get close."

By now, I realized it wasn't that she truly wanted to reconnect with me. Instead, it seemed as though every time I appeared to be doing well, she tried to reestablish contact. She had done the same when I was staying with my father, and now she was doing it again.

I had previously reached out to her on Facebook, just to say hello, but she never responded. Looking back, I believe she ignored my message because she assumed I was still in Jamaica. Perhaps, in her mind, there was no reason to engage if she didn't see any progress on my part. But now, after seeing my post about "smiling into my destiny," she was suddenly reaching out.

I went on to express my disappointment, mentioning that I had messaged her on Facebook before, and yet she hadn't acknowledged it. Her response offered neither an apology nor an explanation. Instead, the conversation took a turn, becoming more heated than I had anticipated. I pressed for an answer. Had she seen my message? And if so, why hadn't she responded? But she refused to acknowledge my questions, sidestepping them entirely.

The Facebook Message: A Moment of Reflection

The exchange with my mother, sparked by my Facebook post, lingered with me long after it ended. When she saw the picture of me in Texas, smiling confidently and seemingly secure in my future, her message about our lack of closeness stood out. It wasn't just a passing comment. It was a reflection of the emotional gap that had been growing between us for years. Her words acknowledged the distance, but they felt more like a resignation than an invitation to bridge it.

Despite the conversation, I felt a mixture of frustration and sadness. Once again, I had reached out, hoping for a different response, but instead, I was met with a blunt acknowledgment of our separation. Her words weren't new, they were a truth I had come to accept over time but hearing them so directly still stung. It was a painful reminder of the years of strained communication, missed opportunities, and unresolved emotional distance that had defined our relationship. As I processed the exchange, the timing of it all seemed to intensify my feelings.

I was fasting that day, seeking a deeper connection with God, and the conversation felt like an intrusion on the peace I had hoped to find. It disrupted the stillness I was trying to cultivate, and while I tried to remain calm and composed outwardly, inside I was grappling with a storm of emotions. I had hoped, perhaps naively, that the physical distance between us could be bridged by emotional closeness, but her response brought the reality of our relationship into sharp focus. Instead of drawing us closer, the conversation left me feeling even more disconnected.

As I reflected on this moment, I began to see our relationship more clearly, not just as it was, but as it had always been. The lack of closeness wasn't just a symptom of the past; it was a reality of the present. For years, I had reached out, trying to connect, trying to heal the distance between us. But no matter how much effort I put in; the gap remained. It wasn't just a matter of physical separation; it was an emotional divide that had been growing wider with time. I had hoped that the changes in my life, the new places I was discovering, the personal growth I was experiencing might somehow create an opportunity for us to reconnect.

I believed that perhaps my transformation could inspire a shift in our relationship. But that day, as I faced my mother's words, I realized that true closeness requires more than time, distance, or circumstance. It requires mutual understanding, a shared desire to bridge the gap. And for all my efforts, it seemed I was the only one reaching across the divide. This realization was painful but necessary. For so long, I had carried the weight of hoping, of trying, of believing that if I worked hard enough, I could fix what was broken between us.

But in that moment, it became clear: relationships only change when both people are equally invested in healing and growth. No matter how much I wanted things to be different, I couldn't force the connection.

The conversation with my mother forced me to examine my own emotional boundaries and needs. I began to see how much energy I had poured into longing for a relationship that always seemed just out of reach. It wasn't an easy realization to accept. I had clung to the belief that if I could say the right thing or show enough love, I could close the gap between us. But now, I was beginning to see that some relationships might never change, no matter how deeply we desire them to.

That day, in the midst of fasting and reflection, I had to confront some hard truths about my relationship with my mother. The silence after I reached out, the unanswered message, and the years of emotional distance weren't isolated moments. They were part of a pattern. A reality I could no longer ignore. It wasn't just about the recent Facebook exchange; it was about the cumulative weight of everything unspoken between us. The emotional baggage we carried and the walls that had been built over the years had created a divide that seemed impossible to overcome.

And yet, amidst the pain of this realization, there was also a moment of clarity. I began to understand that my emotional well-being couldn't depend on her willingness to meet me halfway. I couldn't keep tying my sense of peace and healing to the hope that she would change or that our relationship would improve. My journey had to be about my growth, my healing, and my ability to move forward, regardless of where we stood.

Accepting this truth wasn't easy. Letting go of the hope I had held for so long felt like giving up on something sacred. But I began to see that it wasn't about giving up, it was about releasing unrealistic expectations and finding freedom in accepting what was. I realized I had to prioritize my own emotional independence, even if it meant letting go of the dream of closeness I had always longed for. And yet, in that moment of reflection, a sense of clarity emerged. I realized that my emotional well-being could no longer depend on someone else's willingness to meet me halfway. I needed to prioritize my own healing and growth, regardless of the state of our relationship.

It was a difficult but necessary step toward emotional independence. While it didn't erase the pain of the situation, it helped me understand that holding onto the hope of things magically changing would only keep me stuck.

Conclusion: Moving Forward with Purpose

As I reflect on the journey that took me from the quiet streets of Jamaica to the uncertainties of life in the United States, I see how each challenge, each moment of struggle, became a stepping stone toward the person I am today. Every chapter of my life, though filled with difficulty, has helped shape a resilience within me that cannot be easily shaken. The experiences I've lived through, whether they were moments of disappointment, the pain of distance in my relationships, or the personal trials I faced, have all contributed to a deepening sense of independence and strength.

The challenges I encountered have, in many ways, been the catalyst for my personal growth. I came to understand that true independence isn't just about being physically alone or managing life on my own; it's about having the confidence to make my own decisions, standing firm in my beliefs, and knowing that I am not defined by what I've been through, but by how I choose to move forward. Life's hardships have only reinforced my commitment to myself and to the future that God has promised me.

Through these difficult moments, my faith became the foundation on which I stood. The conviction that God had a purpose for me, even when circumstances suggested otherwise, provided me with an unshakable hope. Whether in the quiet moments of prayer or in the decisions I made, I realized that each step I took was guided by His hand, even when I couldn't see the path ahead. Through this journey, I learned to trust that His plans for me were far greater than anything I could have imagined for myself.

Looking back, I see that I have grown, not only as an individual but also in my walk with God. It wasn't always easy to embrace my faith amid uncertainty, but it was during those very moments that I experienced profound spiritual growth. My independence, once driven by a desire to distance myself from everything I had known, now feels intertwined with my dependence on God's will for my life. I've learned that independence doesn't mean standing alone. It means knowing who I am in Christ and walking in the purpose He's given me.

The distance in my relationship with my mother, the challenges I faced in navigating immigration, and the other trials I encountered were not merely obstacles to overcome; they were opportunities for growth. They taught me lessons in patience, perseverance, and, most importantly, in trusting God's timing. As I move forward, I do so with the knowledge that my past, my struggles, and my faith have all come together to form a foundation of strength that I can carry with me into the future. Each experience has taught me to walk with purpose, knowing that I am not simply surviving, but thriving with the strength God has given me.

Looking ahead, I face the future with confidence, trusting that God's plan for me is unfolding in ways I cannot yet fully understand. With each new step, I embrace His guidance, knowing that my path is already paved with His love and purpose. The best is yet to come, and I am ready to move forward, knowing that I am exactly where I need to be.

CHAPTER 10

Disconnecting from Family

The Breaking Point: The Fear and Uncertainty

I t felt as if the ground beneath me had vanished, leaving me suspended in a void. One moment, I was just another person trying to carve out a path in the world, and the next, I was gripped by the unrelenting fear of being discovered. My immigration status had expired, and though it wasn't something I had chosen or intended, I found myself caught in a precarious, powerless situation. The realization hit me hard like a crashing wave pulling me under, choking my thoughts and leaving me gasping for air.

Fear became my constant companion. It was as though the very air I breathed was heavy with anxiety, amplified by the administration's harsh stance on immigration and the unyielding enforcement of its laws. The presence of police officers loomed over my life like a shadow I could never escape. Walking down the street became an act of courage, one fraught with the terrifying possibility that any officer might stop me, demand to see my papers, and end my fragile existence in this new world.

Uniforms became symbols of my fear, so overwhelming it blurred reason. It didn't matter. whether they belonged to police officers, security guards, or strangers in official attire. The mere sight of a uniform tightened the knot of anxiety in my chest. In those moments, my fear was all-consuming, and there was no space for anything else.

The Weight of Uncertainty

The weight of uncertainty loomed over me like a persistent shadow, a constant reminder of how quickly my life could unravel. It wasn't just the looming expiration of my legal status that consumed me; I was also fighting an invisible battle; one I couldn't fully articulate at the time.

I was caught in a spiritual warfare that drained my energy, left me confused, and made me desperate for peace. These attacks weren't just external, they were internal, intangible forces working against me. Though I couldn't explain these struggles fully to anyone, I confided in a few trusted individuals in the United States, hoping for understanding and comfort.

Some people may have thought I was paranoid, unable to comprehend the intensity of my experience. To me, the attacks were vivid, tangible, and unrelenting, far too real to be dismissed as imagination. From time to time I received prophecies that accurately confirmed what I was going through and even years later, I received a prophetic word that affirmed what I had gone through. The prophet revealed that those spiritual attacks were real. They weren't just a trick of my mind but genuine forces at play. This revelation validated my experiences, proving to me that my struggles weren't imagined. Yet, without the language or support to fully explain what I was going through, I often felt alone in it. That loneliness drove me deeper into myself, seeking solace in solitude, the only place I felt safe.

The isolation became both a comfort and a curse. I had always valued quiet moments, but now the desire to disconnect became overwhelming.

The stress, fear, and emotional chaos in my life formed the perfect storm. I stopped trusting others to understand what I was going through. Even the people I had once confided in, family and friends, seemed distant, like strangers. I couldn't bring myself to share the depths of my struggle, fearing that they wouldn't fully understand, especially since spiritual attacks can't be seen or proven in the physical realm. So, I withdrew further into the shadows, choosing to carry my burdens alone rather than add weight to others and also removing myself from the public eye and from those who were secretly attacking me.

Eventually, I decided to sever ties entirely. I changed my phone number, cutting off communication. Then, I blocked all my family members on Facebook, creating a digital wall between me and the outside world. I informed a few of them about this decision, letting them know they could still contact me through other means if necessary. But one family member's reaction stood out; she was visibly upset, and I couldn't understand why at the time. It wasn't until years later that I would come to recognize the spiritual significance of her response.

Later, I deactivated my Facebook account altogether. It felt like the only way to escape the chaos and regain a sense of peace. I didn't know how long the silence would last, but in that moment, it was my only option. Disconnecting became my defense mechanism, a way to protect myself from a world that felt overwhelming and out of control. Yet, deep down, I knew this silence wasn't sustainable. True peace would only come when I confronted the very world I had chosen to shut out.

The Decision to Disconnect

The decision to sever ties was not one I made lightly. As the weight of uncertainty pressed down on me, I yearned for peace, something that felt increasingly impossible to achieve while staying connected to the chaos of my family life. The spiritual attacks I endured added an unseen layer of stress that compounded my fears about my undocumented status. It felt like I was waging battles on multiple fronts: physical, emotional, and spiritual, and the noise of daily interactions only magnified the turmoil within me. Disconnecting seemed like my only way to regain control and protect the fragile sense of peace I was clinging to.

Taking action required a level of determination I didn't realize I had. Changing my phone number was my first step. It was a decisive move to create space and reduce the flood of communication that had become too overwhelming. Blocking my family on Facebook wasn't driven by anger or resentment, but by self-preservation. I needed a space to think clearly, to breathe, free from the expectations, questions, or judgments that often accompanied my interactions. Eventually, I cut off all remaining digital ties, closing the door completely on anyone who might try to reach me. For the first time in what felt like forever, I had taken control of my own narrative. I created the distance I needed, giving myself room to reflect, heal, and regain perspective.

Yet even as I made these decisions, I couldn't silence the inner conflict they brought. A part of me wondered if this disconnection could be seen as betrayal. Was I abandoning my family when I should have been standing firm? Or was this necessary for my survival, a chance to rebuild myself without interference? Deep down, I knew the answer. This wasn't about them; it was about me. I had spent years trying to bridge gaps, trying to hold things together for everyone else, all the while neglecting my own well-being. The choice to step back, though deeply painful, was an act of self-care. It was an acknowledgment that my spirit needed protection, even if others didn't understand.

The spiritual attacks I faced were an entirely different battle. They left me questioning my every move. Was this disconnection truly helping me, or was it making me more vulnerable to the very forces I was trying to escape? Every step I took toward solitude felt like both a relief and a burden. The silence I created allowed me to hear my own thoughts clearly for the first time in years. I could pray, reflect, and seek God's direction without the distraction of outside opinions. But this silence also carried a weight of its own, a gnawing question of whether I had gone too far. Would I ever find the strength to reconnect, or had I cut myself off so completely that there was no way back?

During this time, my faith became my anchor. I reflected often, turning to God for clarity and reassurance. I wanted to believe that my actions weren't selfish, that they were necessary for my survival. The spiritual attacks I faced felt like a storm no one else could see, and I realized that no one could fight these battles for me. Even when my choices hurt others or caused disappointment, I reminded myself that healing sometimes requires stepping back, even from the people we love most.

Though the disconnection was painful, it gave me moments of solace, an inner quiet I hadn't felt in years. For the first time, I could listen to my own needs without guilt.

The Solace in Silence

In the silence I created, I found myself navigating a delicate balance between solitude and isolation. At first, the quiet felt heavy, almost suffocating. I was surrounded by uncertainty, fear, and the weight of unanswered questions about my future. Yet, as I settled into this space, I realized that silence could also be a gift, a sanctuary where I could truly hear myself think and, more importantly, where I could hear God's voice.

During this time, I leaned into my faith in a way I never had before. With everything else stripped away, I saw the disconnection not as a loss, but as an opportunity to grow closer to God. I used the quiet to seek Him with intensity, dedicating hours to prayer and preaching His Word. Even though my circumstances hadn't changed, my perspective began to shift. I started to see the silence as a tool for refinement, a time when I was being molded and prepared for what lay ahead.

Although I had disconnected from my family, God ensured I wasn't entirely alone. He sent people into my life who offered help and comfort in ways I hadn't expected. Among them was a pastor in Texas who stepped in during a particularly challenging time. His kindness and guidance reminded me that God's provision often comes through His people. There were moments when the weight of my circumstances felt unbearable, but God always provided exactly what I needed. Whether it was through a kind word, practical help, or a simple gesture of support, I felt His presence working through others. These encounters were like rays of light breaking through a stormy sky, affirming that I wasn't abandoned.

In the stillness of those quiet moments, I experienced a peace that only God could provide. My struggles didn't vanish, but I felt His presence in a way that was undeniable. My prayers became intimate conversations, my worship became a lifeline, and my trust in Him deepened with every passing day. In the absence of other voices, His voice grew clearer, guiding me through the uncertainty and giving me strength when I felt weak.

Of course, moments of doubt and emotional strain still arose. Isolation has a way of amplifying fears, and there were times when I questioned whether I had made the right choices. But whenever those doubts crept in, I turned to the Word of God for reassurance. Scriptures like Isaiah 41:10 "Fear not, for I am with you; be not dismayed, for I am your God," became my anchors. Even when I didn't fully grasp it in the moment, those words were a quiet source of strength, reminding me that I was never truly alone.

This period of disconnection wasn't without its challenges, but it became a season of profound growth. The silence gave me the space to confront emotions I had long ignored, to seek clarity about what truly mattered, and to draw strength from my relationship with God. While the path ahead remained uncertain, I emerged with a renewed sense of purpose and an unshakable faith that He was in control.

The Struggles and Growth

The time of disconnection, though fraught with challenges, became an unexpected opportunity for profound personal growth. In the solitude, I found the space to reflect, not just on the circumstances that had brought me to this point, but on the person I was becoming. Both emotionally and spiritually, I grew in ways that might not have been possible without the stillness this season of my life demanded.

One of the most significant realizations during this period was the importance of letting go. Not in terms of forgiveness; I had already forgiven my family long ago. I knew my ultimate goal was to enter heaven, and holding onto unforgiveness was not an option if I hoped to get there. Yet, even though I had forgiven them, the pain from past experiences still lingered at times. It wasn't bitterness or resentment; it was the natural ache left by wounds that heal but leave behind scars. Part of my journey became learning to carry those scars without letting them define me.

Conversations with others added another layer of complexity. People would often ask, "How is your family back in Jamaica?" A simple question, but it always caused me to pause internally. I wasn't in contact with them, but I couldn't bring myself to say that aloud. So, I would smile and respond, "They should be fine," even though "fine" was a word I chose more for their comfort than for the truth of my situation. Even the pastor in Texas, who had been such a blessing in my life, would ask about my family. And every time, my answer was the same: "I believe they are okay."

Over time, I realized this habit of protecting the truth of my situation was a quiet strength. It wasn't about dishonesty; it was about preserving my dignity and guarding my privacy as I navigated a complicated and deeply personal season of life. I came to understand that not everyone needed to know the full extent of my struggles. Shielding myself from unnecessary scrutiny, judgment, or pity became an act of self-preservation, allowing me to focus on healing and growth without the weight of others' opinions.

As I pressed deeper into my faith, I found that this time of solitude was shaping my perspective for the future. I began to embrace the truth that my value was not tied to my circumstances, nor was it defined by my family relationships. My worth was rooted in God's love for me and in His plans for my life. This revelation became a cornerstone of my growth, teaching me that even painful seasons serve a purpose.

The Quiet Before the Storm

As the days turned into weeks and then months, I found myself standing at a crossroads. The disconnection had, in many ways, been necessary. It was a retreat into myself, a quiet period to gather the broken pieces of my spirit. Yet, the quiet was never meant to be permanent. It was the stillness before something greater, before the storm of reconciliation that was yet to come. In my isolation, I learned the duality of silence: its ability to both heal and wound, to create space for reflection while amplifying the ache of unresolved emotions.

I had intentionally stepped back from my family and the world in search of peace. I thought solitude would give me the clarity I desperately sought, and in some ways, it did. But I also came to understand that solitude had its limits. It couldn't give me closure or heal the relationships that, despite all my efforts, still weighed on my heart. I'd hoped that disconnecting would ease my pain, but as I sat in that silence, the weight of what was left unsaid and undone began to surface. The relationships I had tried to protect by withdrawing lingered in my heart, unresolved, waiting for a reckoning.

The lesson I learned during that time was profound: sometimes, to move forward, you have to step back. You have to give yourself the space to heal, to understand, and to grow. It wasn't an easy lesson. The fear of losing connection, of being misunderstood, hung heavily over me. But I began to see that healing didn't always look or feel like peace. Sometimes, it looked like tension, discomfort, and struggle. It was in that struggle that I found resilience, a deeper understanding of myself, and the courage to continue forgiving.

I didn't just forgive my family for the wounds of the past; I also forgave myself. I forgave myself for not knowing how to navigate the complexities of those relationships sooner. Forgiveness became an ongoing process, one that required grace, not just for others but for myself as well.

During this time of quiet, a beautiful and unexpected chapter began to unfold in my life. It was then that I met my husband. Amid the silence, when I least expected it, I found someone who would become my partner, my strength, and my support. My heart, heavy with the burdens of the past, began to open again. The love we shared was a reminder of the beauty that could bloom even in the midst of uncertainty. Our connection brought healing in ways I hadn't imagined, offering the companionship and stability I had lacked during my season of isolation. We got married, and in that union, I discovered a new sense of peace and purpose.

Even in my solitude, I was never truly alone. There were moments when God's presence felt so tangible, it was as if the fear and confusion I carried began to dissolve. In the stillness, I could hear His voice whispering within me, guiding me, preparing me for what lay ahead. That small voice reminded me that it wasn't time to sever ties for good. Reconciliation, though complicated and uncertain, was still a possibility.

Now, as I reflect on those months of withdrawal, I see them not as a setback but as a step forward, a necessary step. That season of silence forced me to confront what I had been running from, what I had been avoiding. And with that confrontation came a choice. A choice to stop hiding, to open the door again, and to face whatever was on the other side. I wasn't sure what that open door would lead to, but I knew it was time to take the first step. The stage had been set, and reconciliation was on the horizon.

The quiet was nearly over. And though I didn't know what would happen next, I knew I was ready. Ready to face the unresolved, to embrace the discomfort of healing, and to move forward with a deeper understanding of myself, my family, and the lessons God had been teaching me all along.

CHAPTER 11

Seeking Independence and Reconnection

Introduction to Struggles with Validation and emotional exhaustion

As I reflected on my journey toward reconnection with my family, I realized it was important to first revisit a period of my teenage years, a time that profoundly shaped my understanding of relationships, forgiveness, and my own resilience. Living with my mother during that period brought its own set of challenges, ones that left lasting impressions on how I saw myself and others. I tried my best to be well-behaved at home and at school, diligently meeting my responsibilities and doing what was expected of me. I wasn't seeking validation or praise; I was simply trying to be myself while staying on the right path. Yet, despite my efforts, I often found myself longing for something deeper, a sense of connection and belonging that always seemed just out of reach.

No matter how hard I worked or how much I tried to follow the rules, my actions were frequently overlooked or dismissed. This persistent lack of recognition left me questioning whether my efforts even mattered. I wasn't asking for grand gestures or constant approval, just a simple acknowledgment that what I was doing was enough. Instead, I often felt invisible, and that invisibility began to weigh on me in ways I didn't fully understand at the time.

The ongoing cycle of striving to do my best and receiving little acknowledgment only deepened the emotional distance between my mother and me. It wasn't just about recognition; it was about being seen and valued for who I was, not merely for what I could do. This left me questioning my worth and wondering whether I would ever receive the understanding I so deeply craved.

As I navigated the typical challenges of adolescence, I was also burdened by a profound sense of emotional isolation. My mother's words and actions, though likely unintentional, often left me feeling as though I was invisible as if no matter how hard I tried, I could never quite measure up to her expectations.

That unspoken pressure, coupled with the natural physical and emotional demands of growing up, created a tension within me that I struggled to shake.

The Math Teacher Incident

I remember one particular day in school during math class. The teacher was struggling with a problem on the board, unable to arrive at the correct answer. Math had always been my strength, so as I observed him wrestle with the equation, I realized he had forgotten the formula. Without hesitation, I quietly offered the solution, and the teacher, after a moment, followed my suggestion. When the problem was solved, the lesson continued, but the moment lingered in my mind.

What struck me most, however, was how this seemingly small, innocent action turned into something negative at home. I'm not sure who told my mother about it. Perhaps it was my sister but somehow, the story reached her. Instead of recognizing that I had helped, it was twisted into something to criticize. My mother's reaction wasn't one of praise or gratitude, but one of accusation. She made it seem as though I had been disrespectful by "correcting" the teacher. It was never my intention to undermine anyone; I had only tried to help in that moment. But to my mother, it was an offense, and this was a familiar response from her. No matter how much effort I put into doing something right, it was often met with suspicion and negativity.

This incident became a symbol of a broader pattern in my life: no matter how hard I tried to do the right thing, my actions were often misunderstood or criticized. It felt as though everything I did was viewed through a lens of skepticism, and I was rarely given the benefit of the doubt.

What should have been a moment of recognition for my quick thinking and helpfulness turned into yet another example of how nothing I did seemed to be enough to earn positive validation from my mother. It added to the confusion and emotional exhaustion that had already settled in my heart. Over time, I began to wonder if my good intentions would ever be truly seen or appreciated, or if I would always be misunderstood.

Emotional Weight of the Tension: The Buildup of Unspoken Issues

The emotional toll of trying to maintain a positive relationship with my mother, despite her constant provocations, was immense. I felt as though I was walking on eggshells, always cautious not to say or do anything that might set her off. It seemed like no matter how hard I tried, the ground beneath me remained unstable, with every word or action under constant scrutiny, ready to be twisted into something negative. The tension in our relationship was palpable, a silent undercurrent that weighed heavily on me.

One incident, much like the math teacher situation, made the emotional exhaustion of navigating our interactions even more apparent. When I helped the teacher solve the problem and it was turned into a point of criticism, it wasn't merely a misunderstanding. It was a clear reflection of the deeper,

288

ongoing tension between us. I never knew what would trigger her or when she would react negatively, and that uncertainty made every exchange feel like a potential landmine. I found myself second-guessing everything I said or did, wondering if I would be accused of overstepping or criticized for something others might see as harmless.

The emotional weight of constantly trying to keep the peace, of striving to be seen for the good I was doing, began to feel unbearable. There was no room for honest communication or resolution. Instead, there was a perpetual undercurrent of unspoken issues, festering in the silence between us. It was as though the tension had built up over time, layer upon layer, without ever being addressed or confronted. And I, the child trying my best, was left to carry the weight of that unresolved emotional burden, unsure of how to navigate the storm.

In my mind, I tried to justify her reactions, convincing myself there must be something I was missing, some hidden reason for her behavior. But with each new incident, like the math teacher moment, it became clearer that the emotional strain of our relationship wasn't a one-time event but it was a constant, ongoing challenge. No matter how hard I tried to maintain peace, the tension lingered, unspoken but ever-present, hanging over us like a heavy cloud.

Unseen Struggles and Unspoken Competition

At one point, my mother mentioned something my sister had said years ago: "Bet she is going to be the one to take care of me." My response was simple: "That's awesome." But the comment struck me harder than I expected. It wasn't my sister's sentiment that stung. It was the way my mother framed it. It highlighted something I had always known but never fully confronted: my sister and I had experienced entirely different versions of our mother.

My sister grew up in the same house as my mother. Unlike me, she remained under her roof, benefiting from a more stable family dynamic. Her father, married to my mother, was present in the household, providing her with a sense of security I never had. She had both parents in her corner, a cushion that made life's challenges feel lighter. For her, home wasn't just a place, it was a foundation. In contrast, I had no such safety net. I left home at eighteen, thrust into a world where I had to fend for myself. Paying rent, juggling bills, and figuring out how to survive became my reality.

There was no one to catch me if I fell. The rejection I had felt from my mother wasn't just emotional, it was tangible. It followed me into every corner of my life. When my mother moved into her new house, my sister joined her. On one visit, I noticed my sister was living in the front room of the house, and my mother proudly shared that my sister had tiled the kitchen herself. It struck me as a stark reminder: my sister had a stake in this home, a sense of belonging I was never offered. When I had asked for temporary shelter, I was denied.

This difference between us, between what we had been given, was undeniable. My sister, with the cushion of my mother's support, had fewer obstacles to navigate. She could afford to invest in their home, in their lives, in ways I couldn't. She didn't face the same financial pressures I did. She didn't have to claw her way to stability. And yet, my mother seemed oblivious to this disparity. It was as though my struggles were invisible to her.

When my sister eventually traveled to the United States, she left from my mother's house, grounded by the stability and support of a strong foundation. She knew that if she ever returned, her place would be waiting. I had no such assurances. I entered the United States with nothing but my faith and determination. No safety nets. No guarantees. I had to build my own foundation, brick by brick, in a foreign land.

Forgiveness and the Burden of the Past: Emotional Struggles and Unresolved Issues

Despite my best efforts to forgive my mother and move forward, the unresolved issues from our past lingered just beneath the surface. Forgiveness is often seen as the final step in healing, but for me, it was only the beginning of a deeper and more complex journey. I had forgiven her in my heart, but the emotional scars remained. Though the pain had dulled over time, it was never fully erased. I tried to let go of the anger and resentment, but the process wasn't always easy. The past, with its layers of hurt and misunderstanding, remained unspoken. It left a heaviness in my spirit that I could never quite shake.

As a child, I had hoped that one day my mother would recognize the weight of her actions. I imagined a moment where she would apologize, where there would be mutual understanding, and we could acknowledge the pain that had been caused. But that moment never came. Instead, I carried the burden of unspoken words and unanswered questions. I tried to convince myself that I was fine, that I had forgiven her and moved on. But deep down, I knew that the unresolved wounds still shaped me. It felt as though I was trying to build a future on a foundation cracked by the past.

I wanted to move on. I worked hard to build a life for myself, to create relationships free from the weight of my history. But no matter how much I tried, the past followed me, like a shadow I couldn't outrun. The struggles I faced weren't tied to a single incident or a few hurtful words. They were the accumulation of years of misunderstanding, harsh criticism, and the silence that followed. My efforts to do right were often eclipsed by my mother's reactions or her inability to see my worth. Even though I had forgiven her, I couldn't escape the feeling that the chasm between us had never been bridged. Much of what needed to be said remained buried, unspoken, and unhealed.

The weight of the past wasn't something I could simply wish away or ignore. It was ever-present, sometimes faint and at other times overwhelming, a quiet reminder of everything unresolved. Forgiveness, while freeing in some ways, didn't erase the pain. It allowed me to move forward, yes, but I still carried the weight of those unresolved hurts. I continued seeking peace, but I was never fully at rest.

The Reconnection and Revisiting the Past: Reopening Communication

After years of silence and emotional distance, I decided to reconnect with my mother. It wasn't a choice I made lightly, and it certainly wasn't without hesitation. The past had left its marks on me, and I knew that reopening communication meant the possibility of reopening old wounds. But I was determined to move forward. I wasn't seeking to dwell on the pain of the past; instead, I wanted to forge a new connection, one built on mutual respect and understanding.

When I reached out, it was with the intention of sharing the updates that defined my present, my marriage, my accomplishments, and the steps I was taking to build a life of my own.

Our early conversations felt almost awkward, as though we were two strangers trying to rediscover a bond that had been dormant for far too long. I didn't want to relive the pain or misunderstandings of the past. I didn't want to dissect what had gone wrong or rehash what had been said. Instead, I focused on the present. I wanted to share the joy found in building my own family and the growth I'd experienced over the years. I wanted to keep the focus on what was happening now, not on the shadows of yesterday. Yet, no matter how much I tried to keep things light and positive, I couldn't ignore the tension that lingered in the air. Beneath the surface, old emotions simmered, unspoken but undeniably present.

Reconnecting with my mother was an act of hope, a decision rooted in my desire to move forward, not to reopen every past grievance. But I soon realized that it wasn't so easy to leave the past behind. Certain conversations seemed to drift back into old patterns, as though the weight of our shared history was always just beneath the surface, waiting to rise again. I wanted to be open, to be vulnerable, and to forge a new relationship with her as the adult I had become, not the wounded child I had once been. Still, it became clear that we were navigating a delicate balance teetering between acknowledging our history and striving to move beyond it.

While I hoped that this renewed communication would bring us closer, I quickly learned that healing isn't instantaneous. It requires time, patience, and a willingness from both sides to let the relationship grow in a healthier direction. For now, I'm taking it one step at a time cautiously reopening the door to a connection I'd long yearned for, even as I recognize that there is still much to work through.

The Tension of Revisiting the Past: The Conversation That Reopened Old Wounds

When I decided to reconnect with my mother, I thought we could begin anew, leaving behind the hurt and misunderstandings that had weighed us down for so long. But I quickly realized that some things couldn't be left in the past, no matter how much I wanted them to stay there. One particular conversation reopened wound I thought I had buried, forcing me to confront the unresolved pain. My mother insisted on revisiting the topic of abuse, something I had long tried to move on from. Years earlier, I had confronted her about it, but she denied any wrongdoing, claiming she hadn't abused me. At the time, I had accepted her denial for my own peace and chosen not to press further. But now, she brought it up again, and I couldn't avoid it.

Over the phone, she said, "You said I abused you, but I didn't abuse you." The years of unresolved pain came rushing back with those words. I took a deep breath before replying, "Yes, you did abuse me." I reminded her of the moments that had left deep emotional scars. I recalled one incident when my sister and I were walking behind her, laughing as children do, only for her to turn around and scold me, saying, "You are the one that something is on to laugh about." Those words cut deeply, making me feel small and insignificant.

I reminded her of another time, on my birthday, when instead of offering kind words, or even a birthday greeting, she had walked into my room and said, "People say you look like me, but you don't, because you're ugly." It wasn't just the words but the way she told them that left me feeling devalued and unworthy. I brought up the countless moments of emotional neglect, how I was expected to wash everyone's clothes by hand as a teenager: my brother's, my stepfather's, my mother's, and my own; how there was often very little lunch money for me; usually left over coins found in her purse; and how my pain was routinely dismissed. Every time I tried to express how these things had hurt me, she rejected my feelings, making me feel invisible.

Her response was blunt and unyielding: "I will never apologize to you." In the same breath, she mentioned an incident involving my sister. She reminded me of a time when I came home from school and told her my sister had skipped school. My mother had beaten my sister with a machete, and she informed me that she had to apologize to her. Hearing this story, right after she told me she'd never apologize to me, felt like salt on an open wound. Why would she apologize to my sister but refuse to acknowledge the pain she caused me? And why would she inform me that she had apologized to my sister just after she said she would never apologize to me. Her words made it clear that she couldn't or wouldn't face the truth of my experiences. Instead, she shifted focus, deflecting blame and invalidating my reality.

I responded quietly, "Well, whatever I did or whatever you said I did back then I'm still apologizing." Over the years, I had apologized repeatedly, even when I didn't believe I was at fault, just to keep the peace. But now, as an adult, I couldn't help but wonder: What does it take for a person to simply say, 'I didn't mean it that way' or 'I'm sorry,' instead of doubling down and dismissing my feelings?

The conversation soon veered in another direction, bringing up something that had lingered in my mind for years: a prophetic word I had once received. A prophet had spoken about witches in the family, claiming my mother had sought protection that unknowingly opened a door to the demonic attacks I had been experiencing. When I asked her about it back then, she denied any knowledge, insisting she had never done anything of the sort. She dismissed the prophet's words outright, but I was left wondering. Was the prophet referring to my grandmother, who had raised me? Or had he been mistaken?

Years earlier, during another prophetic moment, I had also asked her about my umbilical cord or as we call it in Jamaica, the navel cord. The question had come up in connection to a spiritual inquiry, but she brushed it off, saying, "Let the past stay in the past." Now, during this recent conversation, she brought it up again, unprompted, and I couldn't help but wonder why she hadn't forgotten that I'd asked.

This time, she finally gave me an answer: "The navel cord got lost when I was moving," she said, "just like how your little brother got lost." Her words left me more confused than ever. Why hadn't she told me this before? Why did it take so many years for her to address my question? Her answer only deepened my sense of unease, adding yet another layer of uncertainty to our already fraught relationship.

Talking to My Brother and His Involvement: Seeking Support from Family

For a long time, I had chosen not to speak to my brother about anything concerning my mother. Despite visiting his home several times, I always avoided bringing up any negativity. Even years earlier, when she intercepted him in Kingston and shared her side of an altercation we'd had, I refrained from defending myself. I told myself that the past was better left untouched. But now, with my mother dredging up old incidents, claiming I had once walked on a bed with my shoes on (a memory I couldn't recall) among other accusations; I felt it was time to address the situation.

I decided to speak with my brother and his wife, hoping to gain their perspective and possibly their support. Since they were still in Jamaica and in regular contact with her, I thought this might help bring some resolution. During that conversation, my sister-in-law was kind and empathetic. She acknowledged my struggles and said, "Some people don't apologize until they're on their deathbed." Her words offered a small comfort, but even as we spoke, my mother called me on the other line. She sounded upset, claiming that the same people I had been speaking to were saying, "If she can do that to her mother, then what would she do to me?" It became painfully clear that this back-and-forth was heading nowhere productive. Reluctantly, I ended the conversation.

Years ago, I had opened up to her, sharing something deeply personal that she had overheard and asked me about. She used that vulnerability against me. What I had shared in confidence came back to haunt me. I had approached that conversation thinking I could trust and build a bond, not giving her every detail, but enough to show accountability. Even though, if I had gone into full detail, she would have recognized that I was not totally at fault. Instead of honoring that moment, she later shared it with my brother completely out of context. It was not relevant to what we were discussing, yet she brought it up anyway. It felt like a desperate attempt to shift blame and paint me in a negative light. That was something my brother would never have known about otherwise. Rather than using it to promote healing, she used it to reinforce a narrative about me, grasping at straws to find something negative to say as if determined to paint me in a negative light.

There are so many things about my younger siblings that I have never heard my mother repeat. When I was younger, I heard something troubling about my sister and spoke about it. My mother scolded me for mentioning it. Yet years later, someone from our high school informed me that it had been widely known. I had not heard it at school. I heard it from my sister's friend, who said my sister told her. Still, my mother defended and covered for her. Likewise, I have never heard her talk about the many serious troubles my other brother experienced, which I won't mention in this memoir out of respect, but they were significant. Even during those times, she made sure he had cooked lunch to take to work as an adult. She has always been there for them, even into adulthood. But she has never shown me that same level of care.

Shortly after, my brother suggested holding a family Zoom meeting to address everything openly. I immediately agreed. I had nothing to hide and was open to honest discussion. But when he approached my mother with the idea, she called me again, this time adamantly refusing. She dismissed the suggestion outright, saying, "Your brother cannot resolve anything," and adding that she didn't want to "start talking," a statement that implied she had something negative to say about him.

Amid this mounting tension, I learned that my mother had been spreading a narrative about me: "It must have been something wrong she was involved in that caused her to disconnect from everyone." Her words reflected how negatively she viewed me, despite the truth being far different. When I was in Jamaica, none of my family members made any effort to reach out to me. My sister had wished me a happy birthday on Facebook, and that had been while I was in America. I was always the one initiating contact, sometimes after years of silence. Her version of events simply didn't match the reality I knew.

As her frustration grew over my conversation with my brother, her words turned even more cutting. In one particularly hurtful moment, she said, "You asked me about witches in the family. You are the only witch I know." Her accusation stung deeply. I took a deep breath and responded calmly, "I don't think a child of God should be calling another child of God a witch." In that moment, I had the chance to demonstrate the maturity I had gained over the years. I didn't retaliate or dishonor her, even as her words wounded me. I stood my ground with grace, refusing to let her accusations drag me into disrespect or anger. She never apologized for speaking such a cruel word over me.

The Letter to Auntie Colleen: Symbolizing Hidden Feelings

When I lived with my grandmother during my early teenage years, I often struggled to express the emotions I carried. At that age, everything felt amplified, and I saw my grandmother as unbearably loud and overly critical. She always seemed to be scolding or fussing, and like many teenagers, I misunderstood her intentions. One day, overwhelmed with frustration, I decided to pour my feelings into a letter addressed to Auntie Colleen, a popular radio program where people shared personal stories and emotions. The letter wasn't meant to be sent. It was simply my way of releasing the frustrations I couldn't find the courage or words to verbalize.

In the letter, I described my grandmother as "miserable" and vented in the raw, unfiltered way teenagers often do. It felt harmless at the time, just a private outlet for my emotions, a way to navigate the tension of adolescence in a household where emotions weren't openly discussed. I folded the letter and tucked it into my school bag, confident that it would remain hidden. Somehow, though, my mother found it.

Nearly three decades later, she brought up that same letter to my brother, still trying to paint a bad picture of me. Even though it happened so many years ago, she continued to hold it against me, using it as ammunition. Something that had been a private, emotional outlet from my teenage years was now being twisted into evidence to question my character. Or perhaps someone else had discovered it and passed it along to her. Either way, she used it as ammunition, intent on framing it as evidence of some unresolved rift between my grandmother and me. What she refused to acknowledge was that the letter had been written during my early teenage years, a time when my behavior naturally reflected the growing pains of adolescence.

Even my grandmother, years later, had remarked that I had been "a little feisty" as a teenager, but she understood it was just part of growing up. Yet here was my mother, decades later and well into my forties, dredging up a forgotten letter to make a point that no longer mattered. Who does that?

My mother's decision to revisit that letter felt like yet another way to cast me in a negative light. She clung to it as if it were proof of my flaws, refusing to see the bigger picture. What she failed to understand was that the act of writing the letter symbolized something far deeper: my attempt to process feelings I didn't feel safe expressing aloud in our home.

Looking back, my relationship with my grandmother grew stronger over the years. When I eventually left her house, the tension faded, and we began to understand each other better. In fact, my grandmother would later reflect on those years. She admitted that she'd thought I was feisty as a child but came to see that I wasn't nearly as outspoken or rebellious as some of the grandchildren who came after me.

Those children openly challenged her, sometimes crossing the line into disrespect. By comparison, I had only ever grumbled to myself or, in this case, in a private letter.

After my mother brought up the letter, I had the chance to speak with my grandmother about it. She seemed surprised and even confused. "Then who could have told her something like that?" she asked. Her reaction reaffirmed what I already knew, she had never seen the letter, nor had she ever felt disrespected by it. In that moment, I realized just how much our relationship had grown. What had once been a source of tension had long faded into the background, replaced by mutual respect and understanding.

The Continuing Denial and Conflict: Rehashing Old Issues and Patterns

My mother's refusal to acknowledge the truth of the past often left me feeling unheard and invalidated. She consistently twisted events, creating a narrative story that painted me as the one at fault. For instance, when I reminded her of how she used to give me just a handful of coins from her purse as lunch money, she adamantly denied it. She insisted that she had given each of us one hundred dollars, sharing the money that my siblings' father had left equally among us. But if that were true, why couldn't I afford lunch at school? Her version of events simply didn't align with the reality I lived. And yet, she clung to her story with unwavering conviction.

It didn't stop there. When I brought up how I used to wash the family's laundry weekly, scrubbing clothes by hand for my mother, stepfather, and sibling, she dismissed it without hesitation. "What are you talking about?" she asked, claiming she used to pay me for the washing. I was stunned. This was yet another reimagining of the past, one that erased the truth of my experience. The more she redefined these moments, the harder it became to reconcile her version of events with my own memories.

Over time, I came to understand that some people will cling to their version of the truth, even if it means causing pain to the ones they claim to love. For my mother, accepting responsibility seemed too difficult. Instead, she rewrote the past, piece by piece, until her narrative became unrecognizable to me. This lack of accountability deepened the emotional strain between us, leaving me to carry the weight of unresolved hurt.

It wasn't just one or two incidents. It was a pattern. Even after calling me a witch, an accusation that stung more than words could express, there was no apology. The weight of these moments added to the strain between us, but I knew I had to find peace for my own sake. Forgiveness became my only option, not because it was earned, but because holding on to unforgiveness would only harm me. I often reminded myself of the saying, "Unforgiveness is like drinking poison and expecting the other person to die."

Forgiving her without an apology wasn't easy, but I knew I had to do it for my own peace. It required letting go of the expectation that she would ever take responsibility for her actions or give me the validation I craved. Forgiveness didn't mean excusing her behavior. It meant freeing myself from the bitterness that threatened to take root in my heart. It was a process, a decision I had to make daily, to release the pain and choose my own healing.

Yet, the pattern of denial persisted. This wasn't just about lunch money or a single accusation. It was about how these moments accumulated over time, stacking like bricks to form an impenetrable wall between us. I longed for resolution and for her to see and acknowledge the pain her actions had caused but I had to accept that it might never come. And so, I chose to forgive, not as an act of weakness, but as a declaration of strength.

Setting Boundaries: Recognizing Your Need for Peace

Forgiving my mother was a step toward healing, but I soon realized that forgiveness alone wasn't enough to safeguard my emotional well-being. I needed to take a harder, more uncomfortable step: setting boundaries. It wasn't an easy decision. The idea of creating distance from the woman who brought me into this world felt unnatural, even wrong. But over time, I came to understand that boundaries weren't about punishment; they were about self-preservation. I needed to protect my peace, my mental health, and my sense of self.

Even after forgiveness, the cycles of denial, blame, and emotional manipulation persisted. Each interaction felt like it chipped away at the stability I was working so hard to rebuild. I began to realize that by giving her unchecked access to my emotions, I was leaving myself vulnerable to repeated pain, whether or not it was intentional on her part. I had to ask myself: Was I willing to keep subjecting myself to this hurt? The answer, though painful, was no.

Setting boundaries didn't mean shutting her out completely. It meant defining what I could handle emotionally and limiting contact to situations where I felt prepared. It required releasing the hope for apologies or acknowledgment that might never come. Instead of waiting for validation from her, I focused on giving myself the space I needed to heal.

At first, the decision to limit contact felt like betrayal. I worried about how it might be perceived, not only by her, but by others and even by myself. But the more I leaned into the idea, the more I began to understand that setting boundaries wasn't a rejection of her as a person. It was an affirmation of my own worth. I deserved relationships that nurtured and supported me, not ones that left me feeling drained or invisible.

The boundaries I set weren't perfect, and I often second-guessed myself. There were moments when guilt crept in, whispering that I was being ungrateful or unkind. But every time I prioritized my peace, I felt stronger. Forgiveness had been an important first step, but boundaries became the shield that protected the progress I had made. By setting them, I wasn't abandoning my mother or the love I had for her. I was simply choosing to love myself as well.

The Impact on My Current Life: Living with the Consequences of the Past

Living with the consequences of the past, especially in relation to my family, remains one of the hardest parts of my emotional journey. Maintaining boundaries has become essential to my well-being, but it often feels like a constant battle. My family, particularly my mother, still struggles to fully understand or accept my truth. This leaves me in a difficult position, trying to protect myself emotionally while navigating relationships that are still clouded by denial and the lack of accountability. Even when I've tried to communicate openly, my words often seem to fall on deaf ears, leaving me feeling unheard and misunderstood.

I've learned that setting boundaries isn't just about protecting my peace. It's about asserting my right to live in my truth and refusing to let anyone make me feel as though I'm lying or exaggerating my experiences. This ongoing struggle has shaped me in ways I never imagined. It has made me more resilient, yes, but also more guarded. The emotional weight of knowing that the people who should understand me the most don't always validate my experiences has left its mark. While I continue to grow and heal, there are still days when the pain of it all feels overwhelming.

One thing I've come to realize is that healing is not just about moving forward. It's about making peace with the reality that some people, no matter how much you love them, may never fully acknowledge the hurt they caused. I've come to believe that if you hurt someone publicly, you can't simply go to God privately to repent without taking responsibility in the same public space where the harm occurred. True healing requires more than just an apology. It requires accountability. Without it, the cycle of denial continues, leaving the one who has been hurt stuck in emotional limbo.

The refusal to accept the truth, especially when it's rooted in my lived experience, makes finding peace more difficult. But even as I wrestle with this, I've had to keep reminding myself of a simple truth: I deserve peace. I am worthy of living a life free from the burden of unresolved pain and unspoken truths. And no matter how heavy the weight of the past may feel; my healing is my responsibility, and my freedom is worth fighting for.

The Revelation About Family Dynamics: How I Learned to Navigate Family Relationships

The emotional complexity of family dynamics often goes unnoticed until you find yourself caught in the middle of unresolved issues. For years, I believed that love and loyalty should overshadow any wounds or hurts. I thought family ties alone should be enough to sustain relationships, even in the face of pain. But I quickly learned that not all family relationships are built on mutual understanding or respect. My relationship with my mother, shaped by years of unaddressed pain, became a stark example of this reality. I spent so much of my life trying to reconcile the love I felt for her with the hurt caused by her actions. Over time, I realized that true reconciliation could never happen without acknowledgment of the past.

One of the most valuable lessons I've learned is the necessity of setting boundaries. Without boundaries, the cycle of hurt only deepens emotional scars and reinforces unhealthy patterns. I came to understand that I could no longer allow myself to be repeatedly hurt by people who were unwilling to confront their own mistakes. Setting boundaries wasn't about holding grudges or seeking revenge. It was about protecting my emotional well-being and refusing to tolerate disrespect, even from those I love.

This process was particularly challenging with my mother, who often twisted the truth and refused to take responsibility for her actions. As I began to unravel the layers of our relationship, I saw that these patterns were not just about me. They were tied to a larger history of unresolved issues within the family. Understanding this didn't make the pain any easier to bear, but it did help me see the context in which these behaviors existed. Still, navigating this terrain wasn't easy. I often felt the weight of unspoken expectations and societal pressures to maintain family bonds at any cost.

What I've come to accept is that some relationships will never be what we hope they could be. While I longed for a deeper connection with my mother, I had to face the painful truth that she might never offer the acknowledgment and healing I craved. So, I learned to navigate these relationships differently, not by cutting people off completely, but by protecting my peace and establishing clear emotional boundaries. It wasn't easy, and it still is not, but the peace and strength it has brought me are worth the effort.

Conclusion: Reflection on the Journey Toward Healing and Moving Forward

As I reflect on the journey I've traveled, I realize the road has been long, marked by challenges, heartache, and lessons that have shaped me into the person I am today. There were moments when I felt completely alone, when the weight of unresolved family issues felt almost too heavy to bear. Yet, through it all, I've come to understand that it is possible to rise above our circumstances, to heal from past wounds, and to move forward with strength and purpose. The emotional scars of my past will always be a part of me, but they no longer define who I am. I've learned that healing is not a straight line; it's a process that requires time, patience, and grace. Along the way, I discovered the importance of forgiveness, not just for others, but for myself. Letting go of resentment and bitterness wasn't easy, but I came to realize that forgiveness wasn't about excusing what happened. It was about freeing myself from the pain that threatened to

313

hold me captive. Forgiveness, I found, is the key that unlocks true healing.

In 2 Corinthians 12:9, it is written: "But he said to me, 'My grace is sufficient for you, for my power is made perfect in weakness.' Therefore, I will boast all the more gladly of my weaknesses, so that the power of Christ may rest upon me." This verse reminds me that even in my most vulnerable moments, God's grace has always been enough. His strength has carried me through seasons of uncertainty, giving me the courage to face each new chapter of my life.

I also hold onto the promise in Romans 8:28: "And we know that in all things God works for the good of those who love him, who have been called according to his purpose." No matter the hurt or struggle, I trust that God's plan for my life is good and filled with hope. I am no longer a prisoner of my past, but someone who has learned to walk in the freedom His grace provides.

To those who may be reading this and feel as though the weight of their past is too much to carry: I want to encourage you. Healing is possible. Rebuilding is possible. Thriving is possible. The journey may not be easy, but with faith, strength, and the right support, you can overcome anything you're facing. You are not defined by your circumstances;

you are defined by your resilience and the strength that lies within you. Keep moving forward, knowing that God is with you every step of the way.

CHAPTER 12

Honoring Your Parents

What It Means to Honor Your Parents

Honor is a word that carries immense weight, especially in the context of family relationships. Culturally, honoring parents often means showing respect, gratitude, and obedience. In many societies, particularly in Jamaican culture, this respect can translate into unwavering loyalty, silence about familial conflicts, and a lifelong commitment to care for parents, regardless of personal circumstances. It is a concept deeply rooted in tradition, shaping how children are raised and how they perceive their role within the family structure.

From a biblical perspective, however, honor goes beyond cultural expectations. The Bible commands us to honor our father and mother, as seen in Exodus 20:12: "Honor your father and your mother, so that you may live long in the land the Lord your God is giving you." This command is reiterated throughout Scripture, emphasizing the importance of respect and gratitude for the role parents play in our lives. Yet, biblical honor does not demand blind obedience or passive acceptance of mistreatment. In Ephesians 6:4, parents are reminded of their responsibility: "Fathers, do not provoke your children to anger, but bring them up in the discipline and instruction of the Lord." This balance reveals that honoring is a two-way street, requiring mutual respect and accountability between parents and children.

In this chapter, I seek to redefine what it truly means to honor one's parents, bridging the gap between cultural traditions and biblical truth. Honoring parents does not mean staying silent in the face of abuse, nor does it mean carrying the weight of pain without seeking healing. Parents are entrusted by God with the sacred responsibility to nurture and protect their children, not to harm them under the guise of authority.

Writing this memoir brought me face-to-face with difficult questions about honor. At one point, I hesitated, wondering if telling my story would dishonor my mother or other family members. The cultural narrative that discourages speaking out was deeply ingrained in me, making me question whether sharing my truth could be seen as an act of betrayal. But over time, I realized that silence perpetuates cycles of pain. Breaking that silence was not an act of dishonor. It was an act of courage, faith, and a commitment to healing. I came to understand that honoring parents does not mean ignoring past wounds but rather confronting the truth with grace and a desire for restoration.

317

This chapter is dedicated to exploring the true meaning of honoring parents, a definition rooted in love, truth, and godly principles. It is my hope to encourage others to seek healing, embrace their voice, and walk in the freedom that comes from breaking unhealthy cycles. Honoring parents, as God intended, involves accountability, respect, and forgiveness. It requires holding onto truth while extending grace and allowing space for healing, both for ourselves and for those we love.

The Cultural Perspective: Silence as Honor in Jamaican Culture

In Jamaican culture, the concept of honoring one's parents is deeply rooted in a code of silence. Children are often expected to carry the weight of parental actions, good or bad, without complaint. To speak out against a parent, particularly about harm or neglect, is considered the ultimate dishonor, a betrayal that reflects poorly on the child rather than the parent. This unspoken rule traps many in a cycle of pain, unable to confront their wounds or seek healing.

Growing up in Jamaica, I witnessed how this cultural norm shaped everyday life. A child who dared to express their feelings about mistreatment was often met with rebuke rather than support. "Big people business," as it's often called, was strictly off-limits to children, even when that "business" directly affected their well-being. Parents held absolute authority; their actions were deemed beyond reproach. In such an environment, children learned to suppress their pain, bury their emotions, and accept their reality in silence.

This cultural perspective is especially evident in the way abuse is justified or minimized. A parent disciplining harshly might defend their actions by saying, "A fi mi pickney, mi can do what mi want," meaning, "It's my child; I can do what I want." The underlying message is clear: parents wield unchecked power, and children have no voice. This belief perpetuates cycles of harm, as children who grow up in such environments often carry unresolved trauma into adulthood.

One poignant example of this dynamic played out publicly a few years ago when a Jamaican man, known for his talent on a popular platform, spoke out about the abuse he endured from his mother. Despite not growing up with her or benefiting from her care, she sought reconciliation with him after he won a significant amount of money. He chose to break his silence, detailing the neglect and abuse he had suffered. In response, his mother defended herself, claiming he had been "rude" as a child, a familiar narrative used to justify harsh treatment.

His decision to speak out sparked widespread debate. Some criticized him for airing "family business" in public, accusing him of dishonoring his mother. Others praised his courage, recognizing the importance of transparency and healing. While the conflict seemed to subside over time, it remains unclear whether true reconciliation ever occurred. This incident highlighted the cultural tension between the expectation of silence and the necessity of addressing past wounds.

The silence enforced by Jamaican culture comes at a great cost. Children raised without the freedom to express their pain often carry that silence into adulthood, where it manifests as unresolved anger, depression, or difficulty forming healthy relationships. The belief that speaking out is dishonorable traps individuals in cycles of shame, isolating them and invalidating their experiences.

For me, breaking this silence was a critical step toward healing. It wasn't an act of rebellion or dishonor; it was an act of survival. I realized that staying silent only perpetuated the pain and allowed harmful narratives to persist unchecked. Speaking out became an act of courage, a way to reclaim my voice and challenge the cultural norms that had silenced me for so long.

The idea that honoring parents means remaining silent about their wrongdoings must be reexamined. True honor is rooted in love, accountability, and respect. It is not rooted in fear or blind loyalty. Parents, too, are called to honor their children by nurturing, protecting, and guiding them in ways that reflect God's love. When they fail in these responsibilities, silence does not serve anyone. It only deepens the wounds.

Ephesians 4:25 says, "Therefore, each of you must put off falsehood and speak truthfully to your neighbor, for we are all members of one body." While this verse speaks to relationships within the body of Christ, it also applies to family dynamics. Speaking the truth is a vital step toward fostering healing and reconciliation.

As I share my story, I hope to encourage others who feel trapped in this cultural expectation of silence to find their voice. Breaking the silence is not easy. It requires strength, faith, and often the support of others. But it is a necessary step toward healing, not just for the individual but for future generations. By addressing the pain and speaking truth, we can begin to dismantle cycles of harm and create a legacy of love, accountability, and understanding.

Breaking the Silence: Speaking Out as Courage

Speaking out is not an act of dishonor; it is an act of courage, a step toward healing, and a way to uplift others who may be enduring similar struggles. The decision to write this memoir was not an easy one. For years, I wrestled with whether sharing my story would implicate others or be seen as dishonoring those involved. Jamaican culture, with its deeply ingrained expectation of silence, weighed heavily on my mind. Could I speak my truth without being judged as disloyal or ungrateful? These questions lingered, holding me back from what I now recognize as a divine calling.

For years, I received prophecies about writing books, affirmations that my life's experiences were meant to serve a greater purpose. These were not vague, generalized messages; they were clear, direct confirmations that my testimony could be a vessel for change. The first book that came to mind was a memoir. Yet I hesitated, questioning whether I was ready to confront the past and commit it to paper. I feared that sharing my experiences might reopen wounds that others were not prepared to face and perhaps wounds that I wasn't sure I was ready to fully examine myself.

What ultimately pushed me forward was the realization that this story is not just about me. It is about ministry. As prophesied, I came to understand that young people were waiting for my testimony. My experiences, painful as they were, held the power to inspire, encourage, and guide others who might feel voiceless and alone. Keeping silent would have meant withholding a gift that God intended for others. This memoir became a way to serve, to minister, and to remind others that healing is possible.

Writing this memoir also became a way to redefine what it means to honor others. True honor is not found in silence or in the suppression of truth. It is found in love, in respect, and in the courage to address what has been broken so that it can be restored. When parents harm their children, whether intentionally or unintentionally, silence only allows the harm to fester. By speaking out, I am not seeking to dishonor anyone. Rather, I hope to create a space for healing for myself, for others who have endured similar experiences, and perhaps even for those who caused the harm.

This process of writing has been an act of courage. It has challenged my fears and pushed me to confront societal norms that have long silenced so many. But this is not about placing blame or pointing fingers. It is about reclaiming my voice and my narrative. It is about showing others that they, too, can face their past and find a path toward healing.

As I reflect on this journey, I've come to understand that breaking the silence is an act of service. Many, especially young adults, are carrying the emotional scars of their upbringing while grappling with cultural expectations that demand silence and submission. By sharing my story, I hope to offer a roadmap for healing and a reminder that they are not alone.

Proverbs 31:8-9 says: "Speak up for those who cannot speak for themselves, for the rights of all who are destitute. Speak up and judge fairly; defend the rights of the poor and needy." While this passage often refers to advocating for justice, it also calls us to give a voice to those silenced by societal norms. Speaking out about personal pain and injustice is a way to honor this call. It allows me to stand not just for myself, but for others silently enduring similar struggles.

This memoir is a testament to the power of resilience and the necessity of courage. Confronting the past is never easy, especially when doing so challenges cultural norms and risks backlash. But it is necessary. Healing begins when we acknowledge what has been broken and take steps to mend it. Silence may feel safer, but it does nothing to address the pain or create meaningful change.

Romans 8:28 reminds us: "And we know that in all things God works for the good of those who love him, who have been called according to his purpose." This verse has been a source of strength for me throughout this journey. It reassures me that even the painful parts of my story have a purpose. God can use every experience, no matter how difficult, to bring about healing and growth, not just for me, but for others as well.

To those grappling with perhaps to speak out about their own experiences, I encourage you to seek God's guidance and trust His timing. Speaking out is not about seeking revenge or validation; it is about finding freedom and allowing others to find freedom through your testimony. It is about breaking cycles of pain and building a legacy of healing, truth, and love.

A Sacred Responsibility: The Role of Parents

Parents are entrusted with the sacred responsibility to love, Nurture, and protect their children. This responsibility is not merely a cultural expectation or societal norm. It is in fact a divine mandate. In Ephesians 6:4, the Bible instructs: "Fathers, do not provoke your children to anger, but bring them up in the discipline and instruction of the Lord." This verse highlights the importance of parenting with care and intention, avoiding harm while guiding children toward growth and righteousness.

When parents fulfill their role with love and integrity, they create a foundation of trust, security, and emotional well-being for their children. However, when this responsibility is abused through neglect, harsh discipline, or emotional manipulation, it leaves lasting scars. Children raised in such environments often carry wounds that affect their self-esteem, their relationships, and their ability to trust others. The impact of parental abuse runs deep, shaping how children see themselves and the world around them. In many cultures, including Jamaican culture, parental authority is often viewed as absolute. The parent's word is final, and any questioning or criticism is considered disrespectful. This dynamic can foster an environment where abuse is justified under the guise of discipline or tough love. However, authority is not a license to harm, but it is a responsibility to guide and nurture with wisdom and compassion.

The Bible makes it clear that parents are called to reflect God's love in their parenting. Psalm 103:13 says: "As a father has compassion on his children, so the Lord has compassion on those who fear him." Compassion is the cornerstone of godly parenting. It requires patience, understanding, and a willingness to prioritize a child's well-being over pride or frustration. Unfortunately, some parents misuse their authority, prioritizing control or cultural expectations over the emotional and spiritual health of their children. This misuse of power often manifests in physical, verbal, or emotional abuse. While discipline is a necessary part of parenting, it must always be balanced with love and respect.

Discipline that shames or harms a child violates the trust that God has placed in parents to care for His children. The consequences of such abuse are far-reaching. Many adults carry unresolved pain from childhood, struggling to reconcile the love they feel for their parents with the hurt they endured. This internal conflict can lead to strained relationships, difficulty in setting boundaries, and a cycle of pain that continues across generations. Yet, healing is possible not only for the child who was hurt but also for the parent who caused the harm. Accountability is a critical step in breaking this cycle. Parents must be willing to acknowledge their mistakes and seek forgiveness, both from God and from their children. This act of humility and accountability is not a sign of weakness; it is an act of strength and love. It reflects a commitment to healing and to restoring the trust that may have been broken.

In Matthew 18:6, Jesus issues a stark warning: "If anyone causes one of these little ones those who believe in me to stumble, it would be better for them to have a large millstone hung around their neck and to be drowned in the depths of the sea." This powerful imagery underscores the gravity of a parent's responsibility. Children are not possessions to be controlled; they are individuals to be cherished, nurtured, and guided. Healing within family relationships requires effort from both parents and children. It begins with open communication, where both parties feel safe to express their feelings without fear of judgment or retaliation.

Healing also requires a willingness to forgive, not to excuse the harm that was done, but to release the burden of resentment and create space for reconciliation. Parents who have caused harm whether intentionally or unintentionally have an opportunity to model God's grace by seeking forgiveness and making amends. Likewise, children who have been hurt can find freedom in forgiveness, even if full reconciliation is not possible.

As I reflect on the role of parents, I am reminded of Proverbs 22:6: "Train up a child in the way he should go; even when he is old, he will not depart from it." This verse reminds us of the enduring impact of parenting. The way a child is raised lays the foundation for their future for better or worse. Parents have the sacred responsibility to sow seeds of love, faith, and wisdom, knowing that these seeds will bear fruit for generations to come. Ultimately, parenting reflects God's relationship with His children. It is a role that requires humility, patience, and steady commitment to love. When parents fulfill this role with integrity, they not only honor their children but also honor the God who entrusted them with this sacred responsibility.

Personal Reflection: Writing the Memoir

Writing this memoir has been a journey of faith and self-discovery, one that challenged me to confront my past with honesty while leaning on God for strength. The decision to share my story was not made lightly. It came with moments of doubt and countless prayers for guidance. I sought clarity through prayer, trusting that if it was God's will, He would give me the strength to share my experiences for a greater purpose. I understood that telling my truth could stir uncomfortable emotions, not just for me, but for others involved. Yet, as I prayed and sought clarity, I realized that this process wasn't solely about revisiting my pain. It was about uncovering the lessons God had been teaching me all along.

The act of writing became deeply reflective. As I pieced together the chapters of my life, I began to notice patterns, moments where God's grace carried me through even when I couldn't recognize it at the time. Every tear, every struggle, and every unanswered question became part of a larger narrative, one that revealed His plan for my life. This memoir became less about recounting events and more about aligning with God's purpose for me: to use my story to inspire and encourage others.

One of the greatest tests of faith during this process was confronting the possibility of criticism or rejection. In Jamaican culture, speaking out about family struggles is often met with resistance, especially when it involves parents. I wrestled with the fear of being misunderstood, labeled as disrespectful, or causing further rifts. Doubt crept in, and I often questioned whether I was making the right choice. But in those moments of uncertainty, I remembered the prophecies spoken over my life, words that declared young people would find healing and hope through my testimony. Those prophecies became my anchor, reminding me that my story was part of a bigger picture, far beyond my personal struggles.

Amid this inner turmoil, I reached out to a trusted friend, a leader in the church and a social worker, to seek her advice. I asked her, "Do you think I should share my story?" Without hesitation, she responded, "Yes, you need to share your story. It's your story".

Her words resonated deeply, even though she didn't elaborate on the impact my story might have on others. I knew in my heart that sharing my journey could bring healing and hope. Her affirmation gave me the courage I needed to move forward. It reminded me that what I had endured wasn't just for me, it was for others, especially young people who might find themselves in the same place I once was.

As I continued to write, I wrestled with the question of how much to share. I turned to my husband for his thoughts, unsure of whether expressing certain feelings or details would be appropriate. His response was always steady and reassuring: "It's your experience; it's part of your story." His words encouraged me to embrace the truth of my journey, even when it felt uncomfortable to face. Writing became not just about recounting events but about honoring my experiences, no matter how painful or difficult they were to relive.

The support I received from both my friend and my husband reminded me that this was my truth, and it was worth telling. Their encouragement gave me the strength to press on and to trust that my story could make a difference.

The writing process also deepened my understanding of forgiveness and grace. Revisiting moments of hurt forced me to confront emotions I thought I had moved past. But instead of reopening wounds, I found myself leaning into God's promise of healing. Through His Word, I was reminded that forgiveness doesn't erase the pain, but it releases its power to control us. Forgiveness allowed me to approach this memoir with a spirit of reconciliation, not bitterness.

Reflecting on my calling, I realized that sharing my story was more than an act of obedience, it was an act of trust. Trust in God's timing, trust in His purpose, and trust that the lives He wanted to touch through my words would be reached. Writing this memoir became my way of saying "yes" to His will, even when the path seems unclear.

Ministering Through Experience

Throughout my life, I've come to understand that my story isn't just my own, it's a testament to the transformative power of God's grace. While my experiences often felt isolating and painful, I now recognize them as stepping stones toward a greater purpose. Sharing my struggles isn't merely about recounting hardship; it's about revealing how God works through even our darkest moments to shape us into vessels of hope for others.

I've learned that when we are transparent about our challenges, we give others permission to do the same. Vulnerability becomes the bridge that connects hearts, creating a space where healing can begin, not just for the one who shares but for those who listen. It is in those moments of shared humanity that God's presence becomes most evident, reminding us that we are never truly alone.

I often think about the young people I've encountered, those who feel weighed down by burdens they believe are too heavy to carry. When I share my story, my prayer is that they see themselves reflected in it. I want them to know they are not alone, that their pain is not the end of their story. No matter how bleak their circumstances may seem, God has a plan for their lives. He has taken my pain, my struggles, and even my triumphs, and used them to mold me into someone who can speak truth into the lives of others. My journey is proof that no experience is wasted when placed in God's hands. I've come to realize that my ministry isn't just found in the words I speak but in the experiences that have shaped me. Each step of my journey has been part of a bigger picture, one that serves to lead others toward healing, purpose, and hope in Christ. By being transparent and honest about my own struggles, I hope to inspire others, especially young people, to trust in God's timing and his perfect plan for their lives. There is hope, even in the darkest moments, and God is always at work, turning our trials into testimonies.

Conclusion: Honoring Through Truth and Growth

Honoring our parents is a concept deeply rooted in respect, love, and understanding. True honor, however, goes beyond passive compliance or remaining silent in the face of harm. It calls for an honest acknowledgment of our experiences, a willingness to confront the truth, and the courage to break free from cycles of dysfunction. On my journey, I have learned that honoring parents authentically does not mean accepting abuse, ignoring the pain of the past, or stifling our voices to maintain a façade of harmony. Rather, it involves recognizing the complexities of our relationships, acknowledging the hurt, and choosing to heal.

Authentic honor begins with confronting the truth of what we have lived through, how those experiences have shaped us, and how they can propel us toward growth. Honoring parents in this way does not equate to dishonoring them. Instead, it reflects a profound reverence for our own journey, our pain, and our resilience. For many, this process requires unlearning harmful patterns that may have persisted for generations. As we work to shed these patterns, we create the opportunity for healthier relationships, not just with our parents, but with ourselves and those around us.

Breaking these cycles of harm is far from easy.It demands immense courage and vulnerability. It also requires forgiveness, not as an act of excusing the wrongs committed, but as a way of releasing the past's grip on our present. Forgiveness is a gift we give ourselves, allowing us to step into a future unclouded by bitterness or regret. Reconciliation, while not always possible in the way we might hope, can still offer profound freedom when both parties commit to healing. Even if relationships are not fully restored, the act of pursuing peace grants us the ability to move forward, untethered from unresolved pain.

The hope I carry is this: no matter how painful our past may be, we always have the power to grow, transform, and create new legacies. By embracing truth, extending forgiveness, and committing to personal growth, we can break generational cycles of harm and establish a foundation of love and understanding for future generations. True honor lies in becoming the fullest version of who we are meant to be. In doing so, we not only honor ourselves, but also offer a new vision of hope and healing to those who come after us.

Honoring our parents is not about blind obedience or enduring mistreatment. Instead, it involves recognizing their role in our lives while maintaining our integrity and well-being. As Exodus 20:12 reminds us: 'Honor your father and your mother, so that you may live long in the land the Lord your God is giving you.' This command emphasizes respect and reverence but does not require us to accept harm or neglect our own needs. Similarly, Proverbs 22:6 teaches us: "Start children off on the way they should go, and even when they are old, they will not turn from it." This wisdom reflects the importance of nurturing others with love and guidance. True honor, then, is rooted in love, care, and responsibility.

CHAPTER 13

Mother's Day and birthday: Setting the Stage

Mother's Day and birthdays were the occasions when my mother and I most often reached out to each other. These milestones, marked on the calendar, became rare moments our voices touched, separated not just by miles but, more profoundly, by emotional distance. Birthdays, in particular, were brief exchanges: a simple "Happy Birthday," perhaps with a few emojis and a short note. The connection felt routine, almost obligatory, like a box checked off a list.

But Mother's Day was different. It felt like a ritual, a gesture I performed out of duty rather than celebration. I would send my greetings, perhaps a message or a phone call, but the act often felt hollow. Beneath the surface, I struggled to truly honor the day. It unearthed the weight of years marked by absence and silence, years where our relationship had been defined more by the things left unsaid than by what was spoken.

The simple phrase "Happy Mother's Day" carried a heaviness I couldn't ignore, as if the unspoken years lingered in the air, clouding the moment. In those moments, I often found myself reflecting on what motherhood meant to me and whether it was something I could genuinely celebrate. These occasions, while outwardly mundane, stirred deep emotional undercurrents. They became reminders of the longing I carried for a connection deeper than the obligatory exchanges we shared, a connection that had often been met with silence. The ache of those unmet expectations lingered, turning simple greetings into reflections of all that was missing.

A Mother's Day of Reflection

There was one Mother's Day in particular, when my emotions reached a breaking point. I had been reflecting deeply on what it truly meant to honor my mother, and the more I thought about it, the clearer it became: my mother had not fulfilled the role I needed her to play. She carried me for nine months, and for that, I would always be grateful. But beyond that, the nurturing, care, and presence I longed for were painfully absent. In contrast, my grandmother had stepped in to fill the void.

With her quiet wisdom and unwavering care, she became the mother figure I needed. She offered me the love, understanding, and stability that my heart had always yearned for. The stark difference between the bond I shared with her and the bond or lack thereof I shared with my mother was impossible to ignore. My grandmother embodied the nurturing spirit I craved but never received from my mother. That Mother's Day, I couldn't bring myself to say, "Happy Mother's Day." It wasn't an act of cruelty; it was an act of self-preservation. The years of unmet needs, the emotional distance, and the silence that had defined our relationship weighed heavily on me. Offering her those words would have felt dishonest, a hollow gesture that betrayed what I truly felt in my heart. It wasn't about disrespect, it was about finally being honest, even in silence, in a relationship that had been filled with so many unspoken truths.

Choosing not to reach out that year wasn't easy, but it felt like the only way to honor my own feelings. Still, the guilt lingered. I questioned whether I was wrong for withholding my greetings, for not fulfilling what seemed to be an expected duty. But deep down, I knew the truth: my decision wasn't about defiance or blame. It was about my need for more than just words, it was about seeking a genuine connection and the love of a mother, something I had never truly received.

The Consequences of Silence

That year, I chose silence, a silence that carried more weight than words ever could yet left me tangled in guilt and confusion.

It wasn't the silence of apathy but the silence of a deep, internal struggle that I couldn't easily articulate. Deciding not to reach out to my mother on Mother's Day wasn't an act of malice; it was an act of honesty. For years, our obligatory greetings on birthdays and holidays had only masked the truth: the emotional connection between us had been severed long ago.

After Mother's Day had passed, my mother was upset that I didn't call to share any Mother's Day greetings. She was especially hurt because she found out that I had called my brother, her eldest son to be a blessing to him and his family. I can't clearly remember whether she called me herself to express her hurt or if my brother was the one who told me, but either way, I found out that she was deeply bothered by the fact that I reached out to him but hadn't contacted her.

The weight of her pain was evident. Her tone, whether in her own voice or in what was relayed to me, carried sharpness, confusion, and anger over the missed acknowledgment. It wasn't just disappointment I sensed; it was the expectation of being honored, of being celebrated in a way I couldn't bring myself to offer because I didn't feel she had earned that place in my life. But her reaction wasn't only about a missed phone call. It was about the years of unmet needs and emotional gaps that had quietly built up between us.

In that moment, I struggled to find the right words, not because I didn't understand her pain, but because I was thinking about how she had not truly been a mother to me over the years. How could I make her understand that this wasn't about forgetting a holiday? It was about years of silence, years in which her role as a mother had fallen short of what I needed. This wasn't a wound that could be healed with an apology or mended with a single conversation. It was the kind of pain that had been festering in the spaces between us, growing deeper in the absence of real connection.

I felt guilty, but not in the way she might have thought. I didn't feel guilty for not calling because I knew my silence wasn't born of cruelty or indifference. I felt guilty because, deep down, I knew that my decision had broken a long-standing pattern. My silence was an unspoken acknowledgment of the emotional distance between us, a silent confession that our relationship had never been what it should have been. That truth weighed heavily on me, even as I tried to stand by my decision.

As I meditated on the words told to me, I felt as though I was caught between two opposing worlds. On one side was the world of expectation, where a mother should be celebrated without question. On the other side was my reality; a fractured relationship that I couldn't bring myself to celebrate.

Her reaction wasn't just about the missed phone call. It was about the unraveling of a dynamic that had long been out of sync. She didn't understand, and I wasn't sure she ever would. The truth was too complicated, too painful to condense into words she could hear or accept.

I was left with a swirl of emotions: guilt, frustration, and an aching kind of grief. It wasn't the loud, messy grief of loss, but a quiet grief that settled deep inside me. I couldn't tell whether I was mourning the relationship we never had or the one we had lost along the way.

What I did know was that the silence I had chosen, the silence I thought would give me space to process my feelings, had its own consequences. It didn't heal. It didn't bring clarity. Instead, it amplified the tension that had been quietly growing between us for years.

Later, as I reflected on that moment, I came to a difficult realization: this silence wasn't mine alone. It was a shared silence, one that had existed between us for far too long. My mother's disappointment wasn't just about my absence on Mother's Day. It was about the unspoken truths that defined our relationship: the years of neglect, the unmet emotional needs, the distance that had grown between us while we both pretended everything was fine.

In many ways, her hurt mirrored my own. That moment, that silence, became a turning point for me. It forced me to confront the truths I had avoided for so long not just about my mother, but about myself. I realized that silence had been my way of coping, a way of protecting myself from pain I wasn't ready to face. But silence doesn't heal wounds. It only hides them, leaving them to fester in the darkness. And sometimes, the only way to move forward is to face those wounds, no matter how deep or raw they may be.

The Decision to Reconnect

The following year, as Mother's Day approached, I stood at a crossroads. The silence I had maintained the year before still lingered, heavy and unresolved. Yet, somewhere deep within me, there was a shift, a quiet pull urging me to reach out. It wasn't a decision I made impulsively. It came from long moments of reflection, grappling with my emotions, and, most of all, a desire to prevent the distance between us from growing irreparably wide.

It was a complicated step, one that felt like venturing into unfamiliar terrain. Still, it was a step I knew I needed to take, if only to keep my heart from hardening completely to the idea of reconciliation. By then, I had spent enough time reflecting on the events of the previous year. I understood why I had chosen silence. It felt justified in the moment. But I had also realized that silence wasn't a solution. It had only widened the gap between us, leaving old emotional wounds to fester.

I hadn't forgotten the pain of the past, and the hurt hadn't disappeared. But holding on to my confusion and disappointment was keeping me trapped, tethered to the version of myself I no longer wanted to be. I didn't want to remain imprisoned by what was. I wanted something more. I wanted peace, closure, and perhaps the faintest hope of a connection that could one day resemble the relationship I had once longed for.

When I finally made the decision to reach out, the words came hesitantly, each one carefully chosen. But my goal was clear. I didn't expect to fix things or alter the dynamic between us. I only wanted to give her something I knew she valued: a simple Happy Mother's Day acknowledgment. I understood how much that message meant to her, and I hoped it might ease the tension created by my silence.

I wasn't reaching out in an attempt to rebuild what was broken. I simply wanted to fulfill an unspoken expectation, to take a small step toward softening the distance between us. As I composed the message, my thoughts were not on how she might respond. I already knew she wanted to hear from me. My motivation came from a heavier place, the desire to free myself from the weight of unspoken expectations and lingering disappointments.

The emotional stalemate between us had become unbearable, and I was ready to make a move, not out of obligation, but because the silence had begun to take its toll on me. Sending the message wasn't an act of hope. It was an act of release, a way to bridge the growing chasm between us, if only by an inch.

Even in the midst of my uncertainty about our fractured bond, I felt a pull to reach out. Perhaps it was my way of acknowledging that, despite all the pain, she had shaped my life in ways I couldn't ignore. Or maybe it was simply a way to reclaim my voice, not for her sake, but for mine.

Deep down, I understood the reality. We had drifted too far apart for reconciliation to come easily. Still, I extended my hand, however tenuously, as a small affirmation that the bond between us, though fractured, had not been entirely severed.

When I finally pressed send, I felt a quiet release. It wasn't a sense of peace, not quite. It was more like a fragile resolve, a faint assurance that I had taken a step to soften the sharp edges of our estrangement. The relief I felt was unexpected. I knew the message wouldn't transform our relationship or erase the years of pain. But that wasn't the point.

In reaching out, I had reclaimed a small piece of my agency. I was no longer standing still, immobilized by the unresolved tension between us. I had chosen to take a step forward, and that decision felt like an act of courage. It wasn't about her anymore. It was about me. About my own healing.

It's difficult to articulate the emotions that coursed through me in those moments. A mixture of hope, anxiety, and quiet determination settled in my chest. In some small way, I wanted her to see me more than the version of me shaped by old wounds and misunderstandings, but the one willing to try.

Reaching out wasn't about pretending the hurt didn't exist. It was about showing her, and myself, that despite everything, I still cared. That I still wanted more than silence.

Ultimately, though, I knew this choice wasn't entirely about her. It was about breaking free from the chains of a past that had held me captive for far too long. I was done letting neglect and disappointment define my emotional life.

Reaching out wasn't a cure-all, nor was it a promise that things would suddenly improve. But in that moment, I felt like I had reclaimed control over my story. I wasn't erasing the pain or pretending it hadn't shaped me. Instead, I was choosing not to let it dictate my future.

What came next was uncertain. I didn't know if this small gesture would lead to a deeper conversation or simply become another moment in the long, winding history of our relationship. But what mattered was that I had taken a step, however small, toward healing. And that was enough.

Preaching on Mother's Day

The Balance of Motherhood: Honoring Both Joy and Pain on a quiet Sunday morning, as I stood at the pulpit, a sense of purpose settled over me. I felt compelled to address the complexities of motherhood, both its beauty and its heartbreak. The Lord had placed a specific word on my heart, one that deviated from the usual Mother's Day sermon. Instead of focusing solely on celebration, my message sought to encompass the full spectrum of emotions tied to

347

this sacred role.

Drawing inspiration from the story of Mephibosheth in 2 Samuel 4:4 and 2 Samuel 9:3–7, I wanted to speak to those rejoicing and to those mourning, bringing healing, balance, and understanding. Motherhood is undoubtedly one of the most impactful roles in a child's life. A mother nurtures, teaches, and loves, shaping the person her child will become. Her influence is profound, her presence irreplaceable, yet not everyone shares the same experience. For many, the relationship with a mother is not a source of comfort but a reminder of pain.

On this day, social media is filled with glowing tributes to mothers, sacrifices and love, but beneath those tributes lies an unspoken reality. For some, Mother's Day is a day of grief, rejection, or unresolved hurt. I took a moment to acknowledge the silent pain that often accompanies this day. I spoke to the child mourning the loss of a beloved mother, the person estranged from their mother due to conflict or neglect, and the mothers themselves who carry wounds of rejection, low self-esteem, or mental illness.

My intention was not to overshadow the joy of celebrating good mothers, but to extend grace to those who often feel forgotten on this day. My message was a reminder that even in brokenness, there is hope. Even in the shadows, there is comfort to be found.

The Impact of Rejection and Loss

Mephibosheth's story resonates deeply with the pain of being "dropped." As the son of Jonathan and grandson of King Saul, he was born into a lineage of royalty, but tragedy forever altered the course of his life. In her desperate haste to flee, his nurse dropped him, leaving him crippled for life. The Bible offers no mention of his mother, leaving us to wonder: Would she have been more careful? Would she have sacrificed herself to protect him, ensuring his safety at all costs?

Similarly, some of us have been "dropped" by the very people entrusted with our care. Mothers, who are called to provide love, stability, and guidance, sometimes fall short of fulfilling their role. Whether through intention or circumstance, their neglect or rejection creates deep wounds that leave lasting scars, shaping a child's identity and their sense of worth.

Some mothers reject their children as a result of their own struggles. Mental illness, unresolved trauma, or bitterness tied to the child's father can cloud their ability to love fully. For others, envy may creep in, distorting their perception of their child as competition instead of a blessing. Unplanned pregnancies, too, can lead to rejection that begins in the womb. The rejection may feel intangible at first, but it takes root, growing into a spirit of unworthiness that can follow a child into adulthood, manifesting as cycles of exclusion, self-doubt, and repeated feelings of being unloved.

But on that day, as I stood before the congregation, I declared this truth with unwavering conviction: Every cycle of rejection is broken by the power of God in Jesus' name.

Lodebar: A Place of Brokenness

Mephibosheth was carried to Lodebar, a barren land of forgotten people, a place symbolic of hopelessness. His lameness was not just physical; it was emotional as well. Many of us, dropped by those we trusted, find ourselves in our own Lodebar spaces where we feel forgotten, rejected, or unworthy of love. Yet, Mephibosheth's story doesn't end there. King David, remembering his covenant with Jonathan, asked, "Is there anyone left of the house of Saul, to whom I may show the kindness of God?" When Mephibosheth was found, David didn't see his lameness or his brokenness. Instead, David restored his inheritance and invited him to dine at the king's table, a place of honor and acceptance.

This is God's promise to us. Even when we've been dropped or rejected by those who should have loved us, God remembers us. He calls us out of our Lodebars and sets a place for us at His table, covering our brokenness with His abundant grace.

The Two Sides of Motherhood

In my sermon, I sought to honor the mothers who have selflessly sacrificed for their children. These are the mothers who embody love, resilience, and strength. Women who teach values, nurture character, and guide their children into adulthood. Their efforts deserve recognition, not just on Mother's Day but every day. Their impact is immeasurable and worthy of celebration.

However, I also addressed a more painful reality: not all mothers fulfill this role. Some children bear the weight of toxic or narcissistic relationships with their mothers. Others have endured abandonment or neglect, carrying wounds that cut deeply and often persist across generations. These experiences create cycles of pain that can feel impossible to break.

Mothers, too, are not exempt from suffering. Some endure rejection by their children, whether due to misunderstandings, unresolved conflicts, or spiritual attacks. Others carry heavy burdens of guilt and shame for their perceived or actual failures, wrestling to reconcile their past actions with the present. The pain runs both ways, often leaving scars on both sides of the relationship.

I emphasized the importance of forgiveness for mothers and their children alike. Forgiveness is not about excusing the harm or pretending it didn't happen. Rather, it is a deliberate choice to release the hold that pain has over us. Unforgiveness cripples us, much like Mephibosheth's lameness, and it prevents healing. It closes us off to God's blessings and keeps us trapped in cycles of resentment. Forgiveness, however difficult, is the key to breaking free.

Restoration and Hope

I reminded the congregation that rejection does not define our worth. Just as David invited Mephibosheth to his table, God invites us into His presence. He sees our pain, our brokenness, and offers us healing and restoration. If you've been abandoned by your mother or by others, remember, God has not forgotten you. He has a plan for your life, and your story is still unfolding.

The key to unlocking that plan is forgiveness. Release the pain, trust in God's timing, and allow His love to mend the wounds.

I concluded by urging everyone to honor their mothers, even in the face of hardship. Honoring doesn't mean overlooking the hurt, but it's about recognizing their God-given role and choosing to respond with love and forgiveness. If you've been blessed with a nurturing mother, celebrate her. And if your journey has been difficult, lean into God's love and the family of faith He surrounds you with.

Reflecting on the Message

As I preached that morning, I felt the Holy Spirit guiding me to speak directly to every heart in the room. I could feel the weight of unspoken pain in some, contrasted by the joy of those who had been blessed with loving mothers. My own journey reminded me of the need to address both the beauty and the challenges of motherhood. Social media often presents an idealized version, but the reality is far more nuanced. My message wasn't just about celebration or grief, it was about finding a balance and recognizing the wide range of experiences motherhood brings.

In reflection, I am deeply grateful that the Lord led me to speak with both compassion and truth. The response from the congregation confirmed the importance of this message. Some experienced healing as they released their pain to God, while others found a renewed sense of appreciation and love for their mothers. Above all, I pray that this message served as a powerful reminder of God's limitless love and His power to restore what is broken. Perhaps celebrated or forgotten, abandoned or cherished, God's kindness touches each one of us.

Conclusion: Embracing the Complexity of Mother's Day

Mother's Day is often celebrated as a day of joy and gratitude, a moment to honor the love and sacrifices of mothers. Yet, for many, it also stirs unresolved emotions, complicated memories, and unhealed wounds. It serves as a reminder of the intricate nature of human relationships, particularly the mother-child bond.

Like birthdays, Mother's Day evokes a mix of emotions. For some, it's a time of heartfelt celebration, filled with loving gestures and cherished moments. For others, it is a day of reflection, marked by grief, disappointment, or even anger, a reminder of loss or strained connections. As someone who has wrestled with these feelings, I've come to realize that the day doesn't need to be defined solely by joy or sorrow. It can hold both.

Throughout my journey, I've learned that honoring a mother doesn't mean dismissing the pain or pretending the past was perfect. It doesn't require rewriting history to make it easier to accept. Instead, honoring a mother can be an act of personal growth and understanding. It involves recognizing her role, however flawed, while working to heal the parts of ourselves that were hurt along the way.

To those who find Mother's Day difficult, I want to offer hope. Healing is possible, even in the context of complicated relationships. Reconciliation with your mother may not always be an option, but reconciliation within yourself is. We can embrace new forms of family, love, and support that fill the gaps left by unmet expectations. If navigating these emotions feels overwhelming, seeking therapy or guidance from a trusted spiritual leader can help bring clarity.

In the end, moving forward means trusting in the Lord's love, which is greater than any pain we've endured. His love empowers us to forgive, to heal, and to open ourselves to joy once again. On Mother's Day, and every day, we can find peace, not in perfect relationships, but in knowing that love and healing can coexist with our pain.

CHAPTER 14

The Gift of Self-Discovery: Embracing My True Self

The greatest gift I received on my journey was discovering my true self. No longer weighed down by the expectations of others, I finally stood fully in the light of my own identity. This revelation didn't come overnight; it emerged from years of reflection, healing, and growth. I learned to love myself for who I was, not for who others expected me to be. It was a profound shift, one that allowed me to release the heavy burden of chasing standards that were never mine to uphold.

Healing and forgiveness were vital parts of this process, but equally important was embracing the new opportunities life brought my way. This journey wasn't simply about leaving the past behind; it was about transforming into the person I was always meant to be. In that transformation, I found peace, purpose, and a renewed sense of hope for the future.

Realization of Self-Worth

Over the years, I gradually came to understand the true meaning of self-worth. Those years, though marked by pain and moments of doubt, also imparted some of life's most valuable lessons. I realized that while I couldn't change my mother's feelings toward me, I had the power to change how I viewed myself.

My worth was not determined by her words or actions. I was more than the sum of her criticisms and unmet expectations. Embracing this truth wasn't easy; especially when the person I longed for unconditional love from seemed incapable of giving it. Her rejection often felt like a mirror, reflecting and magnifying my deepest insecurities. Yet, over time, I unearthed a quiet strength within myself, a strength that enabled me to rise above the negativity. I began to see my worth through a new lens; one shaped by faith, resilience, and a determined spirit to grow.

Letting Go of Expectations

Releasing the expectations placed upon me became one of the most liberating experiences of my life. For so long, I carried the weight of trying to prove my worth, constantly seeking approval that always seemed just beyond my grasp. But as I redefined my own sense of value, I realized I didn't need validation from others to feel whole. This journey wasn't about denying the pain or pretending it didn't exist; it was about acknowledging the hurt while choosing not to let it define who I was. I had to unlearn the deeply rooted belief that my worth depended on how others treated me or whether they deemed me enough. Instead, I began to honor my strengths, my achievements, and the person I was becoming.

Transforming Pain into Strength

Pain shapes us in ways we don't always anticipate, but it doesn't have to break us. For me, the pain of feeling unloved and unvalued ignited a spark of growth I hadn't known I needed. It forced me to examine where I had been compromising; settling for less love, less respect, and less belief in myself. That confrontation was painful but necessary. In the process, I unearthed a resilience within me that I never thought possible.

But the journey was anything but smooth. On many days, self-doubt became an unwelcome companion, whispering insidious lies about my worth and potential. Yet, even on my darkest days, I clung fiercely to one truth: I was more than the sum of my circumstances. Rejection didn't define me. Instead, my identity was forged in how I chose to rise above it.

Embracing Healing and Forgiveness

Healing and forgiveness became cornerstones of my self-discovery journey, though neither came easily. Forgiveness didn't mean excusing the actions that hurt me; it meant freeing myself from the suffocating grip of bitterness and resentment. In releasing that anger, I made space for peace to return and joy to take root.

Equally important was self-forgiveness. I had to let go of the times I doubted my worth, when I let the opinions of others dictate my self-image, and the mistakes I made while struggling to find my way. That forgiveness wasn't about erasing those moments but about granting myself the grace to grow beyond them. It was an act of liberation, a release from the weight of regret that allowed me to move forward freely.

One day, as I shared parts of my story, someone said, "You need to heal and forgive." I responded with calm honesty: I already have. Speaking about my experiences didn't mean I was holding onto the hurt; it was a way of acknowledging my journey. Healing doesn't erase scars; it transforms them. The wounds may have closed, but the scars remain as reminders of where I've been and how far I've come. Psychological studies, particularly those on post-traumatic growth (PTG), affirm that healing doesn't mean erasing all traces of pain. According to Dr. Richard Tedeschi, one of PTG's pioneers, healing after trauma can foster new strengths, deeper insights, and emotional resilience; even while scars linger.

Healing isn't a destination; it's a journey. It doesn't mean you'll never feel pain again, but rather that pain no longer controls your life.

Healing doesn't mean forgetting, nor does it mean you're impervious to moments of hurt. Sometimes I still feel the ache of disappointment or regret. That doesn't mean I haven't healed or forgiven; it means I cared. It's a reflection of the love I gave, the hopes I held, and the dreams I once cherished. These feelings are valid. They don't define my healing, but they are part of my story. Healing is an ongoing process of learning to carry your past without letting it define your future.

Rediscovering Joy

As I healed, I began to rediscover joy in the simplest moments: the laughter of a child, the golden hues of a sunrise, or the stillness of a quiet morning. These weren't just fleeting moments of happiness; they were anchors, reminding me of the beauty and goodness that still surrounded me. Each of these experiences became a gentle nudge, encouraging me to embrace life again; even after enduring seasons of pain and loss.

A Renewed Sense of Purpose

In reconnecting with myself, I uncovered a renewed sense of purpose. The pain I had endured no longer felt meaningless, it transformed into proof of resilience and faith. I came to understand that my story carried the potential to inspire and uplift those navigating similar struggles. This newfound purpose became my motivation to keep moving forward, growing stronger, and sharing my truth with courage and authenticity.

Looking Ahead

As I reflect on this journey, I realize that self-discovery is not a destination; it is a continuous, evolving process of growth. It's about learning, transforming, and embracing who I am becoming. The journey has taught me that true self-awareness lays the foundation for a future filled with hope, love, and purpose. This chapter of my life has been a preparation for the next: the journey of faith. Through faith, I have found the courage to face uncertainty, trust in God's plan for my life, and step forward with confidence into the future He has designed for me. The gift of self- discovery is a blessing I now carry with gratitude, guiding me as I step into the next phase of my story.

CHAPTER 15

Journey of faith

For years, I have received prophetic words that shaped my vision and ministry. I can vividly recall the first time this happened, back when I was living in Jamaica. Prophets and ministers, many of whom I had never met spoke with a conviction that I didn't fully understand. They declared a future where I would travel the world, preaching the gospel to nations and walking in the miraculous power of God. They spoke of signs and wonders following me, of healing and deliverance being central to my calling.

One prophecy, in particular, was strikingly specific; I was told I would preach in African nations. I didn't know how or when this would happen, but the words planted a seed of faith and expectation in my heart. I was also prophesied to that I carried a heavy deliverance ministry, though at the time, I didn't even know what deliverance ministry entailed. It wasn't widely discussed or practiced as it is today. Still, those words resonated deeply, even if I didn't fully grasp their magnitude.

The prophetic words didn't end there. Time and again, I was told I was called to be a prophetess. It wasn't a title I sought, nor was it a role I anticipated, but confirmation came repeatedly often from people with no knowledge of my life or what others had already spoken over me. Each declaration stitched together a sense of purpose in my heart. Even when I doubted my own ability, I could never doubt God's power to fulfill His word. At first, I wrestled with the enormity of these prophecies. How could someone like me, someone who had endured so many struggles and uncertainties be chosen for such a high calling? But over time, I began to see that faith and obedience were my only ways forward. The prophecies didn't just describe a distant future; they called me to action, to trust God even when the path seemed impossible.

Looking back now, I recognize that God's hand was at work, even in those early moments when I first heard His call. Faith isn't just believing in a promise, it's walking in obedience, even when fulfillment feels far away. As I share these experiences, I am reminded that the journey of faith isn't about my strength but God's. The prophetic words I received were never just for me; they were for the countless souls waiting to hear the gospel, to witness signs and wonders, and to experience the transformative power of God's

363

love.

Signs, Wonders, and Miracles

Throughout my ministry, I have personally witnessed the power of God revealed through signs, wonders, and miracles.

These experiences not only strengthened my own faith but served as living testimonies to others that the God we serve is still a miracle-working God today.

One of the most profound experiences in my ministry has been watching people receive the gift of the Holy Ghost, evidenced by speaking in tongues just as described in Scripture. Acts 2:4 declares: "And they were all filled with the Holy Ghost, and began to speak with other tongues, as the Spirit gave them utterance." This passage has come to life countless times before my eyes. Guided by the Holy Spirit and through the laying on of hands, I would pray for individuals to receive the Holy Ghost. Time after time, I saw them begin to speak in tongues, their lives transformed as God's overwhelming presence filled them.

Another constant testimony in my ministry is God's healing power. I have seen people delivered from stubborn physical ailments that medical treatments couldn't shake. In one instance, I was invited to pray for people at a church.

Afterward, the pastor shared a powerful testimony of a woman who returned to her doctor, only to discover that her condition had vanished entirely. Even outside church walls, God's healing touch continued to manifest.

At work, I sometimes pray for colleagues who are going through pain or struggles. I remember one woman who had been suffering from persistent fluttering sensations in her stomach. I prayed with her, and immediately, the fluttering stopped, leaving her astonished by God's undeniable power. When I taught young children, the Lord continued to demonstrate His healing through my hands. If a child in my class became ill, I would pray for them, laying my hands upon them in faith. Time and time again, I witnessed them recover. What amazed me even more was how the other children would sense God's presence at work. They would come to me with their own belly aches and small pains, asking me to pray for them too. It was as if they could recognize God moving, even at their young age.

Deliverance ministry has also been a vital and deeply humbling part of my calling. The first time I witnessed the power of God delivering someone from demonic possession involved two sisters, shortly after a church service had ended. The preacher had finished speaking when one of the young women began manifesting signs of possession.

No one moved to help her. But I felt God's unmistakable call in that moment. I knew this was His work for me. By His power and authority, I prayed over her and her sister, commanding the demonic forces to leave. God delivered them both. Since that day, I have had many opportunities to serve in deliverance ministry. I worked closely with a pastor at a deliverance church, assisting in freeing others from spiritual bondage. On one occasion, while visiting a church, I prayed for a young woman, and as soon as I placed my hands on her, the demons within her began to manifest, even declaring their names. The battle intensified, but the environment wasn't conducive to full deliverance. Eventually I took her to another church where the demons were completely casted out.

These moments of deliverance and healing have been profound not only for me but for those touched by God's power. Witnessing people receive healing, deliverance, or the Holy Ghost rekindled their faith, reminding them that God is not distant or inactive. He is present, powerful, and compassionate. For me, these experiences have been humbling and awe-inspiring. They stand as constant reminders of what God can do when we walk in obedience to His calling. The truth is, signs and wonders are not confined to the early church or the ancient pages of Scripture. They are alive today. Through my journey, I have seen how God continues to transform lives, heal the brokenhearted, and set the oppressed free. Each miracle is a witness to His infinite glory and a reflection of His deep, abiding love for His people.

Seeing God's provision through prophetic dreams!

During my university years, my friend and I often faced significant financial challenges. There were moments when she didn't know how she would manage to sit for her exams because she couldn't afford the fees. Some nights, she would go to bed uncertain about how the money would come through, but I would pray, asking God for guidance.

Many times, I would wake up with a prophetic vision, vivid and clear. I could see her seated in the exam room, calmly taking the test. I would assure her, saying, "You are going to take this exam. I don't know how, but God will make a way." And sure enough, each time, God provided. On the morning of the exam, the needed money always came through. She was able to sit for every test.

Over time, my friend came to trust the accuracy of my visions deeply. She once joked, "I wouldn't want you to see when I'm going to die." Her words were lighthearted but carried a deeper truth, she believed in the strength of my prophetic gift. It was a reflection of the trust we shared and the clarity with which God had been speaking through me.

On several occasions, I experienced intense visions of deliverance. These were not just fleeting impressions but vivid, powerful encounters where I saw myself actively freeing people from demonic oppression. In one vision, I even confronted a madman and delivered him completely by God's power. Each vision left an indelible mark on my spirit, deepening my understanding of the deliverance ministry and confirming the calling I had sensed within me. Though these visions didn't always indicate specific moments in time, they served as a constant reminder that God was preparing me. Each vision was His way of guiding me to step boldly into the ministry of deliverance, confident in the power and authority He had given me to set others free.

Preaching the Gospel from the Pulpit to Television: Early Beginnings in Jamaica

A few years after I gave my life to Christ, I began preaching the gospel. Over time, a minister friend recommended me to preach at other churches. That opportunity opened new doors and marked the beginning of a new chapter. I started preaching regularly in various churches across Jamaica that I was connected to. These early experiences planted the seeds of my calling and became the solid foundation on which my ministry would grow. I was later appointed and ordained as an evangelist in Jamaica. I was also sent to plant a church alongside another evangelist, which we successfully did, and we served together as the head for a period of time.

Ministry Expands to the United States

After beginning my preaching ministry in Jamaica, I was eventually invited to speak on a prayer line in the United States. That invitation became a turning point in my journey, leading to a personal call to travel and minister abroad. It was a pivotal moment that opened new doors, allowing me to spread the gospel to a wider audience. As I preached in various churches across the United States, my ministry grew with each step of faith I took, expanding far beyond what I had first envisioned.

Preaching on Television

As my ministry grew, I was blessed with the opportunity to preach on television. It was a significant milestone, enabling me to share the message of hope and salvation with a broader audience. This experience felt like a powerful step forward in fulfilling the prophetic words spoken over my life, a reminder that God's purpose was unfolding before me.

Starting a Ministry and Navigating Challenges

Before the COVID pandemic, I began a ministry of my own. Without a building to call our own, I struggled to sustain it amid numerous challenges. When COVID struck, the situation worsened. The pandemic's economic toll made it impossible to continue, forcing me to pause the ministry. Despite this, I held onto my faith, trusting that God's plan was still unfolding, even if it required enduring these hardships for a season.

Prophetic Fulfillment and the Journey Ahead

Reflecting on my journey, I recognize the fulfillment of many prophecies that were spoken over my life, particularly in the areas of preaching and ministry. Some of these prophecies have already come to fruition, while others are still unfolding. This evolving process has not only shaped my sense of purpose but also broadened my vision for what the future may hold.

Ordination and Titles: A Prophet to the Nations

The journey toward ordination was a transformative moment in my ministry, yet it brought with it significant internal conflicts. I was recognized as a pastor and evangelist, but the process of being acknowledged as a prophetess was far more nuanced. While I had received clear prophetic confirmations of my calling, I understood that ministry was never about titles or positions, but it was about serving others and fulfilling God's will.

At a critical moment, I made the decision to pause the ordination process as a prophetess. It wasn't because I doubted my calling; instead, I felt a deep conviction that ministry is fundamentally rooted in service, not in titles or recognition. Titles do not define us. It is the lives we impact and our obedience to God's direction that ultimately matter.

Over the years, prophetic words have affirmed and solidified my calling to the nations. These words, combined with personal experiences and growth in ministry, have deepened my understanding of the weight of the prophetic role I carry. I came to realize that God's plans for me far exceeded anything I could have imagined. The responsibility of the prophetic calling on my life was not something I could approach lightly.

Reflecting on ordination and titles reminded me that God's calling is not about accolades or recognition. It is about obedience to His will and an unwavering willingness to serve in the capacity He has assigned. My ministry is not defined by a title. It is defined by a heart devoted to serving God and His people.

Transitioning into the Next Chapter: Preparing for God's Perfect Will

As my husband and I step into this new season, we find ourselves in a time of transition that demands both patience and unwavering faith. After years of ministry, overcoming challenges, and experiencing personal growth, we feel a profound sense of purpose in the direction God is leading us. We believe we are on the brink of settling into the place He has prepared for us, where we can not only serve wholeheartedly but also flourish in alignment with His will.

Aligning with His Purpose

The prophetic words spoken over our lives have been unmistakable: ministry is at the core of what God has called us to do. While we are filled with excitement, we are equally mindful of the importance of being in the right place at the right time, fulfilling what God has perfectly ordained. This journey isn't solely about answering a calling; it's about aligning ourselves with His divine purpose and walking fully in His perfect will. I am determined to ensure that wherever we choose to settle, it's not based merely on our own feelings but on the assurance that it is exactly where God wants us to be.

Equipped for the New Phase

Looking back on our journey, the challenges we faced have prepared us in ways we never could have foreseen. The struggles, setbacks, and moments of uncertainty shaped not only our faith but also our resilience and ministry, equipping us for this new phase. Every trial and each season of waiting have strengthened us, building the foundation we need to step into the next chapter with confidence and an unshakable trust in God's promises.

Excitement for What Lies Ahead

We are filled with excitement for the opportunities that lie ahead and the lives that will be transformed through our ministry. My heart is prepared and fully committed to stepping into whatever God has planned, carrying with me a deep sense of anticipation and devotion to His will. This new chapter is not solely about us; but it's about fulfilling God's purpose and making a lasting impact for His glory. As we navigate this transition, we do so with a profound sense of peace, trusting fully in His guidance every step of the way.

The Price of Glory

Ministry is not for the faint of heart. The call to serve God and His people often comes with a cost; one measured through both physical and spiritual battles. Over the years, I have encountered countless challenges that have tested my faith and perseverance in ways I could not have anticipated. There were moments when the weight of these trials felt overwhelming: demonic attacks, witchcraft, and even attempts on my life. The enemy sought to silence me, to push me to give up. But through it all, God stood as my refuge and my steady source of strength.

The Spiritual Warfare

I have experienced firsthand the intensity of spiritual warfare that accompanies answering God's call. At times, the attacks have been relentless, manifesting as physical illness, emotional turmoil, and threats from forces beyond the natural realm. Yet, with every battle, I have gained an invaluable understanding of perseverance. I now realize that the cost of walking in God's glory is significant, but the rewards surpass the sacrifices in ways that only eternity can fully reveal.

God's Faithfulness in the Midst of Trials

God's faithfulness has been unmistakable at every turn in my life. Despite relentless opposition, He has continually preserved me. There were times when the enemy's attacks felt overwhelming, but I stood firm, fully trusting in the promises of God. It wasn't fear for my life that guided me; it was an unwavering reliance on His word that sustained me. Time after time, God intervened and protected me. By His grace alone, I am still standing today, equipped to continue the work He has called me to do. These challenges have not only refined my character but also deepened my trust in His plans for my life.

The Importance of Perseverance and Trust

Through it all, I have learned to trust God on a deeper level. His faithfulness never wavers, and even when the path feels arduous, I am confident that He is walking beside me, giving me strength for the journey. To anyone carrying the weight of their own struggles, my message is this: stay the course. Trust God, even when the odds seem insurmountable, because His faithfulness never fails. The cost of walking in His purpose may be great, but the victory is eternal.

CHAPTER 16

Embracing New Opportunities for Growth

With each passing day, I grew more confident in my ability to create the life I had always envisioned. As I began to heal from my past, I opened myself to opportunities that had once felt beyond my grasp. I embraced each chance for growth, whether in my personal life or professional endeavors. I stepped outside of my comfort zone, taking on challenges that had once filled me with fear. With every challenge I faced, I discovered a strength and capability within me that I had never fully realized.

My life was no longer defined by the rejection and pain of the past. Instead, it was shaped by my resilience, my willingness to heal, and my determination to live fully. The opportunities that came my way were no longer barriers to overcome but gifts to be received and cherished. I came to understand that life offered far more beauty, possibility, and promise than I had ever imagined.

Reflecting on Personal and Spiritual Growth

Through the struggles and triumphs of my journey, I've come to understand that my growth is not defined by external

376

achievements but by a profound internal transformation. Each challenge has fortified my faith and deepened my understanding of who I am in God. As I began to heal from the wounds of my past, I embraced the opportunities before me with renewed strength and confidence, trusting that God had prepared me for this season of growth.

There were moments when I stepped into unfamiliar territory; perhaps it was taking on a new ministry opportunity, building new relationships, or taking risks, I would have once avoided. Each step became evidence to the work God was doing within me, shaping me into someone who could move forward not with fear, but with hope and expectancy.

As I grew spiritually, I realized that true success is not measured by worldly standards but by my ability to serve God and fulfill the purpose He designed for me. This revelation shifted my perspective, allowing me to embrace the future with peace and clarity, one that transcended any external accomplishments.

The Power of a Name: Embracing a New Identity

One of the most transformative steps I took toward healing and embracing my future was changing my name. There were many reasons behind this decision, but the most significant was the realization that my name, which meant "victory" or "conqueror," might have been tied to some of the battles I faced in life. As its meaning suggested, victory often required a battle, and conquering came with hardship. Over time, I began to question whether the weight of that name, constantly associated with struggle, was keeping me tethered to past challenges and difficulties.

Much like the biblical examples of name changes, I saw this as a symbolic step toward releasing the past and stepping into a new future. When Jacob wrestled with God, his name was changed to Israel, signifying transformation and a new identity. Similarly, Abraham's name change marked the beginning of a new covenant and journey with God. In my case, changing my name was an act of faith. It was a way to shed the old layers of identity, break free from the weight of past struggles, and move forward into the person God had called me to be.

This decision wasn't just about letting go of the past; it was about embracing the future with hope and clarity. My new name, meaning "God's favor," was a declaration of trust in the divine purpose unfolding in my life. It reflected a shift in my mindset from identifying with constant battle to embracing a future filled with grace, favor, and peace.

By changing my name, I took ownership of my new identity, one no longer defined by the hardships I had endured but by the promise of God's goodness and favor that awaited me.

Embracing the New: A Step Toward the Future

As I reflect on this chapter of my life, I realize that changing my name was far more than a personal decision; it was a spiritual declaration. It marked an acknowledgment of how far I had come and a bold step into the person I was becoming. It symbolized the truth that as we grow and heal, we are not bound by our past or by the label others may have placed on us.

With each new day, I am learning that true growth is not defined by external accomplishments, but by the internal transformation that brings peace, confidence, and purpose. The name I now carry reflects the abundance and favor that God has prepared for me. It serves as a daily reminder that I am no longer defined by the struggles of my past, but by the grace and favor that fill both my present and my future. Embracing this new identity has empowered me to move forward with renewed strength and unwavering faith, knowing that I am walking in the purpose God has designed for me and that His favor is with me every step of the way.

CONCLUSION

As I bring this memoir to a close, I am reminded that healing and understanding are not linear processes. The journey is a winding road, at times painful, often uncertain, but always leading toward transformation. In sharing these pages of my life, I have come to realize that the brokenness I once carried no longer defines me. Instead, the strength I have found through God, forgiveness, and my own willingness to embrace the truth has shaped the person I am today.

For years, I questioned what it truly meant to honor my parents. Was it simply about respect? About following the rules? Or was it something deeper, a call to recognize the humanity in others, to see beyond flaws and mistakes, and to love even in the face of hurt? As I reflect on my relationships with my mother, my grandmother, and all those who shaped me, I now understand that honoring them doesn't mean ignoring pain or pretending everything was perfect.

Honoring them means acknowledging the lessons I learned, recognizing the growth that came from our struggles, and cherishing the love that was shared, however imperfectly.

In writing this memoir, I have discovered that forgiveness is not solely for those who wronged us; it is for ourselves. Forgiveness brings the freedom to release the weight we carry, to let go of bitterness, and to move forward. It is a choice, a deliberate act to break the cycles of hurt and create new patterns of grace and understanding. I have learned that healing begins with truth: by speaking it, living it, and accepting it.

I hope that in reading these pages, you have found reflections of your own story, whether in the moments of heartache or in the moments of triumph. My prayer is that this memoir inspires you to find your voice, confront the pain in your life, and embrace the possibility of healing and growth. No matter how deep the wounds, we are all capable of transformation. Through the power of love and faith, we can find our way to peace.

In the end, honoring is not about striving for perfection; it is about grace. It means accepting imperfections in others and in ourselves and moving forward in love. As I continue this journey, I do so with deep gratitude for the lessons I've learned, the people who have been a part of my story, and for the hope that the future holds. The road ahead may not always be easy, but I walk it with faith, strength, and the understanding that every step forward is a step toward healing.

EPILOGUE

As I write these final words, I find myself standing at a crossroads between who I was and who I am becoming. The story I have shared is not one of perfect resolution, but of a journey one that continues to unfold with every new chapter of my life. I have learned that healing is not a straight path, but a winding road filled with twists, turns, and moments of uncertainty. Yet, within each of those moments, I have found strength. I have found peace.

The scars of my past, though still present, no longer define me. They are a part of my story, but they are not the story. Today, I stand in the knowledge that my worth is not determined by the abuse I endured or the silence I once kept. I am not the sum of my past; I am a reflection of the choices I make today, the forgiveness I offer and the healing I continue to seek.

I now know that I have a voice, a voice that matters. I speak for those who feel silenced. I write for those who are still learning to tell their stories. If there is one lesson I have learned on this journey, it is that our stories, no matter how painful or imperfect, deserve to be told. By telling them, we begin to break the chains that have kept us bound in silence.

As you reach the final pages of this book, I hope you understand that this is not just the end of my story; it is the beginning of a new chapter. A chapter rooted in truth, healing, and purpose. I now walk in the light of my truth, embracing the woman I was always meant to be. While the past will always remain a part of me, I no longer allow it to hold me back.

To anyone reading these words, I want you to know this: you, too, have the power to choose your own path. No matter where you've come from or what you've been through, there is always hope. Healing is real. Change is possible. Your story is not over; it is only just beginning.

AUTHOR'S NOTE

Writing this memoir has been an extraordinary journey of self-discovery, healing, and hope. By sharing the story of my life, the struggles I endured and the triumphs I achieved, I hope my words resonate with those who feel silenced by their past, burdened by unspoken pain, or trapped in loneliness and despair.

This book is for anyone who has ever believed their voice didn't matter or felt invisible. It is for the young person suffering in silence, wondering if anyone truly understands or cares. It is for the adults still wrestling with childhood scars that linger into the present. And it is for anyone who has endured abuse, neglect, or emotional distance and is seeking a path toward healing and peace.

Though this story is deeply personal, it reflects struggles shared by many. Behind closed doors, countless individuals face pain, often without recognition or support. But this is also a story of resilience, a testament to the strength found in adversity and a reminder that our past does not determine who we are. By sharing our stories, we can dismantle the barriers of silence and move toward healing and connection. To my family, friends, and mentors: thank you for walking alongside me, even when my journey was difficult to understand. To my husband: your unwavering love and encouragement have been my constant source of strength. Your presence is a gift that words alone cannot capture. As you turn these pages, I hope you not only see a reflection of my life, but also recognize parts of your own story within them. May this book inspire hope, foster healing, and encourage you to live authentically. It is my belief that, no matter what we've endured, there is always room for growth, redemption, and new beginnings. Thank you for allowing me to share my heart with you.

www.ingramcontent.com/pod-product-compliance
Lightning Source LLC
Chambersburg PA
CBHW021700120626
46545CB00004B/1323